HARD KNOCKS

This book draws on interviews carried out over a period of eight years, as well as novels, films, and domestic violence literature, to explain the role of storytelling in the history of the battered women's movement. The author shows how cultural contexts shape how stories about domestic abuse get told, and offers critical tools for bringing psychology into discussions of group dynamics in the domestic violence field.

The book enlists psychoanalytic-feminist theory to analyze storytelling practices and to re-visit four areas of tension in the movement where signs of battle fatigue have been most acute. These areas include the conflicts that emerge between the battered women's movement and the state, the complex relationship between domestic violence and other social problems, and the question of whether woman battering is a special case that differs from other forms of social violence. The volume also looks at the tensions between groups of women within the movement, and how to address differences based on race, class, or other dimensions of power. Finally, the book explores the contentious issue of how to acknowledge forms of female aggression while still preserving a gender analysis of intimate partner violence.

In attending to narrative dynamics in the history of domestic violence work, *Hard Knocks* presents a radical re-reading of the contribution of psychology to feminist interventions and activism. The book is ideal reading for scholars, activists, advocates, and policy planners involved in domestic violence, and is suitable for students of psychology, social work, sociology, and criminology.

Janice Haaken is a Professor of Psychology at Portland State University. She is also a clinical and community psychologist, documentary filmmaker, and social justice activist. An interdisciplinary scholar, Haaken has published extensively in the areas of psychoanalysis and feminism, gender and the history of psychiatric diagnosis, group responses to violence and trauma, and the psychology of storytelling.

"In an accessible, direct and compelling manner, this impressively scholarly text surveys the full array of recent debates tackling the complexities of gender and violence. Janice Haaken's voice has become pivotal in the rethinking of domestic violence literature and research, ensuring that this book will become an essential text across the social sciences in all areas where gender is discussed." – **Lynne Segal, Psychosocial Studies, Birkbeck College, University of London, UK**

"This book is pioneering and courageous, employing psychoanalytic concepts to subvert those aspects of (white) feminist activist orthodoxy on domestic violence. The power of storytelling in shaping and transforming women's lives is evoked with reparative narratives which are explored to exhilarating effect." – **Paula Nicolson, Professor of Critical Social Health Psychology, Royal Holloway, University of London, UK**

"Janice Haaken – feminist researcher, clinician, and activist – grips us with her analysis of the stories we tell ourselves about family violence. Whether probing the complexities of victim narratives or examining the different ways feminists and activists narrate domestic violence, Haaken is a pioneer in extending psychoanalytic-feminist theory into the tough terrain of anti-violence politics. Essential reading for activists and gender studies theorists alike." – **Lynne Layton, Assistant Clinical Professor of Psychology, Harvard Medical School, USA**

WOMEN AND PSYCHOLOGY

Series Editor: Jane Ussher

School of Psychology, University of Western Sydney

This series brings together current theory and research on women and psychology. Drawing on scholarship from a number of different areas of psychology, it bridges the gap between abstract research and the reality of women's lives by integrating theory and practice, research and policy.

Each book addresses a "cutting edge" issue of research, covering such topics as post-natal depression, eating disorders, theories, and methodologies.

The series provides accessible and concise accounts of key issues in the study of women and psychology, and clearly demonstrates the centrality of psychology to debates within women's studies or feminism.

The Series Editor would be pleased to discuss proposals for new books in the series.

Other titles in this series:

THE THIN WOMAN
Helen Malson

THE MENSTRUAL CYCLE
Anne E. Walker

POST-NATAL DEPRESSION
Paula Nicolson

RE-THINKING ABORTION
Mary Boyle

WOMEN AND AGING
Linda R. Gannon

BEING MARRIED, DOING GENDER
Caroline Dryden

UNDERSTANDING DEPRESSION
Janet M. Stoppard

FEMININITY AND THE PHYSICALLY ACTIVE WOMAN
Precilla Y. L. Choi

GENDER, LANGUAGE AND DISCOURSE
Anne Weatherall

THE SCIENCE/FICTION OF SEX
Annie Potts

THE PSYCHOLOGICAL DEVELOPMENT OF GIRLS AND WOMEN
Sheila Greene

JUST SEX?
Nicola Gavey

WOMAN'S RELATIONSHIP WITH HERSELF
Helen O'Grady

GENDER TALK
Susan A. Speer

BEAUTY AND MISOGYNY
Sheila Jeffreys

BODY WORK
Sylvia K. Blood

MANAGING THE MONSTROUS FEMININE
Jane M. Ussher

THE CAPACITY TO CARE
Wendy Hollway

SANCTIONING PREGNANCY
Harriet Gross and Helen Pattison

ACCOUNTING FOR RAPE
Irina Anderson and Kathy Doherty

THE SINGLE WOMAN
Jill Reynolds

MATERNAL ENCOUNTERS
Lisa Baraitser

WOMEN AND DEPRESSION
Michelle N. Lafrance

UNDERSTANDING THE EFFECTS OF CHILD SEXUAL ABUSE
Sam Warner

THE GENDERED UNCONSCIOUS
Louise Gyler

HARD KNOCKS

Domestic Violence and the Psychology of Storytelling

Janice Haaken

Routledge
Taylor & Francis Group
LONDON AND NEW YORK

First published 2010 by Routledge
27 Church Road, Hove, East Sussex BN3 2FA

Simultaneously published in the USA and Canada
by Routledge
270 Madison Avenue, New York, NY 10016

Routledge is an imprint of the Taylor & Francis Group, an Informa business

Typeset in Times by Garfield Morgan, Swansea, West Glamorgan
Printed and bound in Great Britain by TJ International Ltd, Padstow, Cornwall
Paperback cover design by Terry Foley

This publication has been produced with paper manufactured to strict environmental standards and with pulp derived from sustainable forests.

British Library Cataloguing in Publication Data
A catalogue record for this book is available from the British Library

Library of Congress Cataloging in Publication Data
Haaken, Janice, 1947–
Hard knocks : domestic violence and the psychology of storytelling / Janice Haaken.
p. cm.
Includes bibliographical references and index.
ISBN 978-0-415-56338-3 (hbk. : alk. paper) – ISBN 978-0-415-56342-0 (soft cover : alk. paper)
1. Abused women–Services for–Citizen participation. 2. Family violence–Prevention–Citizen participation. 3. Storytelling–Psychological aspects. 4. Feminism. I. Title.
HV1444.H33 2010
362.82'92019–dc22
2009047293

ISBN: 978-0-415-56338-3 (hbk)
ISBN: 978-0-415-56342-0 (pbk)

FOR MY PARTNER, TOM BECKER,
WITH DEEP LOVE AND GRATITUDE

CONTENTS

ACKNOWLEDGEMENTS

In the decade of carrying out research and writing related to this book, I have had the joy of seeing many of my students receive their graduate degrees. Over the course of this project, Nan Yragui, Holly Fussell, Kevia Jeffrey, Diana Rempe, Courtenay Silvergleid, Ariel Ladum, and Karen Morgaine completed masters or doctoral projects. They brought ideas, passion, curiosity, and political commitments to the research team in ways that have sustained me and this project. In addition to a series of jointly authored papers, our team presented at dozens of conferences over the years. More recently, Jimena Alvarado joined my research team and helped in the final preparation of the manuscript.

Many close colleagues have sustained me through the history of this project as well. I want to thank Frederike Heuer, who assisted with the interviews carried out in Berlin in September, 2001 and made astute suggestions in developing a structure for the book manuscript. I also want to express my gratitude to Johanna Brenner and Marta Greenwald for their many insightful comments on drafts—and for allowing me to work through my anxieties and ideas over so many dinners and drinks. My colleague Eric Mankowski has been a key source of intellectual and comradely support as well. Working on a domestic violence research team together provided an encouraging place to test out the lines of thinking presented throughout this book.

The Psychology Department at Portland State University has been my intellectual home for the past 30 years, and I am honored to be among so many smart and caring academics who carry out research with the aim of bringing about a more just and humane world. I wish to express special thanks to Sherwin Davidson and Keith Kaufman for their steady support for this and other projects I have carried out through my career in the department.

For the many organizations and individuals who generously contributed their time and insights to this project, I want to express my most heartfelt thanks. Learning about the creative work of advocates throughout the world—so often unrecognized in the academic literature—has kept alive my belief in the power of sisterhood.

And finally, I want to thank my partner, Tom Becker, for his generosity and care in assisting with database management as well as in helping me to hold my life together.

INTRODUCTION

Stories about first experiences are as much about the present as they are about the past. In the course of writing this book, I often recalled my earliest consciousness-raising gathering. It was a divorce self-help group in the early 1970s—made up of mostly young white women, working low-wage jobs while going to school. Many of us had married during a time when college girls were expected to major in finding a good husband. With the dawning of a new age, many of us were now changing our majors. Wandering through the student union building at the University of Washington, I noticed a pink flyer offering the deliverance I was seeking: "For a fifty dollar filing fee, you can write your own divorce documents without the assistance of an attorney . . . come join us and learn together!"

Some in the group told stories of living hell—of having been brutally raped or beaten by their husbands. Others showed more ambiguous signs of suffering that, as Betty Friedan (1963) noted in *The Feminine Mystique*, "had no name." We understood our task, though, of bringing our various marital grievances into compliance with the only legal escape clause available at that time prior to no-fault divorce—*mental cruelty*. In my case, when the judge asked me to explain the nature of the cruelty I had endured, he was met with my tears and downcast eyes. "I don't want to talk about it," I demurred, summoning the evasive modesty accorded to women addressing such intimacies. Lacking a dramatic story, I nonetheless knew the cues. The mental cruelty category encompassed a vast array of female complaints, even as it required a consistently dramatic performance.

By the 1990s, domestic violence had emerged as a "legitimate" container for the unhappiness of women and similarly came to carry considerable cultural freight. In churches, schools, and police departments, groups gathered to discuss the problem of domestic violence and school themselves in the power-and-control motives of abusive men. Even in conservative religious communities, workshops on domestic violence opened space for women to address less readily articulated grievances in addition to physical abuse, from the unfair division of domestic responsibilities to suffering the emotional cruelty of husbands (Haaken *et al.*, 2007).

Hard Knocks builds on my previous work on explaining how stories of familial or domestic abuse acquire complex and varied social symbolic loadings over time (Haaken, 1998, 2002b, 2003). And much like my earlier work, this book enlists a long tradition of psychoanalytic feminist thought to advance a set of political aims. Although psychoanalysis has been used to pathologize women, it also has been used to diagnose those social pathologies that make women feel sick (Benjamin, 1988; Chodorow, 1978; Dinnerstein, 1976; Haaken, 1998; Layton *et al.*, 2006; Ussher, 2003). In their emphasis on the dynamic interplay of rational and non-rational elements of human consciousness, psychoanalytic approaches to social problems challenge rigid categories between rational (coded as masculine) and irrational (coded as feminine). Further, we may be better able to recognize our collective capacities to stir things up. Any force for social change inevitably becomes a fantasy object for the broader culture—a repository for diffuse anxieties, fears, and longings. Just as the oppressed must learn to read between the lines of everyday encounters, so, too, must activists be equipped to read the subtexts of dominant modes of storytelling.

More than other major theoretical traditions in the field of psychology, psychoanalysis places storytelling at the center of human development. As such, it offers a rich legacy of ideas that may be applied to processes of individual and social transformation. Social change involves finding new uses for old stories, and means of breaking out of stereotypical scripts to find alternative denouements. How, for example, do we make use of the intrigue generated by the trope of "behind closed doors" in the domestic violence field and claim cultural space for less dramatic revelations of female suffering?[1] And how do we separate the voyeuristic pleasures produced by portrayals of intimate hidden crimes from their subversive possibilities? These distinctions require that we listen closely to how the story is being told, to the positions of various protagonists, and to recurring themes, motifs, and subtexts in the narrative resolution of the drama.

In attending to storytelling dynamics in the history of domestic violence work, I describe throughout this book recurring plots and sub-plots deployed and chart their migrations across the political landscape. Although many advocates and activists in the domestic violence field are, themselves, battered women, others are engaged in the issue because the bruises and broken bones of women symbolize the broader struggle against patriarchy and sexism.[2] Early organizers of Bradley Angle House in the United States, one of the oldest shelters in the world, describe how their stories of hard living and surviving on the streets aroused less interest than portraits of mothers escaping despotic husbands. At the same time, they recognized how wife beating was "a symbol for what was happening to us" (Bradley Angle, 1978: 44).

Stories recounted here are drawn from over 200 interviews with advocates in the field, as well as from films, novels, pamphlets, and self-help books that were cited in the interviews and in the various training sessions and workshops that I attended over five years of field research. Through this research, I show how storytelling practices became increasingly stereotypical and narrowly scripted as battle fatigue overtook the field. Nonetheless, a rich storehouse of cultural knowledge emerged—much of which has operated "behind closed doors" in the movement itself. Storytelling served as the portal of entry to this background knowledge—what might be termed the *social unconscious* of the movement—and to forms of collective remembering that may be useful in thinking through present dilemmas.

This book takes its title from the idea that fighting for social change requires toughness. Women who have suffered the hardest knocks under patriarchy, whether victims of rape, incest, domestic assault, sex trafficking, or war, occupy special positions in the cultural legacy of grassroots feminism. More than other images of female victims, the stories of battered wives circulate as cautionary tales about the lethal potential of romantic love.

The title of the book also carries the echo of lessons from my childhood. While reverential toward places of higher learning, my father, who was never able to go to college, often described himself as a product of the "school of hard knocks." He protected us from the full scope of his street curriculum, but one lesson was clear: It is important to stand up and fight for what you think is right. I took this lesson into my early feminist radicalism, adopting the principle that those who suffer the direct blows of the system are most positioned to resist it.[3] Radical feminism took up this campaign of wife beating—as well as many other campaigns—with the toughness of a street fighter. And this toughness had its costs, just as it does for other fighters.

The book re-visits four battle zones in the history of this movement where narrative responses to conflicts rigidified over time and where signs of battle fatigue have been most acute. First, there is the conflict between the battered women's movement and the state, and feminist ambivalence over the role of the police as both enemy and ally of abused women. A second front concerns the relationship between domestic violence and other social problems, and the question of whether woman battering is a special case that differs from other forms of social violence. The third conflict centers on tensions between groups of women within the movement, and how to address differences based on race, class, or other dimensions of power, including understandings of what constitutes violence. A fourth involves the contentious issue of how to acknowledge forms of female aggression while still preserving a gender analysis of intimate partner violence. In taking up this last conflict, I address what most advocates wrestle uneasily with on a day-to-day basis: the knowledge that many abused women bring complex psychological dynamics of their own into their embattled attachments (Renzetti, 1994, 1999; Ristock, 2002).

In working through dilemmas that arise in constructing stories about domestic abuse, I make use of one of the oldest rhetorical devices of the movement: the counterposing of *myth* and *fact* (Okum, 1986; Pagelow, 1992). From the earliest consciousness-raising of the 1970s through contemporary educational campaigns, advocates have distributed myth/fact sheets challenging conventional assumptions about abused women. For example, the assumption that "domestic violence is primarily a problem of poor people" may be followed by the "fact" that domestic violence cuts across all class and race boundaries. This coupling of counter-claims transfers the battered woman from the economic margins to the very center of society. The battered wife is recast as Every Woman.

In this book, I counterpose myth and what I term "*counter-myth.*" Rather than presenting feminist rebuttals as facts, I prefer the term "counter-myth" because it suggests a problematic affinity between the two claims. Indeed, the rhetorical dichotomizing of "myths" and "facts" builds on what Roland Barthes (1972: 129) describes as a key founding myth of bourgeois society—the assertion of facts separate from those signifying contexts (and forms of power) that produce knowledge: "The bourgeois class has precisely built its power on technical, scientific progress," set in opposition to myth.[4] Trumping myths with "factual claims" is part of this bourgeois universalizing tendency—the hubris of speaking as if from a position of nowhere.

The mythic disguise—what Barthes (1972) describes as the *metalanguage* of myth—lies in its disavowal of the web of linguistic and cultural signifiers surrounding its claims. The myth both declares a truth and prohibits scrutiny. In the claim that domestic violence is only a problem for poor people, for example, feminists rightfully expose the racist and class associations invoked through such speech acts. But the claim that domestic violence is more common in poor communities may be understood as a fact in either conservative or progressive ways, depending on the contexts enlisted in explaining links between poverty and violence.

My use of the term "*counter-myth*" in describing feminist "facts" does not mean that these refutations are false. In that they do "reveal the political load of the world" (Barthes, 1972: 146), feminist "facts" represent an advance over the claims they counter. But feminist facts operate as myths when they are accepted without question—when truth claims, in the words of Barthes (1972: 148), are "reduced to a litany." Put psychoanalytically, facts may operate as an obsessive defense against ambiguity. And those areas where the lived experiences of women belie feminist factual claims—an issue taken up throughout this book—are precisely those areas where we can see group dynamics at work.

In analyzing dilemmas that have emerged in the history of the battered women's movement, *Hard Knocks* also offers a theory of storytelling, with a particular focus on what I term "*subversive storytelling.*" Many scholars who study the psychology of storytelling suggest that the mind is organized to generate coherent accounts (Gergen & Gergen, 1986; Mankowski & Rappaport, 1995; Nelson, 1989). Novel or emotionally arousing events are particularly ripe for generating stories—for explaining what happened, why it happened, and who was responsible (Bruner, 1990). But not all arousing stories find receptive audiences—a point often overlooked in the social scientific literature that maps this same cultural terrain. My focus on subversive storytelling addresses this political dimension of the problem, where contests emerge over the legitimacy of particular accounts and their social interpretations (Haaken, 1998).

Stories are typically structured around a series of actions: something happens that disrupts the normal state of affairs and a conflict (or series of conflicts) arises that is then resolved by the end of the story. The denouement may be unhappy or ambiguous, but stories are expected to offer some sort of ending. In my work as a clinician, research interviewer, and documentary filmmaker, I am particularly interested in the beginnings and endings of stories. The beginning sets the stage for the framing of the conflict and introduces the protagonists that drive the story forward. The ending brings some form of closure, even as it may "repress" alternative resolutions by appearing as the natural outcome of events. As Mark Freeman (2004: 65) suggests, "only when a story has ended—whether the ending is temporary, as in life, or permanent, as in death—is it possible to discern the meaning and significance of what has come before." Ideological readings of stories require that we uncover the role of social power in this narrative work of the ending and how ruling modes of story production may foreclose on the range of alternative resolutions.

My own ambivalent struggle with radical feminist politics in the 1970s and 1980s, as the strong and uncompromising "mother" of my early political education, informs this project just as it does much of my earlier scholarship on gender dynamics and processes of social change (Haaken, 1998, 1999, 2002b, 2003). Radical feminists—important protagonists in the gripping dramas portrayed in this book—have been much maligned by critics. Donald Dutton (Dutton & Corvo, 2007; Dutton & Nicholls, 2005; Dutton *et al.*, 2009), a leading critic of feminist scholarship on domestic violence, has built a career out of casting feminists as censorious and powerful enough to block scientific advancements at the national level. His characterizing of "the feminist paradigm" casts a wide and undifferentiated net, however, over a complex history of feminist scholarship. Dutton offers that radical feminism "views all social relations through the prism of gender relations and holds, in its neo-Marxist view, that men (the bourgeoisie) hold power advantages over women (the proletariat) in patriarchal societies . . ." (Dutton & Nicholls, 2005: 682). This collapsing of feminist and Marxist categories under the rubric of radical feminism overlooks the complex history of feminist scholarship, including differences in liberal, cultural, radical, socialist, and Marxist feminist positions on conceptualizing violence (Donovan, 1996). In summarily dismissing feminism, Dutton fails to map the very terrain on which he stakes his claims.

Yet it has been difficult for *feminists* as well to critically reflect on practices in the field of domestic violence. Many of the critiques presented here grew out of my social justice activism and work with feminists who attend to the intersections of interpersonal and structural forms of violence such as unemployment, poverty, and the prison/industrial complex (Crenshaw, 1994; Davis, 2000; Incite!, 2005; Richie, 2000; Sokoloff, 2005). Drawing on the moral authority and insights of women of color, I have, as a white feminist, called for more attentiveness to class and race as they shape experiences with and interpretations of domestic violence (Haaken, 2002a, 2008b). I also have been wary of over-reliance on the good female victim/bad male perpetrator typology because women, as well as men, can be cast out of the category of the "good" and viewed as collaborating with the enemy when questioning deeply held tenets in the field.[5]

Cathy Humphreys has pointed out the tendency to rely on "atrocity stories" in advancing the aim of child protection in the domestic violence field (Humphreys & Stanley, 2006: 21). My interest on a political level is to identify the relative *progressiveness* or *regressiveness* of a range of cultural narratives where the drama centers on a domestic abuse scene. Gergen and Gergen (1988, 1997) introduced these terms into narrative psychology to distinguish plots that move the protagonist forward developmentally through the integration of conflict, on the one hand, and those that represent loss of capacities or disintegration on the other. These psychological distinctions between progressive and regressive resolutions of narrative dilemmas may be at odds, however, with political readings of these same narratives. My use of the terms refers to the extent to which the narrative subverts conventional denouements and invites a critical and complex engagement with those human dilemmas at the center of the drama.

PSYCHOLOGY OF STORYTELLING

Any project of social change requires some understanding of human psychology. Alternatives to oppression are not a given but rather must be imagined and this imaginative work requires some theory of mind and of how to change minds. As a psychologist, I spend a great deal of my time listening to stories that are hard to tell, either because the experiences are difficult to put into words or because others are uneasy and therefore stop listening. The accounts of battered women are most certainly difficult to hear, and thus are vulnerable to unconscious structuring—or filling in of the gaps—on the part of the listener (Leisey, 2008).

Although the leading early theorist of the movement, Lenore Walker, is a psychologist, most in the field have jettisoned her work on the *battered woman syndrome* and *cycles of violence*, arguing that domestic violence is a political rather than a psychological problem (Allard, 1991; Bograd, 1984; Ieda, 1986; Pence & Paymar, 1993; Roche & Sadoski, 1996). The rejection of psychology is overdetermined,[6] however, by less readily articulated anxieties in the field. One concern grows from fear that psychology is a zero sum game—that any acknowledgement of pain or suffering in the lives of violent men, for example, means lost ground for women. Further, domestic violence—what is now more commonly termed "intimate partner violence"—seems to generate *too much* psychology to manage politically rather than too little. Domestic violence differs from other social problems faced by women in that it typically takes place in the context of adult relationships. While date rape, pornography, and sex work generally involve younger women, domestic violence is an issue that more often affects women who have been in relationships with men for some time (Lawson, 1989).[7]

In bringing psychology back into conversations about domestic abuse, *Hard Knocks* makes extensive use of psychoanalytic social theory as well as feminist theory—an approach that focuses on group dynamics and how unconscious anxieties and defenses operate on societal levels (Alford, 1989; Nicolson, 1996; Zaretsky, 2004). Working psychoanalytically means that transference processes—how participants bring emotionally charged experiences from the past into present encounters—are important to explore. Although *social* psychology served as the primary lens on this project of looking back on the battered women's movement, most people associate psychology with clinical work. Advocates interviewed over the course of this research generally began by emphasizing how psychologists blame the victim, promote psychotherapeutic change in ways that put women at risk, and redeem men by focusing on childhood trauma rather than on male power and control motives. Psychoanalytic psychology is viewed as particularly suspect, advocates insist, because the focus on unconscious motivation bypasses the political source of the problem. Further, introducing the concept of the unconscious, with its tricky reversals, seems to redeem men and villainize women.

This book represents my long response to those concerns. But in the interviews, I posed the question of why the domestic violence field has been so notably resistive to psychology, even after decades of research and theorizing by feminist psychologists. There is a robust history of critical feminist thought that makes use of psychology to analyze the relationship between social power and gender dynamics (Benjamin, 1988; Butler, 1997; Dinnerstein, 1976; hooks, 1992; Mitchell, 1974; Rose, 1986). Many psychoanalytic feminists have laid claim to the critical methods of Freud as well, including elements of his theory of gender development (Chodorow, 1978;

Harris, 2005; Ussher, 2008). Take, for example, early feminist critiques of Freud's infamous concept of penis envy. In societies where the phallus operates as a symbol of power and signifier of hierarchical differences, girls and women may, indeed, come to resent and envy the "phallus"—which may be any signifier of masculine entitlement or power—and may come to fear their own aggressive impulses as well (Benjamin, 1988; Dinnerstein, 1976; Frosh, 1995).

THE BATTERED WOMEN'S MOVEMENT

Prior to contemporary feminism, men who beat their wives were cast as losers, the degenerate side of the social order. According to conventional thinking, powerful men—those successful enough to inspire genuine devotion in their wives—need not resort to brute force. The popular American television show of the 1950s, *The Honeymooners*, satirized working-class men who tried to show their women "who's the boss." Jackie Gleason played a fat and ineffectual husband who asserted his manhood by threatening to smack his wife. Undaunted by such pathetic displays, his wife vacillated between protecting and puncturing her husband's hyper-inflated ego.

The battered women's movement intervened in this cultural script, recasting the characters on the stage. Rather than a series of isolated tragedies, with each woman coping with her own terrible fate, feminists identified a social pattern in the abuses women suffered in the domestic sphere. The bruises and broken bones of beaten wives viscerally displayed what second-wave feminists advanced in pamphlets and at rallies: the home is a dangerous place for women (Koss *et al.*, 1994; Walker, 1979b).

Feminists also created new denouements to the story of wife beating. Rather than turning to male protectors, women sought refuge in their collective strength. Hundreds of crisis centers and shelters, run by and for women, were established throughout North America, Europe, and Britain in the 1970s (Dobash & Dobash, 1979; Martin, 1976; Pleck, 1987). The claim that all women were equally vulnerable to male violence, which emerged as the rallying cry of the movement, challenged the seductive fantasy that women could individually negotiate their fate and find security in the arms of a good man.

Of all of the campaigns of feminism, the movement against woman battering has achieved incontestable moral victories. No other issue separates old and new world attitudes as decisively as does that of wife beating.[8] More than fights for equal pay, abortion rights, paid parental leave, health care, or gender equality in the household, the campaign against domestic violence has won support across a wide political spectrum. Growing from an underground network of safe houses in the 1970s to national and international campaigns in the 1980s and 1990s, the battered women's movement was a powerful impetus behind the 1993 United Nations Declaration on the Elimination of Violence against Women. In the following year, the movement achieved enough momentum in the United States to secure passage in 1994 of the Violence Against Women Act (VAWA) in the US Congress. This momentous victory also created the Office on Violence Against Women in the United States Department of Justice. VAWA ushered in an unprecedented 30 million dollars in funding for shelters and other crisis services for women, as well as funds for tighter law enforcement (Goldfarb, 2000). Pressed by this initiative and global human rights initiatives carried out by women, in the 1990s the European Union brought domestic violence onto the parliamentary agenda as well, although with fewer binding directives than legislation in the United States (Morgaine, 2007).

The sheer numbers of victimized women and the dizzying array of statistics generated by governmental and non-governmental organizations—with rates ranging from five percent to 73 percent of women reporting domestic assaults, depending on definitions and procedures for counting—ran the risk of overwhelming feminist efforts to frame the problem (Kelly *et al.*, 2001; Klein, 1998). Drawing domestic violence survivors from around the world into a common fold carried the risk of overriding differences in their experiences, as well as erasing from the picture more impersonal or structural forms of violence. For women of color, particularly, there was a painful irony in proclamation after proclamation in the 1990s to "Stop Violence Against Women" as these very same institutions supported economic policies that plowed women down (Incite!, 2005; Kelly *et al.*, 2001; Volpp, 2005).

Although mobilizing around a unifying story of woman battering was an advance, the search for a single voice in resisting male violence in the household also meant that some voices were inevitably shouted down. For women of color concentrated in unstable working-class communities, the combustible atmosphere of family life was not so readily contained behind closed doors, nor was the boundary that separates various sources of bad treatment so distinct (Collins, 1998; Richie, 2000; West, 1999; White, 1985). In her analysis of domestic violence stories in lesbian communities, Janice Ristock (2002) similarly calls for deeper reflection on how feminists frame domestic violence as a social problem. She offers that "we need a much more adaptive, context-sensitive analysis to figure out what is going on" (2002: xi) and that this process can be "anxiety-provoking for feminism" because it is associated with the loss of a gender analysis (2002: 121). Critical space for addressing such anxieties has widened in recent years but so, too, has the movement toward "gender symmetry" in approaching the issue—a movement of considerable concern to feminist researchers in the field (DeKeseredy, 2006; DeKeseredy & Dragiewicz, 2007; Straus, 2006).[9]

In the early 1990s, Kimberlé Crenshaw (1994) introduced the concept of "*intersectionality*" to critique "Eurocentric" feminist models that over-universalize and over-simplify links between gender and domestic violence. She emphasizes the dynamic interplay of systems of oppression in shaping women's experiences of violence—and that any system of domination produces forms of violence. Rather than an additive model, for example, listing the double or triple oppressions of women, feminist models must be extended to include structural forms of violence, such as denial of food, housing, work, and other means of survival, and attend to the combustible contexts where the overwhelming stresses of life can erupt into violence.[10] Crenshaw (1994: 100) charges that the "gag order" within feminism on "discussing higher rates of domestic violence in poor communities" has marginalized the voices of poor women. Beth Richie (2000: 1134–1135) concurs, observing that, however well intended, the initial strategy of downplaying differences in the impact of gender violence in women's lives has been a costly one, particularly for women of color, and has contributed to "a national advocacy response based on a false sense of unity around the experience of gender oppression." Similarly, Ristock (2002: 125) calls for "a language of power that allows us to map the multiple and interlocking nature of identity" and how such identities are enacted in violent relationships. Yet these critiques have not been integrated into the dominant storytelling practices of the field, even as calls for attending to "multiple oppressions" gain currency in domestic violence conferences and trainings.[11]

FEMINIST SOCIAL ACTION RESEARCH

My research continues to be fuelled by the passions that drew me into the field of psychology in the 1970s. During the course of my graduate training, I learned about radical traditions of psychoanalysis and social action research. In calling for researchers to leave their laboratories and enter the field of real social problems, Kurt Lewin (1975, c1951: 169), the founder of social action research in psychology, quipped that "there is nothing so practical as a good theory." I was most intrigued by the Lewin aphorism, "If you want to understand something, try to change it."[12] His program of research was oriented toward practical problems but action research also depended on good theory—ways of seeing and understanding how things may fit together within some explanatory framework.

A primary aim of a series of studies carried out by my research team over a period of five years, a program of inquiry that included interviews with advocates in a number of countries, centered on understanding how cultural and historical contexts shape the elaboration of stories about domestic abuse. As the culmination of that program of research, this book takes up what Amy Shuman (1986) terms competing "*storytelling rights*"—contestations over how stories should be told and who (or which group) has the right to tell them. For social action researchers, the negotiation of storytelling rights is an ongoing process rather than a problem that can be settled procedurally, for example through consent forms (Fine, 1998; Fine & Vanderslice, 1992; Kidder & Fine, 1997). The question of who has the right to tell stories about abused women would include discussion of whether there are sufficient life experiences in common, but also understandings of shared political commitments. Yet commitments and other areas of identity give rise to storytelling in complex ways—a quandary taken up in this book.

Rather than focusing on the accounts of abused women, my research team at Portland State University carried out a series of studies focused on *advocates*—volunteers, staff, activists, and program directors—who intervene in domestic violence situations and assist women in giving voice to their experiences. Much like other social problems, the field of family violence involves a vast array of experts whose job it is to "name the problem" and help victims generate accounts of their experiences.[13] For example, using the term "your batterer" rather than "your boyfriend" (or his name) when women enter a shelter does structure the woman's account. It creates social distance between the woman and her partner, and it confronts her with the seriousness of his behavior. Although this may be helpful for the woman in crisis, women's advocates may be unaware of how such structuring overrides aspects of an abused woman's own account.[14]

Social action research orients knowledge production toward social change. Feminist traditions of social action research, or participatory action research, are intensely collaborative (Fine, 1998; Fine & Vanderslice, 1992; Kidder & Fine, 1997). *Hard Knocks* draws on these traditions in creating a conversation among women's advocates on dilemmas in the history of the movement. My use of the term "*conversation*" is not simply rhetorical. The interviews were carried out very much as conversations—as collaborative engagement on difficult questions. Although there were sets of interviewing questions,[15] the format also allowed for "free associations" with the questions and discussion of the stories that emerged in individual and group discussions.[16]

My approach was to enlist the interviewees, whether as individuals or groups, in a process of analyzing the movement. In this sense, we were a group reflecting on our practices and revisiting some of the emotionally charged terrain where battles had been fought and positions had hardened. In entering this terrain, I sometimes used the analogy of post-traumatic stress to suggest how movements, not unlike soldiers on battle fields, can suffer forms of shell shock. Most of the advocates contacted welcomed this line of inquiry, even though it meant revisiting old questions that many felt had been settled long ago.

In recounting the stories of this movement, *Hard Knocks* brings the *locale* into view—the character of the many places in which women have organized around battering. This book is predominantly structured around conversations carried out with advocates in Berlin, Germany; London and Manchester, England; New York City; and Pine Ridge Reservation in South Dakota, United States. In addition to these four major geographical sites, five separate studies carried out by the research team and interviews with advocates in other locales are integrated into the analysis presented here. The four geographical sites were selected because each had long histories of innovative domestic violence intervention. I weave together scholarly sources on the history of the movement and the oral histories that emerged from the interviews carried out with women, and some men, working on domestic violence in the various geographical settings.

While there is broad agreement that men batter as a means of establishing power and control over women, the consultations reported here go beyond this basic point of commonality to identify areas where women's experiences diverge, and where national history and social identities shape understandings of the problem. I was interested in how the broader political landscape shaped the differing histories of activism and how related social problems, for example, housing politics, welfare policies, child protection services, and immigration rights, influenced the ways advocates thought about the dynamics of family violence. I also was interested in social class as it both brings people together around common interests and struggles, whether as workers, managers, or owning classes, and produces differences in relation to the problem of violence. In the domestic violence field, I have been interested in how class positions shape understandings of what constitutes abuse and violence as well as what should be done about it.[17]

In analyzing transcripts from the research interviews, my research team and I sought to identify junctures where respondents discussed what could be described as a standard "line" in the field. We wanted to unpack these points where defensive stances hardened into stereotypical responses. There are compelling reasons, we understood, for adopting a standard line on a political issue (Kingsolver, 1989). Indeed, social movements require some capacity to unify around shared positions in resisting the status quo. Training materials often provide "scripts" for responding to questions, such as that of why some women stay in abusive relationships. However, as anti-violence activists, many of my students and I shared a concern that the mainstream literature in the domestic violence field had become too narrowly scripted.

In identifying the participants, we adopted an approach where participants in group interviews would remain anonymous in order to allow for greater freedom of discussion. Those who offered to be interviewed individually could choose to either remain anonymous or be cited by name. All advocates interviewed individually did choose to be identified by name.

In presenting the findings, I have attempted to preserve the structure of the stories that emerged as well as the ethnographic feel of the settings.[18]

THE CHAPTERS

Hard Knocks focuses on dilemmas at the level of both theory and practice, and on knowledge that emerges through struggle. Each chapter begins with a myth and counter-myth in order to open up a creative space between two opposing claims. By starting each chapter with a pair of myths and counter-myths, my aim is to create a conversation—to bring together the many intelligent, committed, passionate women (and some men) who participated in this series of interviews. In so doing, it is my hope that their insights will reach a wider audience.

The book is divided into two parts. Part 1, "Dilemmas of theory," focuses on key ideas that have guided the movement through the broad contours of its history. My aim here is to identify recurring sources of group conflict in the movement and show how a feminist psychology can offer insights in addressing those conflicts. Chapter 1 addresses the claim that domestic violence transcends race and class differences. This chapter takes up feminist perspectives that unfold through advocates' accounts of conflicts that arose as domestic violence expanded from a radical feminist to a mainstream political issue. Chapter 2 brings psychology into the conversation, beginning with competing ideas about whether psychology takes the field forward or backward. The chapter goes beyond clinical approaches to family violence, introducing psychoanalytic social theory to bridge individual, couple, and group contexts for understanding violence. Chapter 3 introduces a psychoanalytic cultural theory of storytelling, making use of ideas in the field of literary criticism. In describing three genres that have emerged in the domestic violence field—stories of bondage, stories of deliverance, and stories of struggle and reparation—this chapter offers ways of framing the development of narrative strategies over time in the battered women's movement.

Part 2, "Dilemmas of practice," covers three areas of acute *border tensions* in advocacy work—areas where emotional investments in drawing boundaries between feminist and non-feminist practices are particularly intense. Chapter 4 focuses on the symbolic and practical meanings of shelters (or refuges) for battered women and on group defenses that emerge in women's crisis work. Chapter 5 explores controversies over batterer intervention programs. In identifying dilemmas that arise in working with batterers, I address tensions surrounding the coordination of feminist and criminal justice system responses to violence. Chapter 6 examines the conflicted relationship between child advocates and women's advocates in the field of family violence. A key issue concerns the tendency to cast women as either abusers (as mothers) or victims (as wives) in the choreography of family violence.

The Conclusions summarize the key findings of the book and highlight promising models of collaborative work—models suggestive of the radical possibilities of the women's anti-violence movement. Many of these projects involve minority communities—spaces and places where women, and some men, work at the intersection of gender, race, and class and confront on a daily basis the interdependence of private and public forms of suffering. In gathering up stories and their various plotlines and competing interpretations, I hope to show how the narrative resources of a movement can be as critical to survival as material resources—and sometimes just as hard to defend.

NOTES

1 The metaphor of "behind closed doors" has been used throughout the history of the battered women's movement to signify both the hidden nature of crimes against women in the private sphere and social blindness to the phenomenon. See, as an early example, Straus *et al.* (1980).
2 Linda Gordon (2007) points out how the terms "*patriarchy*" and "*sexism*" are often used interchangeably. She limits the term "patriarchy" to kinship-based modes of production where the senior males—often the oldest males—hold positions of power and authority over group members. In a patriarchal structure, males are subjected to the power of senior males but they also inherit rights to gain access to power or compete for power.
3 Men, like women, are brutalized by patriarchal societies—as casualties of war and exploitive labor under the control of more powerful men. But women have been more apt to resist the system of patriarchy because they are offered fewer compensating rewards. Patricia Hill Collins (1998) suggests that women of color have fewer illusions still about patriarchy because they are not protected in the same way as are white women from the brutality of the system.
4 In rejecting the hubris of modern science, set in opposition to "primitive" or archaic knowledge, anthropologist Micea Eliade (1967: 27) suggests that, "The myth never quite disappears from the present world of the psyche; it only changes its aspect and disguises its operations." Micea credits Freud with exposing the various disguises of the modern subject—how fantasies originating in infancy retain their hold at an unconscious level on the subject even as he (or she) enters adulthood. He also contrasts the Platonic idealism of Jung's collective unconscious, with the psyche as storehouse of fixed archetypes, with Freud's focus on psychic instability and the infantile substrate of fantasies that find their way into the symbolic social order, for example, religious systems of thought.
5 In her autobiographical accounts, Erin Pizzey, founder of the refuge movement in Britain, offers many stories of how she was persecuted and villainized by feminists who were critical of her positions on domestic violence, and particularly her stance that women could be as violent as men. See http://www.erinpizzey.com
6 The psychoanalytic concept of "overdetermination" is related to the notion of multiple causes, particularly in bringing into focus more historically remote and

less consciously accessible determinants of consciousness (Davis, 1988). This same concept has been taken up in critical social theory, particularly through the work of Althusser (1969).

7 This claim is complicated by findings that abused women are more apt to seek help when children become involved (see Stubbs, 2002).

8 Wife beating occurs in countries throughout the world, including in Western countries, as have campaigns organized by women in opposition to this and other forms of violence against women. A central focus of this book, however, is the symbolic resonances of the issue, including its associations with traditional and delegitimized forms of male power.

9 See, for example, the special issue on "The Development of a Theory of Women's Use of Violence in Intimate Relationships" in *Violence Against Women*, *12*, 2006. Swan and Snow (2006: 1039) call for the "study of women's violence within social, historical, and cultural contexts" and greater attentiveness to both "risk and protective factors that appear to be related to women's use of violence with male partners." While acknowledging such contexts, they do not take up the theoretical and political task of addressing where such considerations conflict with earlier feminist formulations. The result is more of a listing of factors than a re-theorizing of links between gender and violence.

10 In *Domestic violence at the margins: Readings on race, class, gender, and culture* (Sokoloff, 2005), contributors draw on Crenshaw's concept of intersectionality to critique Euro-centric feminist universalizing models and widen the social and cultural contexts for thinking through feminist interventions.

11 In most of the volunteer trainings that I attended, materials included a focus on "white privilege," "heterosexual privilege," as well as "male privilege." These multiple presentations tended to be presented additively rather than integrated into a coherent analysis, however, so that one evening one might learn that "women are rarely perpetrators of domestic assault" and the next week that "lesbian battering is a hidden epidemic," with no attentiveness to the apparent contradiction between the two claims.

12 There has been some controversy over the source of this widely cited quote by Lewin and its authenticity.

13 In *Dangerous passage*, Constance Nathanson (1991) analyzes shifting discourses in the United States over teen pregnancy and how such discourses register broader cultural anxieties over challenges to social boundaries and how youth, and females paticularly, operate as sites for a range of projected anxieties..

14 For analysis of battered women's ways of understanding abuse based on qualitative research in a range of countries, see Klein (1998).

15 For a list of interview questions and protocols, contact the author.

16 For discussion of psychoanalytic methods of research interviewing, see Devisch (2006) and Hollway (2004).

17 The stratification model is often used in the social sciences to introduce social class as a variable. For Marxist frameworks for understanding class formations within capitalism, see Ehrenreich (1989) and Thompson (1966).

18 The interviews were audio-taped and took place over four or five days in each of the settings, with group interviews comprised of six to 12 advocates from a range of domestic violence organizations in the region. Although groups included individuals holding a range of positions, from volunteers, line staff, lawyers, program directors to probation officers, I use the term "*advocate*" because all of the interviewees described themselves as women's advocates, a role that conveys political alliances with women as well as provision of specific crisis services. In addition to the group interviews, which lasted approximately two hours, I visited

a number of the programs in each of the regions and sought out women of color who played key roles in domestic violence programs. Between four and six individual interviews took place in each site, each of which was approximately an hour long.

Part 1

DILEMMAS OF THEORY

1

HARD GROUND: FROM SOLITARY SUFFERING TO SISTERHOOD

Myth: Domestic violence occurs primarily in poor communities.
Counter-myth: Domestic violence cuts across all race, ethnic, and social class boundaries.

Stories about beating and being beaten are common in the folk psychology of everyday life. One such story operates as a parable: A worker is humiliated by his boss. This worker then goes home and beats his wife, who then hits her child, who then kicks the dog. It is a simple story but one that carries a potent psychological idea about the dangers of displaced aggression and how feelings of powerlessness and rage are readily displaced from an original source of anger onto a less threatening person or object. The story also illustrates how family hierarchies operate as shock absorbers in the world of work, since the story begins with deference to an abusive boss.

While this story contains a kernel of folk wisdom, the plotline may obscure important differences in forms of power that operate at various sites where aggression is displaced from one object to another. For the man who submits to the power of a boss, home is indeed a place where he can retreat and recoup his injured pride. Further, the release of aggression does not offer the same return for the wife, the child, or the dog as it does for the man. Whatever cathartic value in the displaced aggression of the wife or the child, there is less cultural entitlement for them to make someone pay for their misery. Feminists in the battered women's movement struggle to restructure such tales about family violence and to show how gender operates as a site of unequal emotional and economic exchange (Dobash & Dobash, 1979; Martin, 1976; Schechter, 1982; Yllo, 1993). In some feminist re-tellings of the parable, the wife/child/dog trio occupies the position of the subjugated, with the husband as lord and master. From this perspective, there is only one story to tell: The man beats his wife.

While this feminist re-telling interrupts the chain of perpetually displaced responsibility for aggression, it represses the many variations in women's stories about family violence, as well as the problem of displaced aggression in oppressed communities. In *Pedagogy of the oppressed*, Paulo Freire (1970, 1999) describes this defense as part of the destructive legacy of colonization. Friere explains how developing critical consciousness requires some understanding of how the oppressed may turn a hated part of themselves, the bitter psychic toll of colonization, onto others among the oppressed.

This chapter draws out the dilemmas feminists confront in theorizing commonalities and differences in women's experiences with violence by tracking those dilemmas through the history of the movement. This historical context sets the stage for subsequent chapters and a more careful reading of conflicts that surfaced. By working at the borders of group defenses in various locales and recognizing how defenses have a range of effects, both protective and destructive, we may be better able to analyze the impasses that emerged. One key question guiding this inquiry into the history of the movement centered on the development of social identities for advocates in the various settings. How did women come to identify with the issue of woman battering? And how did historical contexts shape the stories that emerged around woman battering?

In mapping the terrain of feminist identities that emerged in the various locales, I began with the assumption that women confront many of the same dilemmas as do men in monitoring in-group/out-group boundaries. Vamik Volkan (2009) argues that emotional investments in "us and them" distinctions form the central axis of large group identifications. Drawing on the object relations tradition in psychoanalytic theory and his own research in conflict zones around the world, Volkan suggests that humans are predisposed to projection and externalization of threats through their long period of early dependency. In recognizing that the loved maternal object is the very same as the object of its terrifying rage, the infant manages anxiety through an early form of splitting—of separating representations of the "good mother" (gratifying images or sensations) and the "bad mother" (disturbing or anxiety-provoking images and sensations). By keeping images of the bad object separate from the good object, the infant is able to preserve a good self/good object representation that protects against overwhelming anxiety. In the course of human development, children increasingly are able to integrate the good and the bad in themselves and in their primary attachments. Volkan suggests that periods of social crisis, whether threats of war or social upheaval, revive these infantile anxieties and forms of splitting associated with their management.

Sometimes, however, there really *is* an "us" and a "them." Defensive distortions may take the form of minimizing or denying threats as much as they take the form of amplifying them. Groups may face actual enemies—in the power of oppressors—and they may at the same time come to depend on images of the oppressor in the maintenance of feelings of internal wellbeing. Further, chronic crises may produce forms of hypervigilance and a readiness to perceive threats.

By attending more closely to stories about the history of the movement, we may be better able to understand sources of group conflict that arose in fighting male violence. As a starting point for accounts that unfolded in the interviews, the following section opens with a story about the first global summit of the movement and the uprising of international organizing that followed—a powerful event often lost in the collective memory of the movement.

A TALE OF MANY CITIIES

In 1976, over 2,000 women from 33 countries attended the International Tribunal on Crimes Against Women in Brussels, ushering in a dramatic moment in the early history of the campaign against woman abuse. Breaking from the traditional role of weeping wives, women cried out in a chorus of outrage. In combating woman battering, the women called for the "complete restructuring of the traditional family." Diane Russell describes the radical demands women voiced at this historical event:

> Until the division of labor in the family is transformed into one of equal responsibilities for rearing children, caring for the home, and providing for the family financially, women will be relatively powerless both in the family and outside of it, and violence against women will continue to be a problem.
>
> (cited in Martin, 1976: xii)

Whether liberal, radical, or socialist in their politics, feminists shared a critique of the patriarchal family (Donovan, 1996). Founded on principles of human rights, specifically the right to be free of terror and torture, the animus of the anti-battering campaign was its foregrounding of the home as a dangerous zone for women (Dobash & Dobash, 1979; Martin, 1976). The contract under patriarchy in the capitalist era offered women protection and economic support in exchange for services provided in the context of marriage. The battered women's movement exposed this contract as fraudulent, pointing out that women were at greater risk in their homes than on the streets (Koss *et al.*, 1994; Walker, 1979b).

Achieving economic independence from men was a shared premise, but feminists diverged in their analyses of the obstacles women faced once they crossed the threshold of the household and entered the labor force. While some feminists viewed patriarchy as the basic problem and gender as the prototype of other systems of domination, other feminists argued that gender oppression varied historically and worldwide, and that social class was more fundamental than gender in structures of domination (see Donovan, 1996; Schechter, 1982). Still other feminists introduced *dual systems* models in situating the oppression of women. In one of the seminal texts on woman battering, Del Martin (1976), for example, combines a critique of capitalism and a feminist analysis of the patriarchal family, arguing that capitalism benefits from the free labor performed by women in the household, just as individual men benefit from the domestic services of women. Advancing this economic analysis, Martin (1976: 41) explains that "If society succeeds in pressuring women to remain in the home, the labor market is cut in half, and competition for jobs, money, and power is therefore cut in half." Upper-class women exert power over working-class men, many socialist feminists pointed out, as well as over working-class women, for example, as household servants (Schechter, 1982).

The large-scale entry of married women into the waged workforce in the wake of the women's movement of the 1970s did open ground on the domestic front for resisting abuse. Even in low-wage or part-time jobs, women could achieve a degree of independence from men. Women were no longer expected to stoically endure bad treatment from men, in part because more economic options were now in sight. The ideal of the patriarchal nuclear family ideal, with a male breadwinner at the helm and a female nurturer at the hearth, had been destabilized as had the notion that traditional gender roles were natural (Brenner, 2000; Gordon, 2007).

The very prospect of greater options for women intensified, however, the stigma attached to battered women. As Lenore Walker (1979a) notes in her introduction to *The battered woman*, money is no guarantee of protection against male violence. Women stay in abusive relationships, not because they are masochistic but "because of complex psychological and sociological reasons" (1979a: ix). This early recognition of complexity soon encountered a wall of resistance, however, as feminists took on the state. Through a feminist lens, "psychological reasons" could be viewed as code for locating grievances of women in an over-reactive female psyche. The social symbolic power of the battered woman for many feminists was in her capacity to display hard evidence of the brutality of patriarchy.

In breaking down the barrier separating private and public life, a barrier that allowed men to abuse their wives behind closed doors, women's groups argued that the unwillingness of the state to enforce laws against assault and battery was a form of sexual discrimination (Goldfarb, 2000; Schneider, 1994). Further, this discrimination had a direct economic impact on women. Since much of the labor women performed was carried out in the household, and this labor contributed indirectly to the market, the federal government had an obligation to intervene on the basis of protecting women from domestic abuse (Schechter, 1982). With the criminalizing of wife beating and the reframing of the problem as one of *woman battering*, the gendered character of the crime was introduced. And in forging a linguistic and legal connection to battery, a felony, feminists were able to argue that it was a serious social problem that required intervention on the part of the state

(Schneider, 1994). Abused women would no longer be left to fend for themselves in managing the violent men in their lives.

Yet the question of how the state should intervene on behalf of women, and the role of feminist organizations in negotiating with the state, emerged as a new site of conflict. In taking up this conflict, a program in Duluth, Minnesota developed a model that became the international standard in the 1990s for domestic violence intervention. Indeed, there are few products of feminist inquiry that have circulated as widely throughout the world as the "Power and Control Wheel," published in 1993 as part of the Duluth curriculum for batterers. Developed by Ellen Pence and Michael Paymar (1993), the Power and Control Wheel was on display in most programs visited by members of my research team.

Later chapters discuss in more detail the Duluth model and the storytelling generated through this framing of the problem. Key premises behind the model are important to review at this juncture, though, in explaining how the Duluth model facilitated the transition of domestic violence from a radical feminist to a mainstream political issue. In interviews with advocates in the various settings, a key question concerned how the Duluth model functioned as a narrative framework and defensive boundary for feminist intervention.

A cornerstone of the Duluth model is its resolute rejection of therapeutic approaches to couple violence (Pence, 1989; Pence & Paymar, 1993). In ingroup/out-group terms, psychotherapy was cast as the enemy—the bad Other of a movement that had by the late 1980s expanded its borders considerably on the international front. Clinical work with batterers—whether in the context of individual, family, or group treatment—became associated with coddling abusers (Goldner, 1985; Gondolf, 1993; Kivel, 1996; Pence & Paymar, 1993). Therapeutic approaches distract attention from the political aspects of the problem, advocates insisted, by focusing on psychological dynamics or deficits.

As an alternative, the Duluth model frames battering as a direct consequence of patriarchy. In patriarchal societies, men develop a sense of entitlement to control and dominate their female partners. From this perspective, assaults on women are not seen as episodic but rather expressions of a systematic exercising of power over another person, which are highly reinforcing for the abuser. In addition to physical violence, tactics for subjugating women include emotional, economic, sexual, and verbal forms of abuse. Framed in this way, battering is intentional and a result of individual choice. Rather than a loss of control, violence is an assertion of control. The stated goal of the Duluth model is to hold men completely accountable for their violence. In the introduction to *Education groups for men who batter*, Pence and Paymar (1993) describe the acute need for educational programs for batterers after changes in the law led to a wave of mandatory arrests. "The courts refused to impose jail sentences on first

Figure 1 The Power and Control Wheel

Source: Domestic Abuse Intervention Project. 202 E. Superior Street, Duluth, MN 55802. 212-722-2781, www.theduluthmodel.org

offenders without first giving them an opportunity to rehabilitate themselves" (1993: xiii).

In addition to groups for batterers, the Duluth model is associated with the movement toward "coordinated community response" (CCR) to partner violence. Part of CCR involves disallowing the testimony of the victim in adjudicating cases of domestic violence. The most consistent effect of this change in procedures was that the abuser's fate was no longer in the woman's hands: "The prosecutor would (now) not interpret a woman's request to drop charges as a sign that she was safe but as a sign of her vulnerability" (Pence & Paymar, 1993: 17–18). Controlling the behavior of batterers was now a community responsibility rather than that of abused women as individuals. Advocates of the CCR approach pointed out that the man's behavior represents a threat to other women as well as to his present partner. In moving toward mandatory arrest and rehabilitation programs, the authors call for "increasingly harsh penalties and sanctions on men who continue to abuse their partners" (1993: 18).

Court-mandated groups for batterers worked a compromise between these calls for harsher penalties, on the one hand, and concern over the broad sweep of the mandate, on the other (Feder & Dugan, 2002; Feder & Wilson, 2005). A key premise of the Duluth model, however, is that batterer intervention groups must be integrated into a broader criminal justice response. As an alternative to jail time, men are required to attend a series of groups where their progress is monitored by the courts. Some cases are adjudicated through criminal courts while others are adjudicated through family courts, depending on a range of factors, including whether children are involved and the severity of the abuse.

The early feminist critique of the criminal justice system focused almost exclusively on the *passivity* of the state—the failure of the state to intervene on behalf of women (Goodman & Epstein, 2008). In confronting rape and battering, activists charged that the police both covertly and overtly supported male violence by refusing to take the complaints of women seriously. As historian Suzanne Pleck (1979, 1987) argues in reviewing this same history, however, sanctions against wife beating have been an important feature of the cultural and legal landscape in the United States since the early colonies. Even though women have had little in the way of legal recourse throughout much of this history, they have been able to enlist community support against husbands who beat them.[1]

Feminists in the United States enlisted growing tough-on-crime measures in the 1980s to intervene on women's behalf—a development where border tensions have been palpably intense (Crenshaw, 1994; Davis, 2000; Incite!, 2005; Price, 1999; Williams, 1994). The Duluth model served as a bridge between grassroots feminist organizations and a new era of negotiations with the state, and particularly with the police, although the terms of those negotiations differed in various parts of the world. The following reports (based on interviews in Berlin, Germany; London and Manchester, England; New York City; Pine Ridge, South Dakota; and Portland, Oregon) provide insights into the strategic dilemmas that arose with this new mandate.

THE BERLIN INTERVENTION PROJECT

The first set of interviews was conducted in early September, 2001, with Friderike Heuer, who also translated and assisted in analyzing the interview material. Most of the women interviewed were affiliated with the Berlin Intervention Project Against Domestic Violence (BIG), an ambitious multi-agency program that began in the early 1990s as the first large-scale women's initiative after the fall of the Berlin Wall. An outgrowth of alliances among women's organizations in Berlin, BIG created seven working groups and a Political Roundtable to establish new policies and procedures for domestic violence intervention, with improving police response and expanding public education key aims.[2]

The feminist principle underlying BIG was that domestic violence was a public problem rather than an individual or family matter, and society as a whole held responsibility for intervening. Yet from the start, feminists bitterly disagreed over whether BIG was a giant step forward or backward.[3] This debate registered longstanding political tensions within the shelter movement, but the fall of the Berlin Wall created a context for a reconfiguration of political alliances. Indeed, the BIG project may be framed as part of the broader reunification effort, since domestic violence was a problem area where women from the former eastern and western parts of the city could come together politically. Much like child sexual abuse, which had similarly been the focus of large Round Table discussions in Germany, almost everyone, from the left to the right, agreed that domestic violence was reprehensible. And just as societal anxieties over sexuality infused public discourse over child sexual abuse in the early 1990s (Burman, 2003; Haaken, 1998; Nathan & Snedeker, 1997), the broader political scene shaped the "uncovering" of domestic violence as a hidden social problem during this same period.

Many of the women in the Berlin group trace their political migration within the left, moving from socialist to radical feminist politics. One advocate reflects on the early history of the group: "Many people came out of the left. But once you got hooked on the feminist movement you isolated yourself and concentrated on that, but now you see a little bit of an opening again." Another advocate feels that left-wing groups were more prone to sectarianism, and that feminist organizations were more open politically. "There are many isolated splinter groups that only focus on their own goals," she explains. "That's the problem—they do something good but they are not connecting." For many of the women interviewed, the BIG initiative represented new possibilities for broadening the movement, and renewed hope that feminists could make a real difference at the national level.

In Germany, feminists have a long history of struggling with questions concerning collaboration with the state. During the 1970s, the German left confronted the history of the repression of the Holocaust in German collective memory and the extensive collusion on the part of everyday people in the barbarism of the Third Reich (Craig, 1996). In the shadow of that history and the wave of repression of left-wing groups in the 1960s and 1970s, German feminists were sensitized to the quandary of how to work in a non-collaborative way with the state. One advocate in the Berlin group describes the position of feminists in the early shelter movement:

"The western women's shelters have a very strict position that they do not want to cooperate with the police because the state and the state agency reprimand and justify the oppression of women. When this first came up, in these houses that grew up in the seventies when we all had an anti-state and anti-police position, there were extremely intense and aggressive discourses and discussions about which side you were on. Houses became more and more isolated, they networked among themselves, but there was no real reaching out to others."

The boundary of early shelter politics was fortified on two fronts. For abused women, the front was in relation to batterers. For feminists, it was in relation to the state, and particularly in relation to the police as the repressive instrument of the state. Although the early shelters routinely enlisted the police to intervene in battering situations, the protocol included making sure that a woman's advocate was present whenever the police were called. This practice of keeping an arm's length—with feminists assuming a quasi-supervisory stance toward the police—became the official policy of early shelters in many Western countries, including in the United States.[4]

Carol Hagemann-White, a researcher with BIG and leading feminist theorist in the domestic violence field (Hagemann-White, 1998), suggests that this stance became rigidified, however, leading to the isolation of women's advocates. Instead of viewing the new responsiveness of the state in the BIG initiative as a victory for feminism, Hagemann-White charges that feminists enlisted the principle of autonomy from the state to resist change. Her interpretation suggests that group defenses originating in earlier realities may have rigidified over time, limiting the group's ability to respond creatively to new political openings.

The debate over working closely with policing institutions parallels another early controversy in Germany, one centered on female ambivalence concerning male power. Hagemann-White looks back on the radical feminist roots of the shelter movement and how her feminist politics shifted to include more of the psychological dimensions of power:

"My thinking was shaped by the radical feminist approach of the shelter movement, which is that domestic violence is a form of control men exert over women. Over the years I've come to see the issue as not only a reality, but also a symbolic issue . . . It's not only a question of asserting power but also a question of gender identity and the re-construction of gender."

Hagemann-White is making a distinction between traditions of feminism that invite reflection on the complexity of gender versus those that oversimplify gendered power relations. From a radical feminist perspective, male violence is rooted in the patriarchal system of domination, a system that is the basis of economies and cultures throughout much if not most of human history (Donovan, 1996). An extension of this stance is that men, like other imperialistic conquerors, will claim and defend as much ground as is within their reach. There are different traditions of radical feminism, however, and the tradition Hagemann-White cites emphasizes the role of *women* in reproducing patriarchal domination. Men do not simply act on women as passive subjects, but rather enlist women in the maintenance of power. The radical feminist analysis that guided the early movement in Germany required self-reflection on the part of women and attending to the ways that women unconsciously collaborate in their own oppression. Hagemann-White continues:

> "Even then, in 1976, because we were coming from a feminist analysis, influenced by Simone de Beauvoir, who was probably the strongest single influence on radical feminism in Germany, it was a notion of women being complicit in a patriarchal tradition . . . Since women are complicit and involved in this, feminism meant recovering or redefining what it means to be a woman . . . (and) taking responsibility for their own life."

Extending this same expectation to abused women generated anxiety, however. Resentments conflicted with the protective ethos of shelter politics, particularly in the early movement when sisterhood included the expectation of reciprocity. Barbara Kaveman, also a researcher with BIG, describes the pressures early feminists faced in organizing, and how difficult it was to incorporate a complex view of abused women—or to acknowledge anger toward women who returned to their abusers. As Kaveman notes, taking a hard line introduced a boundary between feminist and non-feminist positions that served to contain the tension:

> "In the German discussion, there is something very essential to having this one way only of discussing domestic violence. And this means to be on the side of the victim, and nowhere else. And you have to be on the side of the woman if you want to be in the right place. If there is any doubt about whether you are on this side, then you are on the wrong side . . . If you said that women have a problem, you were on the wrong side. It gave you a very simple model of explanation to counter this, and these things have a tendency to live on their own. Once you have it this way, it is quite simple to explain the world."

The psychoanalytic concept of splitting introduced in the Introduction—of managing anxiety by separating a conflict into absolute "good" and "bad" elements and externalizing the "bad" element—may be useful in characterizing this all-or-nothing response.[5] This defensive splitting, where all negative reactions to abused women are located outside of the maternal fold of the shelter, protects the group from destabilizing tensions. But this defense also carries a cost. The group creates a repressive "superego" that prohibits exploration of conflicts that arise in carrying out the work.

Many of the Berlin advocates note that one cost of such rigid defenses is disengagement from the complex realities of women's lives. In suggesting the limits of some of the positions adopted, Beate Leapold, another researcher with BIG, responds that "we have to take the broader social situation into account," while recognizing that women share to varying degrees some vulnerability to male violence. Kaveman adds, "This was the focus of feminist discussion of domestic violence—that every woman can be affected, every woman is a potential victim, and every man can do it."

After the fall of the Berlin Wall in 1989, domestic violence emerged as a framework for a new era of political dialogue as women from the western and eastern parts of Berlin came together to discuss the problem. The issue of violence in the home created a basis for a shared sense of sisterhood, even as it opened up a new site for the return of repressed conflicts.[6] In the context of reunification in Germany, political conflict registered differences in women's experiences with the state. Although my colleague Friderike Heuer and I had anticipated that women in the eastern part of the city would be more wary of the police than those in the western part, the configuration of positions was just the opposite. Women from formerly East Berlin were far more ready to trust the police, particularly in the reorganized state.

How, we asked, was the conflict then resolved? "The western parts of the city have a lot of resistance to working with the police," one advocate offers, "but the eastern parts do not." Several advocates explain that women from the east welcomed the new opening to work with the state and resented being lectured by "old guard" feminists from the west. As one laments, "Interestingly enough, the very first shelter in [western] Berlin does not exist anymore . . . They were one of the hardest opponents in the original position, and just couldn't integrate some of the contradictions, so they unfortunately closed down."

Conflict among feminists over the BIG initiative was overdetermined by international politics as well, particularly the "importing" of feminist models from the United States. The Berlin group describes their first contact in 1991 with Uta Rozeman and Ellen Pence, from Duluth, Minnesota. One concern centered on the strategy of coordinated community response (CCR), a key principle of the Duluth model described earlier. In relieving abused women of the burden of bringing violent men under control, the CCR strategy was to bring protection of women and the force of law together in a hand-in-glove fashion. On a practical level, the CCR approach meant that women's advocates consulted with police and judges to work out guidelines for policies and intervention (Gross *et al.*, 2000; Syers & Edleson, 1992).

The women interviewed are generally positive about the bold thrust of the Duluth program, although with some ambivalence. In characterizing reluctance on the part of many German feminists to embrace the Duluth model, many joke about the German proclivity to be careful and to weigh alternatives before acting, in contradistinction to the American tendency toward impulsiveness. As one woman notes, "We always hear what was supposed to be happening in America." The other women laugh conspiratorially, adding that Germans see things as more "complicated" than do Americans. One woman comments that the German hesitancy to act is a problematic tendency, one now associated with (perhaps projected onto) the older generation of hardline feminists who they view as rigidly averse to change.

As the movement against woman battering achieved impressive moral and legal advances in Germany during the 1990s, radical politics were tempered by the very climate that sustained heady victories. Although critical of hardline feminist positions associated with early shelter politics, Hagemann-White acknowledges her own ambivalence over the mainstreaming of the domestic violence issue:

> "I think that very much of what has happened in Germany—although many feminists wouldn't think of it this way—has been an interactive, inter-relationship between a feminist movement and the state, particularly the ministry of women. Because violence symbolizes women's oppression, and violence against women is something you can unambiguously act on, the government can say . . . 'This is what we're doing; we're doing something for women.'"

Domestic violence may be a starting place for public discussion of women's issues, but it may also serve to collectively repress more controversial feminist campaigns. Women from the former GDR no longer have the childcare once provided by the state, for example, and now find themselves adapting to the policy in western Germany of subsidizing mothers to stay home with their children, a policy generating increasing resistance among younger women. Further, domestic violence programs may be advanced by conservatives as a means of making the family a "safe zone" for women, even as they pursue policies that reduce benefits and social services.

THE WOMEN'S REFUGE MOVEMENT IN BRITAIN

Just as in Germany, areas of cleavage have emerged in Britain between old feminist models that stress the autonomy of women's organizations and new feminist models that cooperate with the state and adopt a more pragmatic course of action. The newer models also are more apt to be viewed by the "older" feminist critics as excessively entrepreneurial, employing fund-raising strategies that play to the lowest common denominator (e.g., pity) in generating support for women. The two strains of the movement have diverged into separate organizational networks, rather than the one overtaking the other, as is the case in Germany. While Women's Aid remains a consortium of independent refuges for women, Refuge owns and operates a growing number of houses for women in London and is based on a more conventional organizational hierarchy and an emphasis on professionalism.

In interviews with advocates at Refuge in London and Women's Aid in Manchester, housing politics overshadowed debates over the police—specifically the role of women's refuge in the labyrinthine and mutating housing bureaucracies. Many of the women interviewed came out of the housing movement, or worked in shelters for the homeless. Indeed, the history of the women's refuge movement in England serves as a powerful reminder of how intertwined domestic violence and housing crises often are (Dobash & Dobash, 1979). Refuge, as an organization, maintains what remains of the first documented women's refuge in the world—the Chiswick Family Rescue house. In response to the acute housing shortage in London, Erin Pizzey organized a group of women in 1971 to establish the Women's Aid Centre in Chiswick, a borough of London. Initially established as a community center for homeless women and children, the center—later named Chiswick's Women's Aid (CWA)—began to offer refuge to battered women who were seeking assistance. Inspired by CWA, women from Britain, the United States, and other countries began to establish refuge houses in their own communities based on this model (Haffner, 1979; Schechter, 1982). Pizzey (1974) noted in her early work that poor health and other conditions associated with poverty, including brain damage, could directly contribute to family violence, and she railed against the punitive practices and insufficient supports provided by the social welfare system.

While waiting to meet with Refuge staff in London, I read the inspiring history of the organization posted on the wall in the conference room. Beginning with Pizzey's commune for homeless women and children, the history told of how women became politicized through working in the refuge movement. Much like 1970s feminist groups in other countries, early consciousness-raising sessions in Britain expanded to include support groups for residents who found a sense of sisterhood with others who had experienced abuse. Battered women were encouraged to join the staff and were respected for their knowledge—expertise derived from direct encounters with violent men.[7]

Sandra Horley, director of Refuge in London, offers a less romantic view of early refuge services in England as she describes the grim situation at Chiswick house under Pizzey's leadership. Horley tells of the furor among feminists over a book Pizzy co-authored (Pizzey & Shapiro, 1982), *Prone to violence*, which takes the stance that women can be as violent as men—a position that emerged early on as an emotionally charged boundary separating feminist and non-feminist positions. Although she concedes that Pizzey was a pioneer who fought doggedly to secure government funding, Horley also portrays her feminist forbearer as egregiously negligent. At one point, according to Horley, 150 women lived in the eight bedroom house under squalid conditions. Pizzey was taken to court in 1976 for over-housing and was found guilty but spared a prison term. Horley recalls that the Queen intervened during that same time to spare the Chiswick house from closure.[8]

Horley recollects how she took the post of director in the chaotic wake of Pizzy's departure, bringing the house into compliance with state health codes. But the path Horley pursued was fraught with controversy and heated debate within Refuge over how to preserve feminist principles of organization within the complex housing bureaucracy. Horley confesses to moments of resentment over being characterized by some women as an "establishment feminist" because of her professional training, adding that "I was homeless at age 14."

The power of the early refuge movement was in the vision of sisterhood it created—one that displaced the patriarchal family as the legitimate protector of women. "But now," Horley adds, "conflicts are more turf battles than ideology." All the organizations are competing for funding, she explains, which comes from the housing department and local authority as well as charitable contributions. Approximately half of the budget of Refuge is from private donations. Some Refuge staff members express concern over the contingencies attached to funding, and whether increased funding is a means of silencing the movement. As one advocate at Refuge describes it:

> "They say, 'Look, we are doing something about it, we have given six million pounds.' Mostly, it is perpetrator programs without any guidelines or methods to see if it will be effective . . . It is like a wave, someone makes noise about it and then there is action. But there is still no coordination or uniform training."

Sandhya Sharma with Saheli, a refuge for South Asian women in Manchester, England, also reflects back on the history of the movement, but from the perspective of her ethnic community. We met at the refuge, continuing a conversation from the previous day over the longstanding practice of spiriting battered women away to confidentially located refuges. I had proposed that the practice of requiring women to maintain the secrecy of the refuge separated women from their own communities, reinforcing the very isolation that made women vulnerable to abusive partners. Sharma concurs, but adds that the confidential location also allows women some distance from relatives who place intense pressure on women to return—an argument advanced by women in other minority communities as well (Abraham, 2000; Ayyub, 2000; Dasgupta, 2000).

Much like in Germany, domestic violence and immigration politics are intertwined in Britain. Whereas in Germany, feminists feel pressure to cooperate with the state, British feminists confront the neglect of the state in providing services for women, and particularly migrant women without legal papers. Confrontations with housing and immigration authorities are commonplace. In competing with other organizations for funding, and drawing a sharp boundary between domestic violence and other sources of suffering in women's lives, the refuge movement risks suffering the same states of helplessness as do battered women themselves. Yet Sharma also tallies the costs of strategies over which the movement has had some degree of control:

> "When we started in 1976, Saheli was a political movement and we were doing something in a political context. I really believe so much of that has been lost. When I look at other organizations, they are doing political and challenging work around young people and mental health, or Asian women and education. I think there is something valuable about it. Our work is so crisis management that we often don't see the politics in the work we do or the bigger picture. You know, how things are shaping around us . . . When we have meetings, it is funding, finance, and development issues."

Since funding for beds is tied to the legal status of residents, moral and practical dilemmas arise over which women secure shelter from the stormy conditions of their lives. The state does not provide funding for undocumented migrant women, although a number of the refuge organizations raise money specifically for migrant women. In appealing to affluent private donors, however, the stories of abused women are often sanitized and brought into compliance with middle-class standards of womanhood. Women who flee from abusive husbands in order to protect their children are more apt to win public support than are women who fail to display feminine virtues of sexual chastity and deference to authority in the course of taking flight.[9]

Operating in tandem with the ideal of the good victim are equally limiting concepts of the good advocate. The good advocate is one who is motivated, in some settings, by the simple desire to help women and, in others, by striving for professional standards. But the term "*professionalism*" also has acquired a pejorative meaning among feminists as it refers to a loss of political commitment (Incite!, 2005; Rodriguez, 1988). Rather than making trouble, good professionals work their way up career ladders and learn to be pleasing to those above them. Professionalism also has meant hiring staff with advanced degrees rather than women who acquire skills through direct experience with domestic violence. Although achieving better services for women is an important feminist aim, some advocates point out that these same services have become over-institutionalized and have lost connections with grassroots organizations. There is also a risk that crisis services devolve into "rescue work" carried out by legions of female volunteers. Sharma describes tensions that arise in Britain in reconciling feminist and labor issues in women's organizations as well:

> "We have a strong management that says all workers should be paid living wages. Starting pay is 16,000 pounds per year . . . This is not just about your commitment or that we as women should be doing this work . . . We always ask women why they want the job when they apply to work here . . . They feel like they have to say 'I am so committed to Asian women causes.' I say, 'Good, you should be. But what about the money? I'm in this job because it pays well in part.' We have to think about what we are saying about the value of women's work when we don't attend to pay . . . All workers get a decent wage. All workers have a chance for development. We have training. Vacation starts at 25 days [per year], then it goes up to 30. I know that in the US that is totally different."

As feminists develop services for women, their own interests as workers emerge as integral to the struggle. Although the Duluth Power and Control Wheel has been imported into many different countries, the model obscures dilemmas that arise for women in negotiating the boundary between defending their own interests as workers and fighting in the interests of women escaping abuse.

NEW YORK CITY AND THE DOMESTIC VIOLENCE GRID

The concept of "coordinated community response" (CCR), a centerpiece of the Duluth model, seems particularly daunting in New York City. Starting with the creation of local shelters scattered throughout the boroughs, feminists since the early 1980s have created a far-flung network of crisis services for women within the various governmental structures that oversee public services. Much like the subway system, the "underground railroad" of services for women spans a vast political and geographical landscape. Shelters are more apt to take the form of set-aside units in apartments throughout the city than separate houses. Also, feminists are more apt to be engaged in legal work than getting women into shelters. This work takes many forms: helping women win exclusions (legal orders for evicting abusive partners) and Schedule Two housing (priority in accessing public housing), and assisting women in fights with the immigration offices.

Sumaya Colman, an African American advocate, describes the situation as a "grid," both in representing the labyrinthine systems women negotiate in confronting domestic abuse and in the tendency of the movement to bracket the problem of woman battering, separating it from the various forces that hold women in check:

> "When I think of the work I have done with women of color, especially African American women—the grid they work through in terms of reporting the violence, staying or leaving, in terms of the issues that are happening in the rest of their world, around police brutality, around the economy. Where else can they go? If not to a shelter, where else can they go? If they are coming from a housing project, where else can they go? It is the total grid, not just 'I should leave.' It becomes a matter of how to leave and of all the different things you have to go through and what comes after leaving. It is not just DV [domestic violence], it is systemic violence and lots of different types of violence in their lives."

The history of the movement in New York City, not unlike in England, is intertwined with housing politics. Sue Loeb, director of Voices of Women, an activist group of battered women, looks back on the early movement and the role of the housing crisis in the current situation in New York City. Loeb elaborates:

> "When I started doing this work in Staten Island in 1980, and the early 1980s, there was still affordable housing when I set up this shelter program . . . In New York City, back in the mid 1980s, you could still find affordable housing in a reasonable amount of time. So the women in our shelter stayed for about six weeks. And then they continued to come to support groups and they got counseling and they got a lot of stuff done in six weeks but they didn't have to be in shelter long term. Now in New York City, women stay six months, nine months, 18 months."

Women tend to stay longer in New York City shelters than in prior decades because the cost of housing has soared—a trend noted by advocates in many other settings as well. Advocates claim that women prefer domestic violence shelters to homeless shelters and that this preference is due to the more respectful treatment and broader range of services they receive. But since women are required to be on public assistance to make use of domestic violence shelters in New York City, shelters are a limited part of the overall coordinated response. Interventions are overwhelmingly directed toward assisting poor women, advocates add, which makes the feminist uncoupling of poverty and domestic violence—the claim that all women are equally vulnerable to male violence—particularly problematic.

Bringing battered women together to identify their own political goals and agendas, Voices of Women was envisioned as a grassroots project in the spirit of the early movement. In the interview with Sue Loeb, I asked about some of the dilemmas that arise as women attempt to find common ground. The position of the movement that domestic violence "cuts across race, class, and cultural boundaries" makes poor women feel "it's not just them and their communities," Loeb explains. But she adds that the groups languish over how to constructively confront differences. She goes on to emphasize that it is important for women to learn that they are all affected by domestic violence, while still acknowledging the vast differences in the resources available to them. A key area where the experiences of affluent and poor women diverge, Loeb suggests, centers on the sense of betrayal in being treated badly by the state: "For white women, it's a real rude awakening. For some of the women of color, it's not at all. They didn't go to these systems expecting to get justice. But the white women do."

Immigration politics and domestic violence work are tightly interwoven in New York City, just as they are in many European cities (Hagemann-White, 1998; Morgaine, 2007). Some advocates frame the issue of domestic violence by invoking the legal rights women have achieved in the United States to be free of male violence. Customary laws and traditional practices are often terribly oppressive to women, advocates emphasize, while adding that some of the freedoms offered to women in the West are illusory. Vickie Gomez, a Puerto Rican advocate with VOW, describes the intense pressures many immigrant women experience to stay with abusive husbands. In entering the United States, women often do enlist laws against domestic violence in negotiating a new path of personal independence. Gomez stresses how important it is to educate immigrant women about the rights they have to be free of personal violence, and recalls one inspiring story of an immigrant woman to illustrate her point:

> "She had been shot in the head. He shot [her] five times. One bullet went through her head and one into her finger. She survived but what she did originally was she took care of her health needs and then she got to the place where she could really pursue it. She went back and she kept track of where he was in this country. She found him and let the police know . . . So they could make the arrest. Throughout the whole time she had to deal with repercussions from the family, once they found him . . . [But] she wasn't backing down . . . Sometimes she would feel badly about him going to jail.

> But she always wanted to hold him accountable throughout. And at the end she did go to court but it was not easy. The whole time she had to stand clear regardless of whether she had the support or not. She had the right because it was on the books. Understand? Because it's on the books."

In repeating the phrase "It's on the books" in her decisive denouement to the story, Gomez underscores the point of how immigrant women make use of new legal rights in crossing national borders. She goes on to tell a story of another immigrant woman—a story with a more uncertain ending. In setting the stage for the dilemma that arose, Gomez reiterates the central principle of feminist organizations—that a woman's choices should always be respected. But Gomez struggles with the principle in this case, as the woman wanted the full weight of the law "down on the head" of her husband:

> "I would say to her, 'There are people out there who will help you deport him, but please don't ask that of me.' But within my job description, if a woman wants to take a man to jail then my responsibility is to advocate. That's my responsibility because those are services that we are saying we are providing . . . Now if it was a case where I had really strong conflicts with it, then I would say to her, 'I have strong conflicts with this and I have to pass it over to somebody else.' . . . But if she needs to use it that is up to her . . . But she should be told ahead of time . . . and that this has implications for other people and it can be misused. There's also immigration politics and anti-immigrant tactics where men can be victims of those politics. It became very clear to me when we had immigration reform and we had welfare reform."

As women's crisis services emerge as the gateway for managing the problems of minority women, the feminist pillars that hold them in place inevitably suffer strains. As Gomez suggests, reconciling feminist stances to "support the woman" sometimes collide with other political values. These are not easy conflicts to resolve, but Gomez stresses the importance of acknowledging and addressing them as part of the work.

Sujata Warrior, a long-time advocate in New York City, offers a more sobering assessment of problems in the movement. She voices concern that the successes of the domestic violence campaign have inhibited broader institutional critiques. In the aftermath of the bombing of the World Trade Center, for example, there was reluctance to criticize the military responses of the United States government. Although there was discussion of militarism in perpetuating interpersonal violence, Warrior adds that no public positions were taken by domestic violence organizations in New York in the political crisis following September 11th. Similarly, the coalitions have not taken stances on immigration issues in spite of the abuse undocumented women experience from immigration authorities. "When you work on the issue of battered immigrant women, starting with welfare reform, the response was 'let's get this through, then we'll get something else through later.'" Warrior laments this pragmatic approach, adding that there are long-term consequences to such tactical choices:

> "Now, the movement is so tied to government money. The movement here does not make a connection between the economic violence committed by the US government and the violence individual women experience. Specialization of various projects within feminism—rape, reproductive rights, battering, trafficking—mean projects that are easier to fund. These issues do not bring into question the power structure here. If we do that, we will lose our funding. It all boils down to funding. But there is a place where you have got to critique."

As a South Asian woman working in the labor movement, as well as a domestic violence activist, Warrior emphasizes economic factors contributing to abuse and the limits of single issue politics. She notes that it has been difficult to advance a gender analysis of violence while recognizing the complexity of the problem and differences in women's relationships to violence. Describing male batterers as "bad men" is the easiest step, Warrior suggests, but it is more difficult to incorporate a complex feminist politics into the picture: "It's a simplistic analysis that allows people to handle the situation," but becomes more difficult in incorporating this analysis into other issues where feminists confront more resistance.

> "Women in this movement were very successful. Rape, because of the way it occurs, happens in a context where it is easier to blame the victim. The subtext is that she invited it. In the DV arena, because of the way the injuries appear, you are able to shift blame to the perpetrator in a way that you are not able to do in the rape movement."

Women in the New York City group interview also struggle with the costs of success. As one advocate describes it:

> "In New York, we were successful in getting government funding so that it shapes our programs. I think it is a bad thing because some people who work in the field don't think of themselves as part of the movement. They think of themselves as feminists who work on this issue."

Yet many advocates express confidence that feminist organizations are more open than other political or social service groups to working creatively between the poles of difference and commonality.

Sue Loeb stresses the importance of continuing to listen to one another. Yet the anxieties and defenses that arise can be quite intense, particularly as women discover that they have different things to say.[10] Loeb calls attention to the potential in social movements to reproduce forms of oppression—to "recreate the world we are trying to change"—but she also finds hope in feminist projects that acknowledge conflict and differences among women. In the absence of feminist analyses that allow space for acknowledging differences, conflicts may arise in a disguised form, for example, as burnout or depressive withdrawal.

PINE RIDGE AND THE SACRED CIRCLE

Many of the women and men with whom I spoke at the Cangleska program at Pine Ridge, South Dakota, started the conversation by telling stories. Two were repeatedly offered—one based on known historical events and the other tied to the more numinous realm of Lakota mythology.

Explaining how domestic violence became widespread in tribal communities, many Cangleska staff members cite the Massacre at Wounded Knee as a key historical reference point. After the successful Indian resistance to the US Cavalry in 1876, led by the skillful young military commander, Crazy Horse, the Cavalry returned to this same area of the Lakota tribe 14 years later, attacking with brutal vengeance. Three hundred Indians were slaughtered at the Massacre of Wounded Knee, many while attempting to flee from the carnage. In telling this story, Cangleska staff members stress the violent destruction of their culture and the trauma that continues to be enacted in the form of family violence. They tell how the aftermath of colonization cuts deeply into the tissue of everyday life, as men attempt to reclaim a sense of power, however illusory, by lashing out against those closest to them.

The second story offers a vantage point beyond the trauma of genocide—a vision of the prior integrity of the Lakota people that remains, alongside the legacy of colonized consciousness. The story recounts the creation legend of the Lakota people—their journey from the underworld to their earthly home. The creator is White Buffalo Calf Woman, the feminine principle and source of early cultural knowledge. In her first encounter with the Lakota people, she comes upon two men—one overtaken with ravishing lust for her and the other approaching her as a source of spiritual wisdom. The first man attacks her and is reduced to dusty bones. The second man continues on the path with her and receives the peace pipe, the symbol of renewal used in the sweat lodge ceremony. The two figures in the story represent the dueling spirits within men, one oriented toward death and domination and the other toward life and human connection.[11]

In explaining what many claim to be epidemic rates of domestic violence on reservations, Cangleska advocates use these stories to work between the two poles of their problem. One concerns the scope of the collective trauma that Indian peoples have suffered.[12] Domestic violence work on the reservation means confronting this history, which includes children forcefully removed from their parents and placed in boarding schools, massive poverty, and violent displacement of Indian peoples (Jaimes-Guerrero, 1997). The other pole of the problem centers on reclaiming strengths and capacities, and the sustaining side of Lakota traditions. Interventions with men include mandatory arrests, but the classes men are required to attend also emphasize healing and reparation. This process involves encouraging men to reconnect with the feminine principle, ritually enacted through prayers to the White Buffalo Calf Woman and the rebirthing rituals of the sweat lodge. Reparation through the feminine principle extends beyond the spiritual and into the material realm, with women claiming leadership roles in the courts and tribal council.

Cangleska, Inc. is also the mother organization for Sacred Circle, the foundation that produces and distributes educational material on domestic violence throughout Indian Country. Drawing on the Duluth program in the neighboring state of Minnesota, Lakota women have brought a historical perspective to the concept of male power and control (Artichoker & Mousseau, 2003). While they share the Duluth focus on male power motives as the cause of domestic violence, they also emphasize solidarity with Indian men in confronting the issue. The Cangleska initiative opened space for women to create their own institutions and to demand more control over the tribal councils. The women successfully secured passage of a measure through the council that provided new leverage in tribal policing and intervention. Cangleska developed its own parole and probation services, and worked to make the tribal police more responsive to women in situations of family violence (Cangleska, 2000).

As I suggested earlier, the feminist shift toward coordinated community response (CCR) opened a minefield of challenges, although they varied by region and political history. On Pine Ridge, advocates repeatedly insist that the tribal police are not the enemy. Rather, they are more apt to be perceived as ineffectual. The tribal courts are where the real problems lie, advocates uniformly suggest, and getting the courts to act in adjudicating cases of domestic violence has been a real challenge. More women have been recently elected as judges, which is a hopeful development since women are viewed as less prone to protect men by dismissing the case or "losing" the file.

Responses of advocates highlight the complex and variable relationships between women's programs and the state, and how bound those relationships are to particular histories and locales. The Justice Department is the funding arm of many repressive police practices in the United States. However, the influx of new funds through the Office on Violence Against Women bypassed many of the institutions historically associated with repressive control over Indian peoples. The Indian Health Services, for example, has been bitterly resented by many Lakota Sioux because the doctors, most of whom are white, live in isolated compounds on the reservations and are often paternalistic. In contrast, funds through the Violence Against Women Act (VAWA) came directly to women's programs, run for and by Indian people. Karen Artichoker, director of one of the Cangleska offices, underscores the importance of how domestic violence funding came into their community:

> "I think when you have the resources from the VAWA that we were able to access, you can take an approach that moves outside the medical model and includes the history of oppression that people have experienced, you're going to have something really dynamic that our people can relate to. We have been immersed in a medical model and a substance abuse model that focus on the individual. Some say that it is our genetics . . . But we are a collective people, and when we are able to combine the personal and the political, it is very exciting for us. Yes, you have individual responsibility, but you also have this other collective part of it."

In taking collective responsibility, women also place some of the moral load outside the borders of the reservation. This contextualizing of the problem makes it possible for women to see men as both good and bad, as both inside and outside the fold of their shared humanity. Male violence is interpreted as an effect of colonization, rather than based on an inherent drive to subjugate women. When men are violent, Cangleska interprets the behavior as a violation of Lakota identity. Men are both abusing women and transgressing a core part of their Indian identity.

There is a memory of an earlier time, advocates explain, when men and women lived together as equals. In this re-visioning of the past, the authority required to maintain social harmony is remembered as supportive rather than repressive. Cecilia Fire Thunder, outreach director of the Cangleska program, summarizes this traditional philosophy, rooted in a sense that the elders, men and women, held vital knowledge on which the community depended for survival:

> "There was a time when if people didn't behave, there were strong consequences. But since colonization, particularly with Christianity, that has changed. Christianity is the reason we are in such a mess . . . The Christians tore away a strong belief system that kept

> everyone in line. It is important to understand the historical context of where we are today. I tell Indian people, 'You are not bad, your son is not bad, we are good people. We're just dealing with the effects of 200 years of colonization.' We are in the process of decolonizing ourselves."

Native American and African American women share an awareness of their unique place in US history and of the twin traumas of the Atlantic slave trade and the destruction of indigenous cultures. Yet minority women also confront differences in their histories that are difficult to acknowledge in the women's anti-violence movement. Explaining how "Christianity almost destroyed us," Artechoker goes on to describe her uneasiness with African American women who want to address domestic violence through Christian churches. "We seem to have more in common with African women," Artichoker adds, "because they have such similar beliefs as ours." Some differences are readily incorporated into a common legacy, while other differences—or perceived differences—arouse tensions that may become pronounced when groups of women are isolated from one another.

Like other sites where I carried out interviews, domestic violence and housing politics are intimately intertwined at Pine Ridge. More than the skyrocketing price of housing in metropolitan areas such as New York City or London, the problem at Pine Ridge is the sheer lack of housing. Three families often live under one roof, and there is a long waiting list for young people to find separate housing. Unemployment is staggeringly high on the reservation, but people are resourceful in finding ways to survive. Most capitalist investment schemes on the reservation have failed, Artichoker offers, in part because the economic structures that accompany them do not mix well with the collectivist values of Indian culture. "Maybe we could use some of that capitalist attitude," Artichoker adds wryly. "We are pretty tired of being poor." One of the poorest in the country, the Pine Ridge reservation depends primarily on production and sale of Indian artifacts, a small local casino, and government grants. Yet much of the revenue from land and mining on Pine Ridge, as well as on other Indian territories, remains in the coffers of the US government.[13]

Many abused women who leave the reservation return because there is such a strong sense of shared history. They may be poor and their horizons may have been blunted by chronic encounters with violent men, but the reservation offers relief from the racist assaults of white society. Further, women on the reservation are able to draw on traditional forms of authority available to women, particularly as they recast the meaning of Lakota traditions—their ethnic culture and language—to include gender equality and the power of the feminine principle.

The challenges of women working on the issue of domestic violence at Pine Ridge are clearly different from those faced by women in large metropolitan areas. Whereas Lakota women share a common set of traditions and a pan-Indian identity, women working in Berlin, London or New York wrestle uneasily with cultural differences.[14] As women from vastly different backgrounds seek shelter, the critique of patriarchy offers a precarious foundation for unity when set against the many forces dividing them. At the same time, women throughout the globe are being displaced by economic policies that simultaneously fragment and unify. And many are finding that escaping the patriarchal family does not inevitably lead to the freedom road.

CONCLUSIONS

Throughout the history of organizing around domestic violence, many feminists have argued that woman battering transcends all social boundaries. In creating a unifying story of the battered woman, feminists have been able to expose the fist behind the glove—the brutality concealed behind various myths of the patriarchal protector. As Barbara Kaveman of Germany notes, "For years it was not possible to say certain groups of women are in more danger than others. It was not feminist."

A radical feminist critique of the patriarchal family, grounded in an analysis of women's economic dependency on men, was vital to the movement's early mobilization. Many women have since achieved victories that were inconceivable a generation ago. Women's crisis services remain a lifeline for women in many areas of the world, but these lifelines are particularly vital for women who are vulnerable as a result of their immigration status or poverty. In invoking the unity of all women, advocates may overlook differences, however, as well as the myriad ways in which the relationship between feminist crisis services and the state replicates the very forms of power and control reported in stories of abused women.

A recurring motif in the histories of the movement centers on divisions between "old" and "new" feminist models. These distinctions represent shifts in feminist politics, and the migration of domestic violence from a more radical feminism to a more liberal and mainstream issue. The wide impact of the Duluth model, and particularly the coordinated community response, may serve as the new unifier in a movement that works closely with the patriarchal state. Yet this model may operate repressively if it sutures over the problematic alliances that feminists have forged with the state.

Most of the advocates steadfastly hold to a vision of social change, even as they struggle with distinctions between old and new models and the costs of professionalism. Further, it is not surprising that feminist identity continues to be forged around some of the simpler elements of early radical feminist positions, particularly the notion that women are uniformly the victims in situations of family violence. This remains the *terra firma* of the movement. But the mandate to be "on the side of women and women only" may also operate defensively, shielding women who have some degree of power from the criticisms of those with far less.

There is a striking affinity between radical feminist perspectives on male violence and some conservative populist campaigns stressing victims' rights and advancing moralistic pronouncements concerning individual responsibility. Even the National Rifle Association (NRA) has found common cause with feminism in defending unregulated production of and access to weapons in the US. *Safe, not sorry: Keeping yourself and your family safe in a violent age*, authored by Tanya Metaksa (1997), executive director of the NRA, was on display in the reading room at one of the shelters where I trained in Portland, Oregon. Like radical feminists, Metaksa stresses extreme cases and the unremitting horror of women's lives. She begins by describing the history of women as the property of men, and as "natural prey of society's criminal element" (1997: xvii). No longer quivering in the shadows of history, modern women now can stand on the strong shoulders of their female forbearers, she exhorts, drawing on Golda Meir, Margaret Thatcher, and Indira Ghandhi as examples. Appealing to women's sense of vulnerability in an "increasingly dangerous world," as well as distrust of the police, Metaksa targets male criminals as the menacing source of uncertainty in the world. "Criminals, predators, people on the wrong side of ethical behavior have values that are completely antithetical to the rest of us," Metaksa warns, "and if you don't know which of these categories you fall into, there is a seventy-five percent chance that at some time in your life a predator will teach you" (1997: 15).

One distinction between feminist and non-feminist analyses of violence centers on the identified threats to women's lives, as well as on the prescribed paths of deliverance. Feminists have subverted the dominant patriarchal narrative, where the world outside the household is cast as ominously dangerous, by stressing that the home is more threatening to women than the streets. Further, feminists tend to stress systematic sources of violence, and how dominant institutions are deeply implicated in the suffering of women. Stories of isolated acts of aggression against women—of lone wolves and predatory outlaws—are woven together to recount the untold tales of patriarchy, stories that expose the societal backdrop of violent encounters.

Yet as increasing numbers of men, particularly minority and younger males, are incarcerated for longer periods of time in the United States, the rhetoric of victims' rights, including feminist rhetoric, must be critically examined. This means breaking up the idea of a unified stock of stories about male violence, while still preserving the critique of gender domination that is at the heart of feminist analysis (Crenshaw, 1994; Davis, 2000).

NOTES

1 Pleck also describes how reactionary groups, such as the Ku Klux Klan, also punished white men who were wife beaters. The story of wife beating signified a crisis in who was the better protector of white women.

2 For history on the Berlin Intervention project, see http://www.big-interventions zentrale.de

3 Barbara Kaveman describes how the BIG initiative began in the face of intense opposition, which included a call for a boycott by the national network of feminist shelters. See panel presentation, "Interdisciplinary European research network on gender, conflict and violence," http://www.skk.uit.no/WW99/papers/Hagemann_White_Carol.pdf

4 See, for example, the history of Bradley Angle House—one of the oldest shelters in the United States.

5 For further discussion of the concept of psychological splitting as it relates to group conflict, see Alford (1989) and Gülerce (2005).

6 I have made use of Freud's concept of the return of the repressed in describing historical dynamics in the recovered memory movement as well (see Haaken, 1998).

7 A number of feminist websites have been devoted to tracking down the first women's shelters, with varying results and no clear conclusions. This historical search is itself indicative of the symbolic importance within feminism of the early shelter movement.

8 From that turbulent period, Erin Pizzey went on to campaign for conservative "fathers' rights groups" (see Dugan, 2008).

9 A number of advocates point out that women with many children confront often insurmountable barriers in getting into shelter, particularly migrant women.

10 In *The battered woman and shelters: The social construction of wife abuse*, Donileen Loseke (1992) presents an analysis of how shelter staff are often caught between cultural demands for particular victim stories and the more varied experiences of abused women themselves.

11 For more background on how these stories relate to narrating domestic violence, see Haaken (2008b).

12 Terms such as "Native American," "First Nations," "First Peoples," "indigenous," "American Indian," and "Indian" hold a range of geographical and political implications. I use "Native American" to refer to tribes within the United States, but also use the term "Indian" where respondents use this term to describe a pan-Indian identity beyond the borders of the colonizing country.

13 For history on Indian resistance to the US control over Indian lands and resources, see Center for Democratic Renewal (1992).

14 It is important to recognize the wide diversity of indigenous cultures in North America, including hundreds of tribal groups with separate languages. At the same time, many identify with a pan-Indian or Aboriginal Peoples movement.

2

BETWEEN A ROCK AND A HARD PLACE: FEMINIST PSYCHOLOGY AND THE POLITICS OF VIOLENCE

Myth: It takes two to tango.
Counter-myth: Men initiate ninety-five percent of incidents of couple violence.

As tales of deliverance from bondage, women's stories of taking flight from domestic violence represent a genre of mythic proportions. *What's Love Got to Do with It*, a film based on Tina Turner's (1986) autobiography, *I, Tina*, is such a drama in that it narrates the dangers and traps set for women as they traverse the distance from nobody to Somebody. Like many American success stories told through Hollywood films, *What's Love* introduces a series of obstacles to be negotiated on the ascent to fame or fortune and moralizes about the corrupting side of the journey.

While the film chronicles the formative events that shaped the life of Tina Turner—whose powerful voice evokes the rough sexuality she knew all too intimately in her violent marriage to Ike Turner—it also casts her dilemmas within a standard plotline for women. While Ike Turner is cast as a degenerate, progressively lost to sex and drugs, and prone to melancholic brooding and violent outbursts, Tina Turner, offstage, is portrayed as saintly—as perpetually good, lacking in vices, and without a trace of egoism, despite her skyrocketing success and entry into the high life. We never see her with a drink or cigarette in her hand, nor is this cinematic portrait of her marred by any unsettling suggestion of female conflict between success and maternal obligation. When she gives birth to a son, it is Ike, rapaciously driven by money and the pursuit of stardom, who extracts the newborn from Tina's arms. As Ike forces her back onto the stage, Tina wails out her postpartum blues in a state of anguish, projecting a defiant sexuality that co-mingles with erotic surrender. Her public success and her private tyranny are fused, obliterating any space in the drama for exploring the protagonist's own conflicting desires.

Many women in the audience may be able to identify with this successful black woman who "sings like a man"—belting out songs aggressively, her movements conveying a bold sexuality—because her private persona conforms to white middle-class standards of womanhood. In the film, Tina Turner is cast as virtuous wife—chaste, loyal, and having the sole tragic flaw of suffering from *too much* virtue. Knowing what it is like to lose someone she loves, having lost her own mother in childhood, she refuses to leave Ike, even as he beats her with increasing frequency and ferocity. At the film's denouement, Tina finds the strength to leave, with the help of a woman friend and her newfound conversion to Buddhism.

The film foregrounds, rightfully, how a woman's success can be terrifying to a man, and how violence can be a means of bringing her down. Yet the narrative structure of this drama sends a reassuring message to white audiences. The pernicious threat to this black woman's survival emanates entirely from her black husband. In this gripping tale of emancipation from abuse, there are no exploitive white people. Whites are cast as respectful, helpful, and generous toward blacks, often aiding Tina in her struggle to escape her demonic husband. Ike emerges as the singular source of evil, the place where the badness in Tina's life (and a sexist society) may be safely located and contained. Through this cinematic working of racial ambivalence, white audiences are able to enjoy the triumph of the good black woman without feeling implicated in her troubles.[1]

At the first of a series of training sessions I attended at a Portland shelter for battered women, we were encouraged to see *What's Love Got to Do with It.* More than other popularized films on domestic violence, our trainer suggested, this film captures the issues women confront in battering situations. An issue often neglected in the domestic violence field, however, concerns the social and cultural forces shaping how stories of family violence get told. The film about Tina Turner's harrowing and heroic struggle with domestic violence inadvertently dramatizes key dilemmas that organizers face, as do women leaving abusive relationships: the female protagonist must meet an extreme standard of feminine virtue in order to be cast as a legitimate victim, and her story must conform to this standard plotline—one that has gained currency in the domestic violence field, as well as within popular culture.

In introducing the problematic position of psychology in the battered women's movement, this chapter builds on conversations that emerged from the field interviews. The focus is on group dynamics and border tensions that emerge in providing crisis services for women, and on the considerable emotional labor required in interpreting stories of women in crisis.[2]

My discussions with advocates over the role of psychology in the movement typically began with the failed romance between women's advocates and Lenore Walker, who introduced the concept of the battered woman syndrome in the late 1970s. Walker's work spans several decades of feminist research and registers the historical shifts in the movement, including the demise of psychological theories in explaining woman battering (1978,

1979a, 1988, 1989, 1999, 2006). Although many advocates have jettisoned Walker's research on the battered woman syndrome (Allard, 1991; Bentzel & York, 1988; Pagelow, 1992), this chapter draws out some of the contributions of her early theory as well as its limitations. As an alternative, I make use of psychoanalytic social theory, and particularly Kleinian concepts, in working between the psychological and the political poles of the problem of partner violence. A key site of border tension—and site of anxiety and defensiveness in the battered women's movement—centers on how to recognize the complexities of women's experiences with violence, including the female capacity for destructive forms of rage, without shifting the load of social responsibility for family violence onto the shoulders of women (Johnson, 2006; Rosen, 2006; Stark, 2006; Straus, 2006).

WHAT'S PSYCHOLOGY GOT TO DO WITH IT?

At a fall, 2000 conference on domestic violence and the African American community, Captain Toni Malliet, a black woman and head of the Division of Domestic Violence and Sexual Assault of the Seattle Police Department, also made use of *What's Love Got to Do with It*. She began her presentation with a story. She described a nervous young girl with chronic stomachaches, a girl who watched helplessly as her mother was routinely beaten by her father. In biblical tones, Malliet told of how this girl grew older and rose up against her father, driving him from the house. "That girl was me . . . But now," she continued with a wry smile, "I don't have to take abuse from nobody. I've got a gun, a license to carry it, and I know how to use it."[3] Malliet went on to acknowledge periods of agonizing doubt over working in an institution that often brutalizes her own community. And she expressed unease over arresting men who have little sense of power or control, other than over the women they are terrorizing. After belting out a few lines of *What's Love Got to Do with It*, Malliet concluded by saying that "love's got a lot to do with it." Until the community learns to love each other, Malliet insisted, the tragedy of domestic violence will continue. During the question and answer period, a woman from the audience asked Malliet what she was doing about a recent incident where police killed two young black men in the Central District of Seattle. This question prompted a discussion of the dangers in relying on the police, and of how domestic violence can't be separated from the broader problem of violence in African American communities.

In contrast to many conferences I have attended on domestic violence organized by white feminists, presenters and participants at the conference where Malliet spoke were able to hold in mind a complex range of stories and explanations for domestic violence. The topic of *female* aggression—whether whipping kids or lashing out against partners—did not elicit a wave of defensive outrage. Discussing the importance of incorporating men into the movement, even those with a history of violence, was not felt to be a threat to female solidarity. Participants were able to explore myriad determinants of violence, including situations of violence where women play an active part, while still holding men accountable.

Psychology often takes discussion of family violence in a conservative direction, however, rather than advancing a more complex analysis (Goldner, 1985; Humphreys & Joseph, 2004; Staeuble, 2005). There is a longstanding tendency in Western societies, the United States particularly, to offer individual therapeutic solutions to collective social problems. Yet in recovering the work of psychologist Lenore Walker from the dustbins of the movement's history, I am attempting to retrieve its important insights. Often overlooked is the fact that Walker's work was more *social psychology* than clinical psychology, even though the battered woman syndrome is her most famous (and infamous) contribution to the field. In the cycle of violence theory she proposed, there are the rudimentary beginnings of a dynamic social theory of partner violence—one that lays the groundwork for a more comprehensive approach than does the Duluth power and control model.

In bringing psychology into the early battered women's movement, Lenore Walker was admittedly political from the start. Published in 1979, *The battered woman* estimates that 50 percent of women in the United States are battered by their male partners sometime in their lives (Walker, 1979a). Much like other estimates of tabooed private behavior not readily open to public scrutiny or verification, this number has been challenged (Dutton & Nicholls, 2005). But the precise number is less relevant here than are the discursive strategies of this fledgling movement. Walker could claim that 50 percent of women had been battered in part because of the definition she used to derive such a number, a definition that she has retained over the course of her work.

> A battered woman is a woman who is repeatedly subjected to any forceful physical or psychological behavior by a man in order to coerce her to do something he wants her to do without any concern for her rights. Battered women include wives or women in any form of intimate relationships with men. Furthermore, in order to be classified as a battered woman, the couple must go through the battering cycle at least twice. Any woman may find herself in an abusive relationship with a man once. If it occurs a second time, and she remains in the situation, she is defined as a battered woman.
>
> (Walker, 1979: xv)

Movements struggling for legitimacy face the challenge of moving from the margins to the center, of shifting the political ground from a minority to a majority concern. They also confront resistances, either in the dominant group's minimization of the injuries suffered or in the disavowal of responsibility for those injuries. Walker argues that a near majority of women are victims of male violence, ritually conducted behind closed doors. Much like changing definitions of sexual abuse (Haaken, 1998), Walker's construction of the battered woman syndrome also enlarges the category to encompass a much broader range of normative male behaviors than did earlier definitions of wife beating. Her definition includes psychological coercion and lack of concern for the woman's welfare, experiences with which vast numbers of women could identify. Indeed, if the definition were literally applied, one would expect that far more than 50 percent of women have experienced coercive demands at least twice in the same relationship. In practice, however, the battered woman syndrome came to connote a more sustained pattern of physical assaults upon a woman. But the broadness of the definition created an implicit sense of sisterhood, a realization that overtly battered women suffered from a sickness generated by patriarchy—one that all women suffered from to various degrees.

In her theory of battering, Walker draws heavily on social psychologist Martin Seligman and his concept of *learned helplessness* (Walker, 1978). Based on research conducted with dogs in the 1970s, Seligman advanced a behavioral explanation for passivity in abusive situations. By administering short bolts of electricity to the animals and blocking their escape, Seligman created an experimental situation that parallels many human experiences with abuse under conditions of captivity. Seligman demonstrated a rather commonsense finding: when animals learn that escape opportunities are not contingent upon their responses, they become increasingly passive, even failing to attempt escape after the experimenters create opportunities to do so.

Identifications are more complex in human development—and perhaps in the development of lower-order animals as well—than Seligman's model would suggest. Rather than a learned helplessness model, it may be more correct to describe the observations that Walker assembles through an *illusion of control* model. A striking difference between Seligman's dogs and Walker's battered wives is in the latter's persistent belief in their own control, despite evidence to the contrary. Indeed, as Walker points out, most women do not consider themselves battered until they have experienced extreme and chronic assaults. Contrary to predictions, Walker suggests, battered women score higher than average norms for adults on internal locus of control. She explains this seemingly paradoxical finding:

> It may be that battered women do believe they control their own lives . . . It may be this sense of internal control that is the hope which allows the battered woman to believe she will be able to

> change the batterer or the environment in such a way that things will get better.
>
> (Walker, 1979a: 79)

Walker closes the distance between the battered woman as the Other and the rest of us by sketching the picture of the battered woman along the outlines of the Good Wife. Walker rejects the conventional portrait of the inadequate woman whose poor coping skills and low self-esteem make her the inevitable doormat of her husband. Rather, the picture that emerges is of a woman actively engaged in realizing her ambition of creating a harmonious family. In her early study, Walker describes the battered woman as a "traditionalist about the home, (who) strongly believes in family unity and the prescribed feminine sex-role stereotype" (Walker, 1979a: 31).

While the term "*syndrome*" implies a cluster of associated symptoms without a known cause, Walker does identify a cause of the battered woman syndrome: a cycle of violence. Much like the common cold, the syndrome is incubated behind closed doors. And much like physical illnesses, the syndrome occurs in predictable phases. These include the tension-building period, the explosive or acute battering phase, and the contrition or "honeymoon" phase, when the man attempts to make reparation with his wounded wife. Phase one introduces the greatest variability in describing the responses of women, including attempts to precipitate a battering episode (phase two). Walker (1979a) describes the woman's behavior during that first tension-building period as "collaborating" in the abuse in that her placating behavior implicitly accepts his entitlement to outbursts. But in describing the honeymoon phase, when the husband becomes contrite and seeks forgiveness from his wife, Walker extends her narrative to include the community. In the aftermath of a beating, friends and relatives often deny what has happened. Bruises and broken bones are interpreted as accidents—as evidence that the woman bruises easily or is clumsy, compounding the woman's isolation and her own tendency to minimize the violence. In contradistinction to conventional scripts on family violence, with their Hollywood happy endings, Walker's battering narrative avoids the false closure of a comforting denouement. The honeymoon phase sets the stage for the repetition of the cycle, for a Nietzschean tragic *eternal recurrence*.

Although the patriarchal family is cast as primary pathogen in this feminist diagnosis of the injuries of women, Walker's reliance on the medical model was a costly strategy. In enlisting medical discourse, the battered woman syndrome gained legitimacy for the problem of wife beating but it also became reified. Even as shifting the discursive terrain from a moral framework to a socio-medical model represented an advance, this same model authorized experts to diagnosis, assess, and contain the problem. Such models typically overlook the myriad ways in which those whose job it is to "name the problem" are also implicated in its very societal reproduction.[4]

Walker's theory did depart from an individual psychology, however, in its focus on relational dynamics. Some aspects of her cycle of violence theory could be framed through the psychoanalytic concept of "*projective identification*"—a concept developed by British psychoanalyst Melanie Klein (1952) and central to contemporary psychoanalytic theory (Alford, 1989; Mills, 2006; Young, 2006).[5] Projective identification suggests a pathological social dynamic where both (or many) people are engaged in a destructive interaction, bound together through the externalizing and internalizing, often in rapid succession, of emotions. A disturbing emotional state (e.g., vulnerability, hostility, envy, arousal) is managed defensively by externalizing that state and perceiving it as a part of another person rather than as part of the self. This concept of projection, also discussed in Chapter 1, has been absorbed into everyday or "folk" psychology—explaining, for example, how bullies conceal feelings of inadequacy by placing someone else in the vulnerable position. The interplay of *projection* and *identification*—a centerpiece of contemporary psychoanalytic approaches—is less familiar.[6] Identification enters the drama when the individual develops a dependency on the object of projection in order to enact some emotional state that the individual refuses to acknowledge as a part of him/herself. In dramaturgical terms, the dynamic is one of vicarious experience, where each protagonist plays a part in the drama by enacting one side of an unbearable conflict (Alford, 1989; Young, 2006).

Walker brought new insights into the field of family violence by reframing wife battering as a choreographed event rather than as a loss of control. In addition to this idea of a dynamic cycle—one that repeats itself because it is never satisfactorily resolved—there are other dynamic concepts that may be useful in interpreting what Walker describes as the battered woman syndrome. From a psychoanalytic perspective, stories about others are, in part, stories about the self—with other protagonists in the drama sometimes registering unconscious aspects of the storyteller's own internal world. The victim's story about an abuser may represent both an objective event and a conflict originating in the past that continues to occupy an important place in psychic life. She may protect the abuser not only because she relies on him for material support but because he represents a vital part of her own internal world, whether the "bad object" of childhood or a dangerous and undomesticated part of her own desires.

In *The battered woman*, Walker (1979a) offers interpretations of women's responses that could be viewed as victim-blaming, but they also suggest the powerful bonds that can form through destructive attachments. In describing the unstable, disturbing mental states that battered women experience in the cycle of abuse, Walker (1989: 69) notes that "Her self-image withers as she copes with the awareness that she is selling herself for brief periods of phase-three behavior. She becomes an accomplice to her own battering." Walker also concludes that rage is a combustible dynamic in abuse situations for women as well as for men: "These women often lose control of their suppressed rage and seriously injure their men" (1989: 69). The honeymoon period, where the man seeks forgiveness, allows for a dynamic reversal of positions where the woman gains the upper hand. For both victim and perpetrator, the cycle permits a revisiting of early traumatic attachments where violence operates as one form of human connection and recognition (see Benjamin, 1988).

Power shapes the denouement, however, just as it shapes the positions adopted in the drama. Those with more power—those who control material resources and the terms of dependency—are more able to enlist the less powerful to accept the transfer of "hot" emotional goods. From a Kleinian perspective, working through destructive attachments requires recognition of these multiple identifications and moving from what Klein (1952) described as the "paranoid schizoid position," the prototypical position of the batterer, who projects his terrors onto the object he both dreads and desperately needs, and toward the "depressive position" where the destructiveness of one's own rage and the power of infantile dependencies can be acknowledged (Gülerce, 2005; Klein, 1952; Young, 2006). The depressive position represents a movement beyond all-good and all-bad categories and paranoia and toward more integrated ethical responses—principles implicit in Truth and Reconciliation Commissions (TRCs) throughout the world.[7]

This chapter turns later to insights about the psychological dynamics of abuse that emerged from the interviews—insights not generally incorporated into the domestic violence literature. Before entering this terrain, it is important to understand how the folk knowledge of scientific psychology has circulated in the domestic violence field. As emotionally charged context for any discussion of psychology, the power of psychological literature provides a crucial backdrop for what we might describe as *group countertransference reactions*—emotional reactions rooted in formative experiences in the past.[8] As much as the batterer, psychology is the "bad object" of the battered women's movement.

SCIENTIFIC PSYCHOLOGY AND BATTERING

Science and feminism find common cause in their persistent search for the correct sources of human suffering. Explanations handed down from one generation to the next are suspect because they rely on traditional (mythic) sources of authority. On yet another front, many feminists regard science warily. Feminist critics point out how scientists are active protagonists in the stories they tell, shaping the very findings that they produce. In reviews of the scientific literature on violence, feminists often object to scientific accounts of violence, pointing out how cause and effect are organized through a patriarchal storyline (Rubin, 2008). In starting with *frustration* as the originating cause of male aggression, researchers in the 1960s, for example, perpetuated the idea that aggression was the natural response (Lawson, 1989; Yllo, 1993). The frustration-aggression hypothesis, as it was called, implicitly reinforced cultural demands on women to provide the necessary relief in managing pressure cooker states of manhood.

Take, as another example, the Conflict Tactics Scale (CTS), the most widely used instrument for assessing levels of family violence. Murray Straus and Richard Gelles (1990), who developed the instrument, have generated the frequently cited statistics on rates of family violence in the United States. In their introduction to *Physical violence in American families*, Straus and Gelles describe the hostility and outrage directed at them by many feminists after the publication of their research findings. As leading investigators in the largest national surveys in the United States on family violence, they have been at the center of a raging controversy over the extent of women's participation in family violence. Based on large samples of respondents in several national surveys, the authors conclude that women are as likely as men to initiate and participate in aggressive encounters with domestic partners, including in the use of physical force. Women report that they commit acts of aggression against domestic partners as frequently as do men, and that most of these acts of aggression are not in the form of self-defense.[9]

These findings are not easy to dismiss on methodological grounds. Whereas previous research on family violence was based on special populations, such as students, therapy patients, or clients in battered women shelters, these national surveys carry greater scientific weight because they are based on a more representative sample of American families. Not only does this research offer a broader glimpse of the actual frequency and forms of domestic violence, but also associated factors, such as the relative contribution of gender inequality and economic conditions.

In their effort to untangle these effects, Straus and colleagues (1980) conclude that gender and violence interact differently in private life than they do in the public domain. Although women are far less aggressive than men and commit only a fraction of violent *public* crimes, this same gender difference does not hold true in the context of the household. While the authors place male supremacy at the root of many forms of violence, they also conclude that women participate in family violence far more extensively than is assumed in the domestic violence field. Indeed, they argue that women engage in as much aggression and violence against spouses as do men, and that their aggressive behavior is not merely defensive. Women acknowledge *initiating* physical aggression against their partners as often as do men. The most important sex difference is in the extent of injuries sustained after a fight and in the readiness to seek help. Women suffer more serious physical injury and are also more likely than men to seek help subsequent to domestic assault.[10] These are important findings, of course, but may readily be lost in battles over the either/or categories of victim and perpetrator.

Some of the criticisms of this line of research are common to survey studies more generally: the superficiality of the findings, the reliance on what respondents are willing to acknowledge in their own behavior, and the tendency to tally behaviors without attending to their multiple meanings or their social context (DeKeseredy, 2006). Since women are more apt to view themselves as responsible for male behavior, women may feel guilty about their own aggression and thus more apt to label it as "offensive." Men, on the other hand, are socialized to externalize responsibility for their own aggression, and to view even extreme acts of violence as defensive. Further, critics argue that survey questionnaires obscure the complex relational and power dynamics of gender, generating a body of dislocated facts (DeKeseredy & Schwartz, 1998; Dobash & Dobash, 1979).

But there are significant constraints on most research findings, so we must be careful not to just shop around for findings that support our prior beliefs. At the same time, this equating of male and female contributors to family violence is very suspicious. We have learned from experience that those in power are never short of scientists ready to do their bidding, to produce findings that naturalize prevailing ideologies. But how do we tell a truer story of domestic violence? Is there a procedure we may follow that circumnavigates the various barriers blocking our view? Further, if the behavior in question is not open to public scrutiny—if it happens behind closed doors—do the procedures of science assist us in getting a better picture of what is going on?

Science, including social science, is best conducted in a context open to impartial scrutiny. Carefully trained observers agree on a set of rules for testing claims and scrutinizing the evidence. Most domestic abuse operates outside the bounds of public observation and behind the backs, as it were, of scientists. The various effects of oppression that women know so intimately in private life may not be readily detected through the tools of science. Further, male investigators, like the police, bring their own blind spots to the investigation, perhaps unable to see the suffering of women even when it is in view.

As feminist researchers Claire Renzetti (1999) and Janice Ristock (2002) point out, studying this terrain confronts a minefield of reactions from feminists and non/anti-feminists alike. Donald Dutton *et al.* (2009), for example, mount a persuasive case based on research studies suggesting that women and men are equally violent in private life. But as Walter DeKeseredy and Molly Dragiewicz (2007) argue in their review, their case against "feminist ideologues" suffers from the very problem they purport to remedy. Their critique is so dismissive of the political aspects of violence that it protests too much in its countering of feminist "excesses."

Some researchers intervene in the dilemma over how women are implicated in family violence by tightening the boundaries between categories circulating in the field, introducing space in the debate for normal fighting. In distinguishing between what he terms "patriarchal terrorism" and "common couple violence," Michael Johnson (1995) argues that the domestic violence prototype does not adequately capture the various expressions of physical aggression in families. Many women engage in controlled outbursts of minor violence, as do many men. Episodes of slapping, throwing things, or yelling may dissipate as quickly as they erupt. It is important to distinguish between these forms of aggression and more sadistic forms—ritualized physical and emotional assaults intended to break down a woman's sense of self and to achieve psychological control over her.

In creating the two categories, Johnson introduces female aggression while preserving a feminist analysis of the problem. This typology also offers a corrective to feminist models that over-pathologize aggression. As advocates enlarged the category of domestic violence to include emotional abuse and verbal abuse, Johnson's effort to distinguish between normative and more oppressive forms was a reaction to this very category crisis in the field. If all bad behavior is subsumed under the rubric of violence, the term loses any capacity to differentiate and collapses under its own etymological weight.[11]

Murray Straus (1973) also began his program of research with the argument that violence in the family has been a norm historically, and that taboos against family violence have developed over recent centuries. As the industrial revolution undermined the household as a site of production, the work of women within the family was economically marginalized. The ideological division between the private and public spheres widened while the middle-class household emerged as an idealized refuge from the harsh competition of the marketplace (Douglas, 1977). Responsible for preserving family harmony, wives held some authority in reigning in male vices and influencing men "behind the scenes" (Epstein, 1981; Gordon, 1988). The ideal of the companionate marriage that gained currency in the United States in the 1920s—largely in the wake of turn-of-the-century feminism—did implicitly confront the double standard and expand the rights of wives (Stanley, 1998). Husbands could expect devotion as well as dutiful service from their wives, but so too could wives from husbands. Women were directed to find fulfillment in heterosexual marriage, just as were men.

As Lynne Segal (1990) argues, sex/gender identifications are complex and dynamic, and masculinity means different things to working-class men than it does to middle- and upper-class men. Working-class men have used their bodies, whether in displays of toughness or shows of bravado, to resist more powerful men. In recent decades of feminist scholarship the focus on gender as performance (Butler, 1990), as dynamic and multi-layered (Harris, 2005), and as a product of history and social negotiation (Gergen & Davis, 1997), works with the idea that gendered forms of power are continuously negotiated. Even in the prototypical patriarchal nuclear family, men often are in the more passive position in ceding control over everyday decisions to women. There is a longstanding tension in the patriarchal family over who "really is in charge," and over the scope and limits of female authority. The domestic violence literature tends to downplay male passivity and the relational struggles that ensue over this passivity. Female aggression does take the form of self-defense—such as hitting, slapping, biting, or kicking in combating male assaults (Browne, 1987). But women may employ aggressive tactics in other contests over power as well. If we begin with the assumption that the causal relationship between gender and violence is not simple and straightforward, we allow for a more complex range of dynamics in framing female reactions to a history of oppression.

SCIENTIFIC FRAMING OF FEMALE AGGRESSION

In returning to the story of Lenore Walker, I provide some context for one of the hottest battle zones in the domestic violence field—the question of whether women engage in non-defensive forms of violence. My aim is to provide some context for understanding the intensity of emotional investments in this question and group defenses that have blunted storytelling strategies in the movement.[12] In addition to the work of Walker, I trace the steps of other feminist psychologists who have ventured into this contested terrain, seeking to forge a path between the myth that women are as violent as men and the counter-myth that women are almost never the primary perpetrators.

The theoretical moves of Lenore Walker over several decades of writing on domestic violence register the signifying power of this issue. Although Walker has consistently framed female aggression as a defensive response to male abuse, her early book, published in 1979, includes discussion of the battered woman's rage, as well as varying degrees of culpability in her own oppression. One case illustrates the outrage that could follow an acute episode of battering:

> I really saw red. I mean, when he hit me, it was like putting a cape in front of a bull. I could hardly see straight, just amazed. I just wanted to kill him. A couple of times, I got to the point where I would pull a knife on him. I don't think I ever would have stabbed him, but I just came darn close to it. I felt like . . . Oh, I just had to do it.
>
> (Walker, 1979a: 85)

By the 1990s, as the movement was gaining momentum, the profiles of battered women underwent notable domestication. There was hardly a trace of anger or rage in the battering narratives that circulated in the domestic violence field, including in the many accounts of battering reported in Walker's (1989) book, *Terrifying love*. Drawing on the dissociation model that acquired currency in the 1980s, Walker concludes that women who respond violently often do so in a hypnotic state. Walker (1989: 41) claims that "Women don't kill unless it is their last resort. They don't want the batterer to die, but rather, they just want him to stop hurting them."

It is understandable that battered women have been valorized within feminism because they do bear—literally and symbolically—the collective injuries of women. They are the fallen soldiers in the war against patriarchy, and particularly heroic if they take up arms against the enemy. However, this form of *defensive idealization* of victims may allow for a decisive resolution of the story and, consequently, greater social disengagement from the dilemmas of the movement and from abused women themselves. Women, as well as men, often turn away from the problem of partner violence out of hesitancy to interfere in someone else's business, or simply because they don't know what to do. The impulse to resolve the conflict quickly by identifying clear villains and victims can find its object in cultural scripts that offer easy denouements. Idealization of the victim may be yet another form of social distance in that it denies the woman the full range of her humanity. In a sense, idealization is a demand; it is a demand that the other be "good" in order to be worthy of concern.

Romantic portraits of women who kill their partners also betray a degree of collective anxiety, including female anxiety, that murderous rage in women *may be* more inhuman, more perverse, than it is in men. Walker falls into this trap in her later work focused on the legal defense of women:

> Almost every battered woman tells of wishing, at some point, that the batterer were dead, maybe even of fantasizing how he might die. These wishes and fantasies are normal, considering the extraordinary injustice these women suffer at their men's hands. But it is equally true that the small number of women who kill their batterers do not necessarily want them dead at the time; rather, they are seeking only to put an end to their pain and terror.
>
> (Walker, 1989: 106)

The lionizing of women who kill their male partners is, in part, a reaction against the demonizing of these same women. Walker points out that men serving on juries find it hard to believe that women who are abused would not want to lash out in anger. "If they perceive a battered woman defendant to be truly angry," Walker suggests, "they are likely to judge her more harshly than if they perceive her to be 'merely' afraid" (1989: 202).

In *Women who kill*, Ann Jones (1980) similarly notes the disproportionate horror aroused by displays of female aggression in the family. Jones also offers a cultural interpretation: "It is entirely possible, albeit entirely unproven, that women who kill their batterers are subconsciously perceived as expressing a collective message from all women to all men: *your days of controlling us are over*" (1980: 218). Yet Jones, much like Walker, retreats from this bold acknowledgement of female rage, emphasizing instead its place as a sequel to violence. Anger is the emotion that follows homicide, Jones explains, "the emotion that is allowed to exist freely only when terror and pain, shame and grief, are washed away" (1980: 219). Jones points out that anger is a source of creative, healing energy, just as it is vital fuel in the fight against injustice. But in affirming the positive side of female aggression, Jones launders it of its destructive potential. Even in a state of homicidal rage, women remain essentially good.

Some feminist psychologists have revisited the topic of female aggression by focusing on gender differences in motivations for violence (Browne, 1987). Anne Campbell (1993), for example, argues that men and women hold different attitudes toward acting out violently. She cites studies indicating that males and females experience similar rates and intensities of anger, but that they differ markedly in their subjective experiences. Women are more apt to view their own aggression as a *loss of control*, whereas men are more apt to view their own aggression as a means of *gaining control*. In other words, men and women have contrary experiences in subjective associations between aggressive acting out and self-esteem. Aggression is more integrated into and constitutive of masculinity, Campbell concludes, just as it is more alien to and undermining of femininity.

Campbell (1993) carries us further than many scholars in making space for female aggression while holding to a feminist analysis of couple violence. Conceding the validity of research suggesting that women can be as aggressive as men in domestic situations, Campbell explains such findings as consistent with available literature suggesting that women are slower to wrath than are men. Placing women's aggression in the context of imbalances in the sexual division of labor within the household, she points out that women have far more *cause* for aggression against spouses than do men. Just cause is not limited to defending against physical assaults of male partners, but includes male refusal to assume their fair share of domestic duties. Whereas men experience the home as a refuge at the end of the working day, Campbell notes, women are less apt to be granted such respite.

As Campbell points out, anger and aggression, like many other human emotional reactions, are not directly proportionate to immediate stimuli, nor are they reliable indicators of objective events. Defensive emotions, whether aroused in men or women, are sometimes rational and sometimes not, at times directed toward actual threats and at other times toward imaginary or displaced ones. It is in the nature of emotions, particularly disturbing negative emotions, that there is some slippage between the emotional state and the target. Anger is object-seeking, and the object may not always take the form of an actual threat. Women are as capable as men of building a case against someone in the course of self-justification.

Campbell takes an approach consistent with cultural feminism in suggesting that female aggression is more *expressive* whereas male aggression is more *instrumental*.[13] Here she uses two widely employed categories in the field, both of which carry some problematic freight. The concept of *expressive aggression* focuses on the internal build-up of tension that precedes aggression. Freud is viewed as the father of this cathartic model, with numerous subsequent versions and modifications. While Freud viewed aggression as a drive, subject to build-up and release, more contemporary psychoanalytic theorists, many of whom reject the idea of an innate aggressive drive, focus on relational motivations and deficits. From the perspective of psychoanalytic object relations theory, which is the dominant model within contemporary psychoanalysis, violent behavior is thought to be a response to emotional deprivation or trauma (Chodorow, 1978; Goldner, 1998). Repeated aggressive or violent behaviors are the result of traumatic attachments. Object relations theorists attend to how aggression binds the self to a real or imagined Other. For example, a neglected or abused child may engage in fights or other anti-social behavior as a means of restoring human connection. Provoking a parental beating may be preferable to being ignored because the beating provides *some* form of human connection and holding—an example of the dynamic of projective identification.

The concept of *instrumental aggression*, on the other hand, places far less emphasis on attachments and emphasizes instead the reward functions of aggression. From this perspective, boys learn to be more aggressive than girls because *it works*. This more behavioral interpretation is less attentive to what is "behind" the aggression than in its observable antecedents and effects. In extending this behavioral model to male development, Campbell suggests that boys acquire aggressive behavior in manipulating the environment to achieve desired ends, and they do it because they can get away with it.

From childrearing practices to global warfare, Campbell depicts women as more expressive and men as more instrumental in their aggressive motives and in their moral reasoning. When women do express aggression, Campbell concludes, it typically follows a long build-up and release of tension. Female aggression is less oriented toward instrumental effects, for women have learned since early childhood that aggressive responses rarely get them what they want. Even when women lash out against their male partners, they are more apt to be indiscriminate in their aggression, erupting in an explosive and uncontrollable way. When men assault their female partners, the aggression is more directed and controlled, even when it leads to lethal damage.

This line of argument is important in that it incorporates female aggression into feminist theorizing while keeping a primary focus on male domination. Campbell avoids the slippery slope that many feminists caution against: that any acknowledgement of female tendencies toward aggression inevitably risks opening the door to the villainizing of women. Campbell emphasizes the rational basis of female aggression as an expression of frustration and overwhelming family responsibilities. Women do finally reach a boiling point—although it is slow in coming—when they sometimes lash out.

Feminist psychoanalytic researchers and clinicians have documented this same tendency in female development in male-dominated Western societies. Intense affective states associated with the body—from sexual desire, hunger, to rage—are often experienced as ego-alien and as a loss of control (Haaken, 1998; Rose, 1986; Ussher, 2008). Women may internalize social prohibitions against "excessive" desires and come to fear their own impulses—a dynamic process that may include re-projection of these prohibitions back onto the external world. This vicious cycle includes a perpetual revitalizing of authority—whether a father, husband, master, or repressive social order—as that authority acquires the capacity to protect against dangerous impulses. Indeed, repressive social orders depend on their capacities to mobilize affective investments in their censoring power (Zizek, 2001). From a psychoanalytic perspective, however, there is always a "remainder" of desire that eludes social regulation—a perpetual return of the repressed—that opens possibilities for transcending a given social order.

RECOVERING FEMINIST PSYCHOLOGY: INSIGHTS FROM ADVOCATES

In carrying out interviews in the different geographical settings, my aim was to enlist advocates in thinking through ways of framing female aggression within the context of a feminist analysis of domestic violence and, further, developing a psychology of violence that attends to cultural and historical contexts. Addressing the role of psychology in the domestic violence field generated discussion of dynamics at three levels: *the individual* (e.g., the battered woman and the batterer); the *dyad* (e.g., couple dynamics); and *the group* (e.g., crisis work, cultural communities, including political communities, and societal responses). Since my project focused on cultural contexts for understanding how stories about family violence get told, the interviews went beyond the contentious issue of diagnosis and counseling, even though this was the starting point for all of our conversations about psychology.

Individual psychology

Initial reactions to the role of psychology in the field centered on clinical approaches to battered women, and particularly on the use of diagnoses that pathologize women. Tawa Witko, a psychologist working with Cangleska, on the Pine Ridge Reservation of South Dakota, suggests that "In the beginning, psychologists were often used as a tool against women, particularly in how they dealt with kids in domestic violence situations." Since psychologists have been involved in family assessments and child protection procedures, Native women expect psychologists to intervene punitively, a fear that has grown out of the early history of whites removing Indian children from their homes and placing them in boarding schools.

Advocates in the four settings are unified in their critique: psychology approaches domestic violence as an individual pathology rather than a social problem and tends to identify the woman on the scene as the person most responsible for family violence. In the Women's Refuge group in London, one advocate tells the story of a psychiatrist in the family violence field who set out to study perpetrators in the 1970s but ended up studying women because they were more "accessible."

> "So he worked with our women, and he came up with typologies that basically pathologized women. In his personality categories he used words like 'go-go Gloria,' and 'Fannie the flirt.' This caused a lot of animosity in the feminist movement and that tension is still around . . . In the medical community women are given drugs to deal with their stress rather than giving the responsibility to the abuser or trying to change the situation."

Psychologists tend to blame women and make "excuses" for men, advocates claim, whether in casting the man's violence as a response to failure on the part of the wife to meet his emotional needs or to failure of a mother figure to provide adequate nurture in his childhood. But as Witko points out, it is possible to interrupt destructive behavior while also addressing the role of childhood trauma in men's lives. Witko and I also discussed the feminist dilemma over whether to view male violence as an ego deficit or ego excess—whether abusive men have too little or too much ego strength.

> "The reality is that it is a little of both—for some it is their insecurities, the little boy in a man's body who is acting out—and for others it's just about power. But even for them, there is this insecurity. We don't teach our men—not just Indian men—how to act and feel when they have a feeling of insecurity, or how to ask for help . . . That's not an excuse for their violence, but if you get right down to it, there is that little boy who doesn't know what to do."

Witko explains that their approach is to "Make men accountable while also creating cultural awareness that woman beating violates traditional native practices, that he can't say he's following the Red Road, and then beat his wife." Women are remapping the Red Road—and the meaning of traditional cultural practices—by interpreting battering as a form of identification with the colonizer. From a psychoanalytic standpoint, this interpretation could be viewed as moving from the paranoid position to the depressive position—what Melanie Klein (1952) describes as a developmental advance from primitive splitting to recognizing one's capacity to harm the loved object (Alford, 1989; Hollway, 2006). Invoking shared ideals works toward building up the "good objects" of the group—nurturing aspects of the Native traditions—a vital part of walking the Red Road to non-violence.

Sumaya Colman, an advocate in the New York group, also makes the point that simply transferring blame from the woman to the man, from defining the problem as her individual pathology to defining it as his power motives, limits understanding of the wider context of family violence. Both responses assume an individual psychology based on an all-good victim and an all-bad perpetrator.

> "What I say is: Do we have to vilify a woman in order to say it's unfair or unjust for her to be a victim? Why do we have to demonize a man in order to make him the perpetrator? When I came into this movement I came in under the white feminist thought and theory and model and all that. But that's not where I learned about violence and how it played itself out in my community, nor in my own household."

Colman, an African American advocate working in the domestic violence field, emphasizes the costs of downplaying the role women play in the dynamics of violence, whether of the expressive or the instrumental types. She goes on to suggest that African American women are less averse to the use of violence in protecting themselves, and this sometimes spills over into actual abuse. In her own community, women are insisting that the movement address this issue. "The more you suppress them, ignore them, it seems like the more it writhes. So I began to say, 'let's talk about it, let's pick it apart, let's listen to it rather than denying it.'"

In the following dialogue among advocates in New York City, a racially/ethnically mixed group of women struggle with uneasiness over how to think about female aggression, and the question of whether female aggression ever spills over into offensive (versus defensive) forms of violence:

INTERVIEWER: "In other areas of oppression you could say, in African American communities, men can be understood as violent in response to their oppression . . . That is one way people cope with oppression. So why has that been so difficult to allow here?"

FIRST ADVOCATE: "Because it's sexist . . ."

SECOND ADVOCATE: "There's sexism underlying the battered women's movement. It's total sexist . . . to define this as a battered women's movement. Because women are the victims [in that definition of the movement] and to me, women have a hell of a lot of strength and a hell of a lot of power."

INTERVIEWER: "If you go that route and allow for the range of women's responses to their oppressions—some of which might be violent—then do you lose the gender analysis? Do you lose that primary way that men feel entitled or granted a kind of empowerment to use violence?"

THIRD ADVOCATE: "I think the problem is that most people don't think in a nuanced way on this issue. You know, we pass this law where you're supposed to do an analysis to figure out who's the primary physical aggressor. Well theoretically that could apply to a heterosexual couple or it could apply to a gay couple. But the problem is that we feel forced sometimes to take very clear positions."

FOURTH ADVOCATE: "I also think that people are starting to understand that in communities of color there are different perceptions about violence and it fits in a different space than it does in the white community. And those are all nuances of the issue. But I frankly agree that there are women who are troubled, who abuse their kids, and who are violent with other women in relationships, or maybe are even violent with men. But I think we get forced into a little bit of a box by the action and by the backlash that is constantly in our face about these laws."

The phobic response to female aggression in many areas of the domestic violence field may signify a collective internalization of patriarchal paranoia—an enactment of a cultural drama where feminists, who bear the heaviest brunt of male anxieties over female power, may find themselves most intent on proving the patriarchs wrong by being the best of daughters. As Sujata Warrior points out, however, the image of the good victim is largely a cultural fantasy: "I feel like systems are black and white and they're always looking for the perfect victim. And there just aren't any of those women." The benefits of abandoning the imagery of virtuous womanhood are not so clear either. Critics who reject the strategic use of stereotypes often overlook the quicksand that awaits us on the other side of the political terrain, including how "gender neutral" approaches to domestic violence undermine services for women (DeKeseredy, 2006). Rather than this forced choices between gender-only and gender-neutral models, we might advance instead an intersectional model that place oppression and hierarchy at the center of analysis of contexts that produce violence (Crenshaw, 1994).

Many advocates adopt an implicitly cognitive-behavioral stance in describing male perpetrators, focusing on the sexist beliefs and rewards men accrue through control tactics. Psychological theories or approaches that focus on the conflicted infantile states of men or their past trauma elicit intense resistance on the part of advocates.[14] Through the personality disorder categories of psychiatric taxonomies, however, individual differences among violent men crept back into the literature in the 1990s (Dutton & Starzomski, 1993; Dutton *et al.*, 1997; Walker, 1999). In contrast to the early feminist organizing around domestic violence, some of which focused on war veterans and violent symptoms associated with post-traumatic stress disorder (Herman, 1993), the new enlistment of psychiatry embraces the concept of personality disorders in explaining male violence. Whereas the post-traumatic stress disorder diagnosis *destigmatized* clinical pathology by emphasizing its context, the diagnosis of personality disorder is highly stigmatizing in its emphasis on fixed attributes that are thought to be unresponsive to the environment.[15]

Neil Jacobson and John Gottman (1998) led the way in generating a new typology of male violence that included personality disorders, but of differing degrees of severity. There are two main kinds of abusers, the authors suggest: the cobras and the pit bulls. Cobras lash out in a methodical way, find violence calming, and are more likely to be sociopathic. Pit bulls, on the other hand, are more impulsive, hot-headed, and more apt to be narcissistic. The latter group also is more amenable to therapeutic intervention. This typology grew out of the recognition in the field that there are differences among men, both in the extent of their violence and in the motivations behind it. Patriarchy socializes men into a culture of violence, but not all men embrace this culture in the same way.

In addressing this typology in discussions with advocates, I expressed my objections to using animals in representing men who abuse. The women of color interviewed were most attuned to this problem, and to the racist history associated with such dehumanizing imagery. As Cecilia Fire Thunder points out, sub-human images of abusive men may readily promote racist stereotypes. "I used to love to make jokes about Indian men," she confesses, "but I no longer do that." Continuing, she adds that "these men are my brothers, and they are really hurting. This does not mean that I need to put up with their abuse."

The debate over labels located at the borders between psychiatry and the law, often expressed by parsing the personality disorders into treatable and untreatable sub-types, may be symptomatic of conflicts within the domestic violence field itself over how to socially distribute blame. If some men are more redeemable than others, hardline stances may soften to allow for more differentiated responses.

Couple dynamics

While enlisting conventional portraits of good victims, advocates have steadfastly resisted the cultural fantasy of harmonious marriage as the norm. In Western psychotherapeutic discourse, the couple overcomes problems through effective communication, facilitated by professional counselors. Yet advocates stand in near unity in their opposition to couples counseling (Edleson & Tolman, 1992; Gondolf, 1993; Orme *et al.*, 2000). Psychologists who draw on family systems approaches, many advocates point out, reinforce the assumption that both victim and perpetrator contribute to the problem (Bograd, 1984; Goldner, 1985; Hansen, 1993; Lawson, 1989). By not addressing power dynamics in the family, couples therapists inadvertently collude with batterers, as well as placing women in greater danger by creating the illusion of safety—a point that Virginia Goldner (Goldner *et al.*, 1998) integrates into her own psychodynamic approach to couples counseling. Her approach is consistent with the Duluth model in confronting defenses of men, and particularly the tendency to separate their sense of self (the good object) from the violent behavior (the bad object). The assaulting partner may say, for example, "I came home and it just started again . . . the fighting just happened." Goldner points out how adopting the subject position of "it" rather than "I" in referencing a violent act operates as a defensive disavowal of oneself as the agent of the act. Goldner suggests how these and other psychodynamic interpretations may be helpful, depending on the relational capacities of clients who have engaged in violent behavior.[16]

Even as Pence and Paymar (1993) reject psychological theorizing, there *is* a theory of couple violence implicit in the Duluth power and control model, albeit one that focuses near exclusively on the batterer. The Duluth model grew out of observations on the part of abused women as they began to list the danger signs: possessiveness, isolation of the woman, including separating her from friends and family, and other controlling behaviors. As a theory of couple violence, the woman is a part of the violence only in the sense that she is blind to the tactics employed by her partner. Yet in teaching her to be a more astute observer, the model may inadvertently promote fixation on the man as the most interesting person on the scene, thus reinforcing her own lack of agency.

Beate Nink, a psychotherapist who directs the hotline for domestic violence in Berlin, suggests that clinicians who have been trained to work respectfully with women may be just as effective as those working with the power and control model. Feminist advocates are more apt to encourage women to get protection orders and disengage from abusive men. Nink explains how she tries to combine both therapeutic and feminist principles:

> "[Our goal is to] tell them what is our experience . . . that their hope that they can change the situation by de-escalating or

> whatever does not work . . . It's not particularly political in that the women in crisis are not needing to hear how society works . . . For some it is giving them another way of looking at the situation, or explaining how cycles of violence increase."

Even though many situations of domestic violence are episodic and relatively stable over time, feminist advocates focus on *escalation* as a central dynamic of couple violence (Walker, 1999). While the issue of whether physical abuse inevitably escalates to more extreme violence is an area of debate in the field (Edleson & Tolman, 1992; Felson & Tedeschi, 1993; Hamberger & Hastings, 1993), the concept of escalation continues to play an important narrative role as a caveat for women. It challenges the tendency for many women to minimize their partner's abusiveness or the dangerousness of their situation. Further, in laying out a roadmap for disengagement and introducing terms such as "your batterer," advocates are attempting to provide women with some observational distance.

Yet the "no couples counseling" stance meets resistance from battered women themselves (Pence & Paymar, 1993). Many advocates describe the conflict between their recommendation that women leave their abusers and the intense desire on the part of many battered women for either couples counseling or perpetrator groups. Batterers' intervention groups represent a kind of compromise. They embody the glove of therapeutic interventions, with their promise of changing hearts and minds, wrapped around the fist of court-mandated supervision. The denouement to the story—the question of which men change, which effects achieve those changes, and what measures are important in gauging change—remains an area of contested claims and counterclaims (Babcock & Steiner, 1999; Daly & Pelowski, 2000; Davis *et al.*, 2000; Feder & Forde, 2000; Gondolf, 2001).

At Pine Ridge, however, the approach is to recognize the range of possibilities in abusive situations, and to avoid making women feel ashamed for wanting to go back. Lea White Bear Claws describes this approach:

> "Even talking with the women, I say your husband isn't always like that . . . We go back for the good reasons, because we are partners and have good times together. But unless he starts to deal with his bad parts, it's going to be like this . . . We do this in a holistic way."

By acknowledging the co-mingling of good and bad representations of the male partner, Bear Claws also helps women to recognize their own conflicted desires. If advocates simply devalue the abuser, the woman may be left to defend him—a dynamic that minority women confront on a quite conscious level as they recognize the shifting positions at play in destructive attachments.

In framing the woman's relationship with an abusive partner, advocates often employ a prototypical recovery narrative. "Often women have to leave eight to ten times before they can finally leave," one advocate reports. "It's just like quitting smoking." While advocates assiduously avoid any language suggestive of blaming women, their use of the addiction analogy suggests an implicit acknowledgement of a psychological dependency. At the same time, the addiction story provides a framework for advocates to tolerate *their own frustration* with women who return to abusive relationships by enlisting the medical concept of natural phases of recovery. The analogy offers a framework for recognizing women's struggles with emotional dependencies that are destructive while containing the anxieties that such recognition evokes.

Tensions between an abused woman and her advocate—as another area of dyadic struggle—figured prominently in the interviews. Although workshops and trainings increasingly acknowledge the emotional responses of advocates to crisis work, these responses are often limited to identification with the victim. There is latitude for discussing countertransference reactions in the form of *vicarious trauma*, but far less latitude for acknowledging anger toward victims or moments when advocates may *identify with the aggressor*. Feminist politics require solidarity with battered women—a position that while vital to the work may disavow feelings of anger that arise, particularly when women return to their batterers—a historical dilemma also taken up in Chapter 1.

Although the dominant discourse in the field emphasizes the tendency of advocates to over-identify with the victim, Colman suggests that there may be a more pervasive unconscious tendency to *dis*-identify with the victim.

> "In terms of the psychology of all that, I think it makes all of us crazy because we are not trying to be her. We are trying to protect her but we don't want to *be her* so we deny all of this stuff that is happening in our lives—not just around DV but the violence that we experience on the planet as it exists today. [We deny it] so that we are not the victim."

Colman interprets this defensive response as a reaction to anxieties in the field that are difficult to openly acknowledge, from the difficulties in locating a precise source of threats to women's lives to feelings of disappointment in abused women themselves. As Carol Hagemann-White suggests, the early movement was based on a common political project that included expectations that battered women would contribute to the feminist movement. These expectations led to bitter disappointments, but nonetheless conflict could be acknowledged. But in the context of crisis situations, political mobilization of clients can be problematic. The expectation that abused women become feminist activists may feel counter to the forms of exchange that guide professional service work. Advocates working in feminist organizations may feel inhibited in encouraging women to give something back to the community.[17]

In the absence of a relational theory of violence, the problem of lesbian battering has been difficult to integrate into feminist models as well (Eaton, 1994; Ristock, 2002). There is growing emphasis in the domestic violence field on the problem of lesbian battering, and data on the problem are widely circulated in volunteer trainings. In a typical series of training sessions at a shelter, one session may focus on domestic violence as a singularly male form of power and control while the next session may focus on the "hidden epidemic" of lesbian battering, without discussion of the apparent contradiction. Also overlooked is the question of whether lesbian battering undermines a vital premise of the movement—that women as a group require special protection from men.

There are ways of working through this question but the tendency is to compartmentalize or split off the two sides of the conflict: that women *often are* the aggressors and that women *rarely are* the aggressors. In her important study of violence in lesbian relationships, Janice Ristock (2002) suggests that women's use of violence is "anxiety provoking for feminism" because it runs counter to the idea that women are pacifistic by nature. Violence in lesbian relationships is often rationalized as mimicking heterosexual domination, Ristock (2002) points out, partly to preserve the fantasy that lesbian couples are harmonious and free of power dynamics—that female violence is a symptom of a (pathological) identification with men. Similarly, Mary Eaton (1994) suggests that lesbian couple violence has been unsettling for many feminists because it requires that we address multiple axes of oppression that burden the dependency ties of personal life. The issue of lesbian battering also has been one area where feminists have been able to acknowledge the role of infantile dependencies in battering situations—how intertwined relationships may produce "intense feelings of rejection or betrayal when one member of a couple asserts her independence or indicates a need for separation" (1994: 207). Men who batter are often notable for their deep dependencies on a woman—as maternal figure—but male dependency has been more difficult to incorporate into feminist analyses than has male power (Adams & McCormick, 1982).

Sumaya Colman, an advocate in New York City, reflects on this same dilemma:

> "It's really tough when I look at how we are approaching DV and we're not answering all the questions . . . in a same-sex relationship one of them is the batterer and one is the victim—and there are two women there. It's almost like we are afraid to address that because it's going to come back to the question about women's abuse of power. And I think we have to own that because we do it. But it

> does not deny or negate that women are overall victims of domestic violence when you look at the global issue of violence against women."

Colman holds onto several concepts at once here, refusing the pull toward either/or thinking. One idea she works with is that the charged issue of lesbian battering is symptomatic of broader anxieties in the domestic violence field over female power. The power of women may be particularly productive of anxiety in that patriarchal societies often portray female power as *concealed*—as the hidden force behind the throne. Colman introduces a global framework for thinking critically about less immediately palpable or visible forms of violence.

Another advocate in the New York group responds to the dilemma over female aggression, adding that women, too, must be accountable for their own violence. The assertion in the field that violence is a *choice* people make—that it's about power and control—means that women make the choice as well. In defending women who are violent, it is tempting to suggest that they had no choice, yet this contradicts the current thinking that violence is always a choice. The advocate goes on to add that "Every other person is supposed to make that same choice that you do not to use violence. We all know that. And if you've worked in this field for two or three years, you know how to use it." The group breaks out in hearty laughter, acknowledging that women, too, identify with aggressive forms of power.

If we go beyond the Duluth model, feminist psychology does offer tools for understanding lesbian battering as rooted in dynamics similar to those that contribute to male violence against women. The fantasy of the redemptive power of romantic love produces bitter disappointments, particularly when such fantasies collide with the failure of the couple to deliver on the promise. While both partners may experience the emotional pain that results from this rupture of a dyadic bubble, the one cast in the maternal position—often a woman—carries a heavier cultural responsibility to preserve the illusion. It is a mistake to view the problem of battering in lesbian relationships as a mere reflection of the heterosexual ideal of a masculine and feminine coupling. But as Ristock (2002) points out, there also may be a tendency in feminism to romanticize intimate unions between women.

There also may be a tendency in feminism to over-pathologize aggression. In criminalizing woman battering, the movement lowered the bar on how the boundary between normal aggression and violence—a morally charged term—was drawn. If we begin from the premise that aggression is a necessary part of human defenses and that regulating aggression is a central part of social and moral development, we may want to focus as much on the *inhibitors* of aggression as on the incidents of violence. Lesbian couples bring many of the same infantile longings and deep disappointments to adult life as do heterosexual couples. The celebration of lesbian relationships should not be framed in terms of their freedom from the tortured side of human bonds, but in the possibilities they provide for resolutions beyond exclusive reliance on men. The finding that violence does occur in lesbian relationships may overshadow findings of overall higher satisfaction among lesbian couples than heterosexual couples (Ussher, 2008).

In downplaying female aggression and focusing exclusively on its defensive functions, feminists may lose sight of cultural contexts mediating resolutions of family quarrels, including whether fights escalate into violence or whether violence is averted. Feminists have worked steadfastly to keep the problem of domestic violence in the public eye. As a result of focusing on documenting the sheer magnitude of the problem, however, we may overlook the role of women (and men) in de-escalating potentially violent encounters.

George Twiss, with the Cangleska program at Pine Ridge, describes how he has gained insight into such dynamics, and particularly conflicts that arise for women in de-escalating family violence. Twiss tells the story of a woman who brings a bottle of liquor home at the end of the month, knowing that her man will get drunk, that they will fight, and that he will become violent. The violence enables her to call the tribal police, who transport him to jail. When the check comes at the beginning of the next month, he is securely behind bars and she is able to use the money to buy things for her family, money that he might otherwise spend on drinking binges. While some might view her behavior as enabling, Twiss focuses on the profound constraints of her situation. He also tells the story to illustrate the ways in which women living in oppressed communities learn to manage the damaged men in their lives.

Oppressed communities vary considerably in the place of aggression in cultural practices, and in how the line is drawn between acceptable aggression and violence. Cangleska staff stress non-violence as central to the Medicine Wheel, symbol of the cultural ideal of harmony. Violence tends to be viewed as an effect of colonization, rather than as indigenous to the culture. Spanking is not part of traditional Native American practices, according to advocates, because children are viewed as sacred. When women enter shelter, Inez No Neck explains, "they are told they can't do that, that children are sacred. Because we believe that children choose their parents and this means children are to be respected . . . When women do hit their children, they feel very bad about it." Just as hitting a woman is interpreted as a form of identification with the aggressor and assault on native culture, so, too, is striking children.

Women in communities of color bring to adulthood many of the same fantasy ideals as do white women, but they are more apt to *recognize* as a fantasy the self-sufficiency of the dyadic unit or the couple. So, too, groups with a long history of being victimized by violence have less of a sense of penetrating the veil of silence in addressing violence. In fighting "the Man," oppressed groups also are more apt to acknowledge how this fight spills over into destructive or self-destructive aggression, or becomes displaced onto those closest to them (Freire, 1999).

Group psychology and crisis work

Drawing on social action research methods and psychoanalytic-feminist theory, Erica Burman (2004) describes how group dynamics shape feminist organizational responses to domestic violence. Groups establish feelings of unity by projecting negative attributes onto outside groups, but they also introject or "take in" broader societal conflicts and may enact these conflicts on a group level. *Reflective practices* in social action and feminist research might be extended to include attentiveness to these unconscious aspects of group life and how the histories of women, as staff and residents, are transferred to the group in ways not readily articulated. Acknowledging these dynamics can help in moving beyond defensive stalemates.

This same acknowledgement may produce new impasses, however, as cultural assumptions about group dynamics collide. Psychoanalytic anthropologist Gananath Obeyesekere (1990) addresses this concern by pointing out how anxiety over cultural differences may take the form of denying the complex subjectivity of the "other" or retreating from the difficulties in probing for points of common ground. In carrying out the interviews at Pine Ridge, I was particularly mindful of this tension.[18] As a starting place, psychoanalysis shares with Native American practices an emphasis on storytelling as the "royal road" to the unconscious—to the burial ground of lost objects that are the site of perpetual return. While the formative stories and modes of talking and returning to the past may be different, these practices share an understanding of human suffering that acknowledges the limits of language, and the importance of how one bears in mind a history of loss and suffering. Psychoanalysis also shares with native practices an orientation to silence that places value on stillness and containment, on human receptivity to voices, whether invoked through the talking cure or through ceremonial practices and meditative prayer. Psychoanalytic methods similarly stress the importance of invoking the past through the disciplined practice of attending to "internal objects"—to the voices and images that constitute the relational past (Obeyesekere, 1990; Zaretsky, 2004). Psychoanalysts and shamans are those granted the authority in their society to preside over this process of conversing with voices or spirits outside the range of everyday hearing.

Fire Thunder tells the story of going on a Vision Quest—an Indian practice of going into the forest or desert for several days of solitude and prayer, seeking guidance from the ancestor spirits. This Quest was part of her own path as a feminist and of coming to understand her anger toward men. Victimization is part of the problem, Fire Thunder explains, but so too is the terrible disappointment associated with being abandoned by men. Because men have failed women so often, women may come to devalue men, just as they have been devalued. Feminism requires connecting with the humanity in men, as well as resisting bad treatment.[19]

> "In my Indian Quest, the men took me up there, because the road was not clear. It was only later that I realized how powerful that was—to let men take care of me. Because I had always been so self-sufficient. They took me up there and took care of me, to check on me and come pray with me. One thing I had to do was ask my father and male relatives for forgiveness. I had two sons, and I had been very abusive to them. I had to ask for forgiveness . . . I made a pledge that when I leave here, I will change my life to be more compassionate toward men. Because all the men who went before me, they are part of me. I promise I will treat men better."

For many feminists in the domestic violence field, women are all too ready to treat men better than they deserve. Indeed, women's consciousness groups offered relief from chronic fatigue as a result of continuous attunement to the pain of men. Feminists engaged in early protests against violence, such as the annual Take Back the Night vigils, staked the conditions of freedom on the ability of women to navigate public space *without* the protection of men. As a movement advances, however, the interplay of separation and connection across the gender divide becomes more complex. The importance of separate female spaces, organized by and for women, remains critical. These separate "breathing spaces," as bell hooks (1984) calls them, are vital to all oppressed groups because they offer relief from the dominant group and serve as testing ground for new forms of self-knowledge. But vital as well are places of rapprochement—areas in public life where men and women come together in solidarity around a common vision of progress, one where men also are willing to take leadership from women.

As I asked about conflicts that arise in the domestic violence field, many advocates lamented the loss of an activist movement, an issue taken up in Chapter 1. Although feminist politics are still at the heart of the work, we discussed some of the differences between seeing oneself as an individual feminist working in an organization and identifying oneself as part of a broader social movement (Davis, 1988; Rodriguez, 1988; Schechter, 1982). Yet as psychologists, social workers, and case managers stake out new roles in the domestic violence field, particularly in the area of child protection, conflict over these competing identities may intensify (Humphreys & Joseph, 2004; Humphreys & Thiara, 2003). The conversation in the New York group focuses on the difficulty in reconciling crisis work and ongoing needs of women in abusive situations, as well as in reconciling psychological and political interpretations of violence. As one advocate laments,

> "If she then needs to spend 10 years in therapy or a support group, great. You know, 'deal with your emotional issues, deal with the fact that you really didn't protect the kid or you beat your kid, or that you were going to kill him, or whatever it was that you were kind of driven to.' That's a therapeutic issue that many of us have and many of us need to work out. But the actual helping someone get out of, or protect themselves, or protect their kids, or deal with the nitty-gritty of it—I don't think the leading edge of that is a psychological answer. I think it's a political answer. I'm very open to psychological ideas but not as an intervention . . . I look at that as a long-term process for healing rather than an intervention for safety. And I'm focused on safety when it comes to domestic violence."

This distinction between the psychological dynamics of abused women, on the one hand, and the political demands of crisis services, on the other, seems a very useful one. Rather than downplaying the complexity of crisis situations, this advocate delimits her role as advocate. By separating the political and the psychological, she is able to draw a protective boundary around her role—certainly a vitally adaptive defense. Yet this same boundary-setting may be deployed to over-compartmentalize and over-simplify the work. Safety measures may be oriented more toward protecting shelter workers from awareness of the complex realities of women's lives than they are in actually increasing safety for women in shelter (Crenshaw, 1994; Davis, 1988; Loseke, 1992). Much like the battered woman, crisis workers may become isolated from their communities and rely on a narrow base of attachments. And women's advocates may adopt a crisis mode of functioning that minimizes the costs over time of strategies of survival.

Lakota women and men alike offer many valiant warrior stories, although such stories tend to be cast in the context of heroic resistance to early colonial domination. At the same time, the more historically recent violent confrontation between FBI agents and American Indian Movement (AIM) activists at Pine Ridge, at the site of the Wounded Knee Massacre of the 19th century, remains controversial. Indeed, past forms of violent resistance in many cultures may be more available for idealization than those closer to the present. Further, many activists in the black power and red power movements of the 1960s and 1970s were killed. Tawa Witko explains that just as most black youth have little understanding of the political goals of the Black Panthers, Indian youth have little connection to AIM. Instead, they identify with the rebellious currents in black youth culture, particularly hip-hop.

> "Kids here identify with hip-hop . . . its that fight, the resistance to authority, fighting oppression . . . But like with AIM, the message of resistance gets lost in the violence . . . And the youth sometimes leave their own culture behind . . . There's a lot of healing that needs to be done here."

Group identifications are often complex and culturally mixed, and elders in many ethnic communities voice concern over the loss of a traditional cultural identity. The Sacred Circle philosophy emphasizes the recovery of a positive group identity, implicitly re-projecting some of the moral load of violence back onto the colonizers. But neither do the women engaged in this project of recovery externalize the problem of violence in the sense of placing responsibility entirely outside of their community.

CONCLUSIONS

Sarah Carney (2004) describes the prototypical survivorship narrative as one of individual triumph. The survivor, "though battered, will 'overcome' or 'move on,' or, best yet, 'triumph' over the trauma" (2004: 202). In the absence of a developed feminist psychology, the only available psychological theory may be in the conventional forms that circulate in popular culture. At many conferences, hardline feminist rhetoric is peppered with personal healing exercises and self-affirmations. Conference participants are warned of "reactivation of trauma"—a term that encompasses a range of disturbing feelings—while decades-old lists of myths and facts about domestic violence are circulated, as though the struggle had just begun. In helping other women, advocates do risk suffering the same states of exhaustion, helplessness, and defeat that are common features of battered women. Typically absent from the psychological discourse, however, are the aggressive currents in women's lives, and the broad range of experiences women have with violence.

Drawing on psychoanalytic theory, we may understand better how women, not unlike men, may enact a historically dislocated drama in responding to their oppression. Early feminist organizing included confronting the various ways in which women participated in the reproduction of patriarchy. Feminist consciousness-raising centered on relinquishing the stance of moral innocence granted to privileged women. Liberation came at a price, as Carol Hagemann-White suggests (Chapter 1), and part of that price is to be conscious of the myriad ways in which women, as well as men, are implicated in systems of oppression. As Paulo Freire (1999) suggests in *Pedagogy of the oppressed*, the colonized often discharge rage against others among the colonized, instead of directing it toward the true sources of their misery.

Women of color have a great deal to teach white women concerning the complex psychological dynamics operating in situations of abuse. Less under the illusion that patriarchy will protect women, women of color are less apt to divide the world into simple victim/perpetrator categories. As Sujata Warrior points out, "if you think of violence as one way of controlling, there also are other means of controlling people, like denying them housing or employment."

The building of strong group identities that encompass a range of class, race, sex, and gender positions opens a stronger and wider space for resisting destructive forces in women's lives, including those beyond the brute at the door blocking their exit. In situating domestic violence in the context of a broader critique of society, it makes it more difficult to compartmentalize or to *domesticate* the problem. But this same openness requires a strong and secure feminist movement to know when to yield ground and when to hold it, and the importance of both capacities.

NOTES

1 In *Black looks*, bell hooks (1992) takes up this line of critique. Drawing on cultural theory, hooks describes the oral incorporative response of white audiences to images of black people on contemporary popular culture.

2 In *The managed heart*, Arlie Hochschild (1983) presents a labor analysis of social service work. She makes use of Marxist theory and symbolic interactionism to explain how the skills involved in emotional labor performed by women are often devalued as they are attributed to a natural orientation toward nurture.

3 Paper presented by Toni Malliet at the meeting of the Institute on Domestic Violence in the African American Community, Seattle, WA, December 2, 2000.

4 This critique of expertise and the role of experts in producing the very social problem they are assigned to vanquish is central to the work of Michel Foucault (see, for example, Foucault, 1995).

5 For feminist readings of the concept of projective identification and its roots in Kleinean theory, see Dinnerstein (1976), Hollway (2006), and Nicolson (1996).

6 Young (2006) discusses variations in how this concept is understood in the psychoanalytic literature.

7 In moving toward a broader social distribution of blame, the TRC has also generated critiques. See Haaken *et al.* (2005), for research on controversies over the TRC in the aftermath of the Sierra Leonean Civil War that raged during the 1990s. Similarly, *restorative justice* initiatives, where abusive men are reintegrated into the community rather than excluded, have been the focus of feminist controversy (see Incite!, 2005).

8 For a discussion of the use of the concept of countertransference in psychoanalytically informed field research, see Molino (2004).

9 For a critical review of studies of gender differences in rates of family violence, see Dutton *et al.* (2009). The authors argue that feminist ideology has overridden scientific data as the basis of governmental policy to the detriment of domestic violence practices. For example, mandatory arrests have been expanded despite evidence that this practice increases recidivism in poor communities; counseling

or psychotherapy for abusive men has been barred from protocols, even though feminist educational groups have not been demonstrated to be effective.

10 Donald Dutton also has generated data in claiming that women are as violent as men within the household (see Dutton & Nicholls, 2005; Dutton *et al.*, 2009).

11 An extensive body of research has developed on personality differences among abusive men with the aim of distinguishing between those who are more and less amenable to treatment (see Dutton *et al.*, 1997; Gondolf, 1985, 1999b; Holtzworth-Munroe & Stuart, 1994).

12 In entering this hotly contested terrain, feminist researchers who attempt to find a middle ground often find their work cited on websites for "father rights" or other anti-feminist campaigns. So there is always a risk of providing succurance to the enemy in working through impasses.

13 O'Neil *et al.* (1986) also enlist these distinctions in describing gender differences in aggression.

14 Even as some feminist psychologists include childhood trauma, they often are quick to add that childhood trauma does not "cause" male violence. Since there inevitably are multiple determinants of human behavior, this caveat signifies anxiety in the field over the boundaries of a feminist analysis.

15 Some feminist psychologists have enlisted the post-traumatic stress disorder diagnosis to explain female violence. The diagnosis focuses on the magnitude of stressors that produce violence reactions in women (see Walker, 1999).

16 For a similar psychoanalytic approach to batterers, see Eisikovits and Buchbinder (1996) and Wexler (1999).

17 Tensions between providing services to women and recruiting them to be part of a broader social movement frequently are introduced under the rubric of "professionalism," often because it is difficult to directly address disappointments advocates experience in working with abused women.

18 For a similar line of argument with respect to cross-cultural research, see Merry (2001).

19 In discussing with Lakota women the importance of storytelling in the anti-violence movement, I noted parallels between psychoanalytic approaches and their own psychology of storytelling (see Haaken, 2008a).

3

DAMSELS IN DISTRESS: POPULAR CULTURE AND STORIES OF DOMESTIC ABUSE

Myth: Woman battering violates modern standards of decency.
Counter-myth: Modern societies conceal the practice of violence against women by making it a "hidden" crime.

Abigail Abbot Bailey, a Puritan woman who lived in a settlement along the New Hampshire/Massachusetts state line, wrote one of the earliest memoirs describing flight from the tyranny of a husband. Published after her death and during the Second Great Awakening of the early 19th century, *The memoirs of Mrs. Abigail Bailey* prefigures modern motifs while conforming to the Christian narrative conventions of her time (Baxter, 1980). Bailey dramatized her plight by invoking a spiritualized discourse of captivity and deliverance—a narrative rife with political intonations. Indian captivity stories held a particular sway over the imagination of colonists. They invoked both the trials of New Englanders in an alien land and the fleshly temptations of believers who discerned in their expansion of the frontier a biblical mandate to subdue "savage" peoples, as well as their own primal impulses. But in Bailey's narrative, a cruel husband is cast in the role of "savage," with Bailey as righteous believer transfigured through her struggle to liberate herself from his diabolical control.

The memoirs combines the religious devotional—as a female genre—and proto-feminist stories of resistance, framed in the context of the American Revolutionary War. Written during the 1790s, the diary tells the story of Abigail's marriage to Asa Bailey in 1767, when Abigail was 22 years of age, and recounts the violence she endured at his hands until she finally divorced him in 1793. While divorce was legal in New England, and wife beating could be entered as a justifiable complaint, it was virtually impossible for women to gain a divorce on the basis of physical abuse alone. Unlike men, who could secure a divorce on the basis of adultery, women needed supplementary complaints, such as violence ("cruelty") or incest (Pleck, 1987; Siegel, 1996).

More than an account of a husband's unremitting cruelty, the diary assumes mythic proportions in registering a larger design and purpose behind her suffering. The narrative begins, as many early American memoirs do, with the protected circle of her childhood, which left Abigail ill-prepared for the evil that she encountered in her husband. As she descends into the hell of matrimony, Bailey initially adopts a stance of stoicism. God allows humankind "sorely to afflict and oppress one another; and not only those who appear as open enemies—but sometimes those who pretend to be our best friends, cruelly oppress" (Baxter, 1980: 56). A recurring motif in the narrative centers on the contradictions of New World marriage—as a union based on friendship, on the one hand, and wifely submission, on the other.

This chapter introduces psychoanalytic readings of narrative conventions available to women in scripting domestic violence. My use here of literary methods has a practical aim. In making the dramaturgical dilemmas of the movement more visible, we may be better able to make distinctions between progressive and conservative plotlines. The chapter draws out the implications of various denouements to the story of a domestic crisis, as well as the range of positions available to protagonists in the scripting of their plights, drawing on novels and films about domestic violence that advocates discussed with me in the course of carrying out my field research. I present three *genres* of domestic violence narratives that emerged from my research: *stories of bondage*, *stories of deliverance*, and *stories of struggle and reparation*.

Rather than suggesting a direct correspondence between fictional and actual cases of domestic abuse, my purpose is to show how fiction and nonfiction converge in their reliance on conventional narrative structuring devices, or tropes, that have acquired social currency (Daiute, 2004). And in attending more closely to fictional portrayals that circulate in the domestic violence field, I show how these cultural resources, alongside more material resources, such as legal and social services, housing, or economic assistance, play a vital role in movements for social change.

The three genres described here also register developmental aspects of collective storytelling. Early on in a movement, idealization of the group and its capacities emerges as a dominant motif in storytelling as a means of casting off the collective injuries of the past. The bad aspects of oneself or one's group, the internalized experiences of dirtiness or dangerousness, are projected back onto the oppressor. The badness is transferred to an external source—the oppressor—in reversing the dynamics of power that allow the powerful to deposit (project) unwanted parts of himself/herself onto the oppressed.

Idealization also may take regressive forms. The virtuous (white) maiden, set against a swarthy villain, has been a conventional plot device in female melodrama, as well as in countless horror, action, thriller, and romantic movies. The denouement relies on the competition between a good man and a bad one in determining the maiden's fate, with the identity of the masculine protector recognized through his capacity to vanquish the villain. But the literature taken up in this chapter centers on *subversive storytelling*—stories that deviate from the standard plotline. These are stories where an active female subject seeks deliverance from domestic bondage, a female subject who awakens to her own capacities and searches for paths of deliverance. It is critical to attend to various denouements, however, in assessing the potential of subversive stories to break new cultural ground.

Before embarking on this exploration of literary texts circulating in the domestic violence field, I begin by reviewing works that have shaped my own thinking about the social and psychological dynamics of storytelling. Although narrative psychology works at the borders between the social sciences and the humanities (Daiute, 2004; Rappaport, 1993), there has been relatively little attentiveness to tensions between literary and scientific representations of abuse in the domestic violence field (Haaken, 2008a).

PSYCHOLOGY AND CULTURAL CRITICISM

Cultures throughout history have transmitted knowledge through storytelling. Yet scientific psychology is relatively limited in explaining this most fundamental of human activities. Stories are bound to the particular, to specific characters, motives, and actions, whereas science is concerned with measurable and lawful effects that transcend the particular. While some psychologists test the truth of a story against known facts or a plausible account, these approaches are limited to concrete details and miss the broader social dynamics of storytelling.

Psychologists, like many people, are most conscious of culture when they confront an "other," when they travel beyond the realm of the familiar (Hays, 2001). As long as everyone speaks the same language, culture may be invisible, at least for those in the dominant group who are able to ignore its effects. In the story of Buffalo Calf Woman introduced in Chapter 1, for instance, psychologists might approach the story in terms of how it corresponds to known facts, or to the alterations in the story introduced in the course of re-telling it. But Native American theorists suggest that such stories serve as cautionary tales—as reminders to youth of their moral obligations to the tribe and their dependency on women as the source of life (Zellerer, 1999).

More than statistically significant findings, people tend to remember findings in psychology through the stories produced, whether it is the tragic fate of Harry Harlow's traumatized infant monkeys, Stanley Milgram's tortured subjects, or Martin Seligman's pathetic dogs. The history of scientific psychology does provide wonderful examples of human dramas staged through both laboratory and field research. As a psychology undergraduate in the early 1970s, I found the bystander intervention studies particularly disturbing—studies that were as much about the dynamics of storytelling as they were about the variables of direct interest. In one of the classic bystander studies of the late 1960s, the Kitty Genovese study, researchers interviewed neighbors in a New York City tenement building who had observed a woman being killed in the street below, inquiring as to why they had failed to intervene or call the police. In telling their stories, most observers of the violence explained that they had assumed that someone else would intervene. The social psychological phenomenon that emerged from this study was termed "*diffusion of responsibility*." After subsequent investigation of the conditions under which people intervene, researchers concluded that the fewer the observers the more likely the victim will receive aid from bystanders (Latané & Darley, 1970).

While powerful in its moral implications, the bystander field research is limited by its relatively static focus on discrete variables, such as the number of observers present, and its neglect of the wider cultural contexts that shape responses to victimization. Public responses to child abuse and domestic violence are key examples of the importance of such contexts. Second-wave feminism shifted moral and political discourse on the family, rupturing the cultural hymen separating private and public life and making intervention in domestic violence a community responsibility. Rather than viewing intervention as a function of the number of bystanders or the distance between victims and bystanders, feminists argued that ideological factors, such as sexism, shaped responses to victimization, including the social distribution of blame (Herman, 1992).[1]

The concept of diffusion of responsibility also overlooks the complex dynamics associated with the bystander position. The bystander intervention studies concluded that the failure to intervene or to provide assistance to a victim resulted from the individual's tendency to transfer responsibility to the group. But observing violence elicits *active* emotions as well as passive ones, from fear and anxiety to sadism and voyeurism. The field of psychoanalytic cultural studies offers many insights into the psychology of spectatorship and the complex identifications between observer and observed (Mulvey, 1988). Anna Freud (1936/1966) introduced the term "*identification with the aggressor*" in elaborating on ego defenses that the child develops in response to states of helplessness and subjugation to adult authority.

Some feminist cultural theorists point out that women are barred from identifications with the aggressor in patriarchal societies (Chodorow, 1978; Hollway, 2006), while other feminists stress the instability of gender identifications and unconscious identifications on the part of women with the position of "master" (Benjamin, 1988; Dinnerstein, 1976; Harris, 2005). In *The color purple*, Alice Walker (1982), like many other black women writers, creates female characters that both suffer at the hands of hardened men and actively participate in the social transfer of cruelty. Celie, crippled by the blows she has suffered, colludes with her husband in prompting their son, Harpo, to assert his manhood and beat his wife, the defiant Sophia.

> I like Sophia, but she don't act like me at all . . . If they ast her where something at, she say she don't know. Keep talking.
> I think about this when Harpo ast me what he ought to do to her to make her mind . . . Beat her, I say.
>
> (Walker, 1982: 42–43)

The first step of the battered women's movement centered on creating a unifying story and demanding that it be heard. Once a social problem has been named and made visible, however, myriad modes for telling the story emerge, as do potential identifications with the plot.

PSYCHOANALYTIC CULTURAL THEORY

Although academic psychology achieved legitimacy in the late 19th century through its affiliation with science, I am one of those psychologists more at home in the humanities. More than other theoretical traditions within psychology, psychoanalysis bridges disciplinary boundaries, from art and literary criticism to history and cultural studies. Psychoanalysis includes many theories and practices, but the early theories of Freud continue to be taken up, including by feminist theorists, because they situate human psychology in storytelling practices. Indeed, at base, psychoanalysis is a theory of storytelling (Haaken, 1998; Spence, 1982). According to Freud, children are little empiricists, observing and testing ideas about the world, but these observations are organized into stories. Part fact and part fantasy, these narratives continue as a substrate of adult life and as a dynamic process of representing self in relation to others—the self as both acting and being acted upon.

Psychoanalytic cultural theory points to unconscious anxieties and defenses concealed within prevailing social scripts. Conflict over dependency and vulnerability, for example, may be anxiously repressed in the dominant tales of manhood. Freud's oedipal theory may be enlisted to describe the male trajectory of development as a perpetual return to the mother he was forced to relinquish in childhood (Dinnerstein, 1976; Frosh, 1995; Hollway, 2006; Segal, 1990). Although puberty rituals and rites of passage symbolically sever the tie of the son to his mother, the young boy, according to oedipal theory, unconsciously refuses to give her up. Indeed, the very severing of the tie to the maternal creates an anxious and defensively organized masculinity, compulsively engaged in maintaining an illusory sense of independence (Chodorow, 1978; Harris, 2005). Collectively and individually, male violence against women enacts an infantile drama—an insistence that women preserve the narcissistic fantasy that the boy may forever remain what Freud (1957/1914) termed "his majesty, the Baby."

This Freudian version of the story of domestic abuse may be suspect for many feminists, however, because male perpetrators are often cast as the tragic figures in such dramas. In beginning the story with trauma or loss of the boy's maternal connection, the perpetrator may easily become the more compelling protagonist. Patriarchal societies have produced a vast storehouse of tales about tragically flawed men—stories of violence carried out by misguided love for a woman.

So what good is psychoanalytic cultural theory to feminists, particularly given its tendency to complicate the drama in ways that redeem ruthless men? One response is to use the tools of psychoanalysis to go deeper—to expose the infantile side of masculine entitlement. Rather than focusing singularly on male power and control motives, subversive storytelling might expose the illusion of masculine autonomy. Refusing the position of perpetual chorus to the tragic heroes, feminists might enlist psychoanalytic methods to shed light on the seductions of male power. We might generate more dynamic models of the interlocking wheels of gender development, with cultural and historical forces shaping their grinding paths and points of breakdown. An advanced feminist psychology goes beyond pronouncing women as good and men as bad and insists on complex accounts of women's lives (Goldner & Dimen, 2002; Goldner *et al.*, 1998).

In working with the concept of the unconscious, Adrienne Harris (2005) brings into view the instability of gender identifications and how each sexed subject unconsciously recognizes some part of the self in the gendered Other—projecting discordant states onto the sexed Other to maintain the precarious borders of gender identity. As Lynne Segal (1990) suggests, aggressive currents take many forms in male psychic life even as they carry different emotional and cultural investments. Many boys and men are drawn to action films because they feel powerlessness in the world (Harbord, 1996). But these same young men may unconsciously identify with the vulnerable feminine protagonist on the screen while holding a more primary and conscious identification with the invincible hero. Young men with blunted aspirations may be particularly drawn to superheroes who rescue helpless maidens.

Similarly, women bound by domestic duties may vicariously identify with rebellious rogues. As Janice Radway (1991) suggests in her analysis of the romance novel, women transport longings denied them in daily life into the adventure stories of romance novels. Identifying with the *femme fatale* who artfully subdues and domesticates the masculine brute, the female reader temporarily escapes the daily reminders of the limits of her powers.

FEMINIST READINGS OF DOMESTIC VIOLENCE STORIES

Science begins with putting things into categories and some form of order, and our research team attempted to do the same. In each of the field studies carried out by the domestic violence research group the interviews included the question, "What is a typical story of how domestic violence happens?" We worked at the boundary between fiction and non-fiction, gathering up stories from pamphlets, training manuals, presentations, and interviews. Turning to these literary materials allowed us to attend more carefully to plot and narrative structure, and to identify morals to the stories that tended to be applied in campaigns to combat domestic violence.

In categorizing the stories gathered in this research, three genres emerged, each of which dramatized a set of dilemmas in the movement against woman abuse. The first genre, *stories of bondage*, centers on the female protagonist's awakening knowledge of the household as a site of danger. From the melodrama to the gothic novel, female literary traditions have located the conflicts of women in a claustrophobic domestic space (Massé, 1992). During periods of feminist mobilization, literary portraits of domestic confinement tend toward the gothic, dramatizing the seductively pernicious trap of marriage and family. Menacing forces surround the female protagonist, as she begins to discern the shadowy figure of her husband in the engulfing darkness. The second genre, *stories of deliverance*, casts the woman as an active agent in plotting her escape. Whereas stories of domestic bondage center on an interior world where the female protagonist creates distance through madness or submission to her beastly husband, stories of deliverance center on the obstacles negotiated in charting a path out of this state of pernicious confinement. The third genre, *stories of struggle and reparation*, dramatizes engagement in ideals that elude full realization and exceed the standard denouements that offer means of containing the conflict. This third genre also gives rise to new ethical demands. From a psychoanalytic perspective, this last genre encompasses a more complex morality. Over time, movements must be capable of generating stories that move beyond idealized conceptions of the victim, set against the villainy of perpetrators, to more variegated dramas that allow for enlarged capacities to engage history and human conditions. While all three genres include conservative and progressive texts, stories of struggle and reparation are particularly important in sustaining the vitality of a social movement in that they acknowledge inter-group conflict as an ongoing human dilemma, rather than as an oppressive state to be simply overcome.

The work of Frances Restuccia (2000) in *Melancholics in love: Representing women's depression and domestic abuse* serves as prime example of border tensions that arise in bridging the worlds of psychoanalytic cultural theory and domestic violence politics. In her exploration of textual representations of domestic violence, Restuccia (2000a) makes use of Tina Turner's autobiography, discussed in Chapter 2 of this book, in describing the prototypical story of a woman caught in a vicious cycle of abuse. In her analysis of Tina Turner's heroic journey to free herself from her maniacal husband, Restuccia introduces a third protagonist: the absent mother figure. Building on the work of Jessica Benjamin (1988), who similarly invites reflection on mother/daughter dynamics in female subjugation to male violence, Restuccia goes beyond literary texts and moves into the rough terrain of domestic violence politics.

The texts recounted in *Melancholics in love* focus almost exclusively on a solitary female victim, unable to break free from a pathogenic mother working (as an internal object or representation) in tandem with a maniacal husband. In submitting to abuse, the melancholic woman attempts to revive a connection with the "dead mother" in her own past—the emotionally absent maternal figure defeated by the patriarchal world around her. This depressive dynamic, where the daughter is unable to make psychological use of the mother, creates a tendency in the daughter to turn to powerful men who offer more holding power. But this same holding power comes to strangle her as she submits to its influence.[2]

Restuccia emphasizes the power of sisterhood in formulating a cure for the female depressive, thus pre-empting the conventional patriarchal cures. Yet this script flattens the cast of characters that inhabit the psyches of women and narrows the variations in the cultural enactments of abuse dramas. Restuccia also downplays the voyeurism that may accompany feminist displays of female suffering: "It therefore seems crucial to keep up the current surge of representations of woman abuse—the more spectacular the better?—in an effort to capture the hold of spectacular violence against women in pain, to keep the public eye riveted on manifestations of such pain" (2000a: 83).

Because representations of woman battering are fraught with painful histories of misrecognition, where psychologists and academics have collaborated in turning away from the corporeal reality of abuse, it is understandable that Restuccia keeps images of battered women center stage. She fails to attend, however, to the variable audience responses to stories of domestic bondage and their disturbing and exciting resonances (Goldner, 2002).

Stories of bondage

Although the battered woman syndrome has been dropped from much of the official lexicon of the field, the prototypical story described by Lenore Walker and framed as a clinical condition continues to circulate in women's folk knowledge about abuse. The most frequently cited literary reference is to Jekyll and Hyde, a reportedly recurring motif in the stories of abused women. Drawing on Robert Louis Stevenson's (1974/1886) gothic novella, *The strange case of Dr. Jekyll and Mr. Hyde*, women enlist this literary metaphor to highlight the two sides of the man closest to them, and their own fluctuating states of hatred and idealization that close off possibilities for escape. One of the Berlin advocates describes the prototype: "A typical story is that the men have two faces, the good guy and the bad guy, or they believe 'he is sick.' They come up with excuses to protect him." As this advocate implies, the two faces may allow women to separate the good man from the bad, the latter of which is managed through a discourse of illness.[3] If the man is ill, there is possibility for a cure.

This narrative device of the double self is suggestive of the defense of splitting in managing conflicting feelings about abusive partners. The Jekyll and Hyde metaphor may express the duality women experience in *their own internal representations* of male partners, as well as the split persona of their batterer. In providing crisis services for battered women, feminists attempt to help women "hold" the memory of the sadistic Mr. Hyde long enough to resist the seductive pull of Dr. Jekyll. Yet the trap for feminist intervention centers on the instability and precariousness of the defense of splitting. If advocates express one side of the ambivalence, focusing solely on the destructiveness of the male partner, women may gravitate to the other side of the conflict, defending Mr. Hyde.

This literary image is perhaps the most popularized and readily accessible of the Gothic novels—a genre that spans several centuries of literature, much of which was written by and for women. The Gothic narrative plot centers on the uncovering of threats to a female protagonist within a perniciously suffocating domestic sphere. In describing the continuing allure of the gothic, Diane Long Hoevelor (1998: 3) suggests that "we, like the characters in the female gothic novel . . . want to find something hidden, mysterious, deep, and esoteric behind the black veil." Hoevelor situates the female gothic novel in the context of the rise of modern capitalism, where the promise of freedom and mobility collided with the narrowing of women's lives to the domestic sphere. Industrial capitalism heightened the distance between the private and the public, and the gender divide separating the two spheres (Gordon, 1988; Hartsock, 1997; Schechter, 1982).

Feminist literary critic Michelle Massé (1992) describes a standard plotline of the bourgeois era where the plight of women is cast within the claustrophobic confines of the domestic sphere. In the *marital Gothic*, texts "begin, rather than end, with marriage, in which the husband becomes the revenant of the very horror his presence was supposed to banish" (1992: 7). Conventional resolutions of the Gothic narrative vary, from languishing in masochistic submission to the disciplinary regime of a despotic husband to falling into the arms of a sympathetic and virtuous young man who passes by and takes pity on her. According to Massé, the Gothic heroine embodies bourgeois femininity: a ghostly domestic presence founded on sexual repression, passivity, and devotion to love and duty. Yet the horror at the center of the Gothic marital novel foregrounds the desires that the genre is thought to keep in check: the female protagonist discovers that her home is not her castle, and that her days of confinement—the old medical term for measuring the progression of a pregnancy—are never over. In placing the Gothic narrative in the context of female economic dependency on men, Massé seeks to unravel the enduring appeal of this plotline and the cultural processes by which the feminine fusion of love and surrender to suffering are transmitted. Massé also shows how the Gothic novel circulates in areas of female culture as a cautionary tale: "The ground of the Gothic is littered with wounded and dead wives whose husbands assure them that their injuries are self-inflicted, caused by some larger [mysterious] force, or negligible because of the husbands' own pain" (1992: 25). There is no escape for the Gothic heroine, but her victory is in her capacity to expose the horror and to face the dreadful evidence of her husband's cruelty and her own moral triumph over him.

In mainstream films, beautiful women routinely bring the marital Gothic to the screen. With a face engraved in every 1960s American girl's mind as the embodiment of a surreal feminine (and white) perfection, Farah Fawcett assumed dramatic roles on television several decades later, displaying the harsh lines born of a life of hard knocks. In a series of films in the 1980s, the cultural icon and model Fawcett starred as an abused woman. *Burning bed*, *Extremities*, and the television mini-series *Small sacrifices*, explored domestic violence from the perspective of a female protagonist. Fawcett's lead role in these movies on domestic violence created a sense of their underlying unity. Her face uncannily projected the tragedy of Beauty, unable to tame her Beasts.

As a tale of domestic bondage, *Burning bed* draws on the female Gothic tradition in casting marriage as a deathly embrace. Fawcett stars as an abused woman caught in an increasingly debilitating violent marriage spanning over a decade. While the husband is overbearing and possessive early on—now recognized as red alert signs—he becomes overtly abusive when he loses his job and attempts to restore a precarious sense of manhood. The film maps the traps for women, caught between appeasing the tyrant in order to keep the peace and defying him at the expense of an escalating round of violence. The wife is cast as insecure but certainly not passive as she tries out various strategies of survival. Leaving is not easy, though, because the centrifugal forces acting upon her, ranging from dependent children to the consternation of relatives, work against the forcefulness of her will. Yet when she finally kills her husband, setting fire to his bed, the instinct for survival and the thirst for revenge are inseparably intertwined. While her children are not directly threatened by the husband's violence, the woman's actions are motivated largely by maternal protectiveness and concern. The denouement occurs as the domestic sphere explodes, ignited by the woman's slow burning rage. Much like other woman-gets-revenge films, *Burning bed* registered a new readiness in mainstream film and television in the 1980s to portray female rage. While tales of explosive women serve as a reminder that women no longer take things lying down, these same tales constrain the political imagination by offering no real social avenues of deliverance. Women are typically burned, along with their beds.

Stories of deliverance

Early histories of the battered women's movement include valiant stories of active resistance to male violence, as well as examples of the seductive snares of malevolent husbands. In *Violence against wives*, Dobash and Dobash (1979) discuss the history of British women's resistance to domestic tyranny and the folk literature that emerged in the 18th century on runaway wives. A British newspaper advertisement by a husband in 1764, for example, forbade any person from giving his runaway wife credit or harboring her. To do so was to risk prosecution. Some wives resisted by placing their own advertisments in newspapers, justifying their right to obtain credit and making clear to the community their reasons for running away (1979: 4). In tracing the history of the domestic violence movement, Elizabeth Pleck (1987) similarly begins with an account that underscores the importance of this storyline to the larger struggle for women's liberation. She tells the story of how Elizabeth Cady Stanton and Susan B. Anthony helped a runaway wife find "safe and secret" lodgings after she escaped from her abusive husband, a state legislator (1987: 61).

The feminist campaign to abolish the chastisement laws in the 19th century followed in the wake of the anti-slavery movement, drawing on the moral rhetoric and imagery of this same movement (Dobash & Dobash, 1979; Epstein, 1981; Stanley, 1998). White feminists were a guiding anima in abolitionism, finding parallels between the institution of slavery and their own "domestic slavery" as white women. And in the context of the 19th century, this rhetorical employment of slavery made considerable sense. Women had no legal status, including property rights or the right of divorce other than under conditions of extreme physical cruelty. Women were legally equivalent to children, with men operating as guardians and public representatives of their interests (Breckenridge & Ralfs, 2006; Goldfarb, 2000; Pleck, 1979).

The paths of deliverance from domestic tyranny have been treacherous for all women, but they also map quite different routes through suffering. During the course of carrying out my field research, *Sleeping with the enemy*, a Hollywood film released in 1991 and widely distributed internationally, often became the focus of conversation. The title of the film draws on one of the key insights of early radical feminism—that women are the only oppressed group that routinely sleeps with the enemy. In using the film to illustrate stories of deliverance, my exegesis draws out the interplay of class and gender in Hollywood representations of women escaping the tyranny of husbands. The film also is enlisted here to illustrate the co-mingling of feminist and conservative elements in the scripting of domestic abuse in popular culture.

The narrative structure of *Sleeping with the enemy* works through contrasting portraits of male authority—the Good Provider and the Tyrant—with each competing with the other to oversee the fate of woman. The film opens with Laura, played by Julia Roberts, adorning both her body and her opulent home in conformity to her dictatorial husband's every wish. She is living in a doll's house, with neither a room nor a mind of her own. Her fabulously rich husband—a stockbroker—is obsessed with his wife, his object of desire and most prized currency. He is a man who, as Karl Marx once said of capitalists, only feels pleasure in relation to the things he owns. As the drama unfolds, each tentative act of self-assertion on Laura's part is met with her husband's brutal fist, literally or figuratively, blocking any path of escape from his totalitarian control. A fateful turning point is reached when her husband takes her sailing, knowing that she is terrified of water and unable to swim. The film employs the metaphor of a near drowning at sea, followed by a resurrection and rebirth of the self, to dramatize the heroine's transfiguration. The protagonist has been taking swimming lessons on the sly, furtively acquiring the skills that carry her dormant strengths to the surface. What appears to be a tragic drowning during a boating accident—ostensibly through suicidal resignation—becomes instead a survivor story. Laura swims to shore and emerges from the sea, like some primordial, evolving creature, with the adaptive capacities that enable her to take flight from her nightmarish marriage.

The journey out of domestic tyranny terminates in her hometown, a setting infused with nostalgic imagery of Americana. Laura's return to this source of her being takes her back to her mother, blinded by a stroke and thus impotent to intervene on her daughter's behalf. As a runaway wife, Laura lives in constant dread that her husband will discover her hidden location and return to repossess his marital property.

This hometown, which provides a tenuous sort of sanctuary, is also the place where Laura finds a Good Man. This good man is, conveniently, right next door—a sweet, boyishly handsome drama teacher at the local college. Much like other good men in Hollywood films, who also often are teachers, this male presence occupies a symbolic space bridging maternal and paternal sides of the social order. While the teacher offers a nurturing (i.e., modern) masculinity, his charms are easily eclipsed, the film implies, by the mesmerizing glitter of the rich man. Throughout the remainder of the film, this good man stands in counterposition to the bad one, narratively repressing alternative avenues of deliverance for the lonely heroine.

Alliances with other women are absent, with the exception of the affectionate tie to the mother, whose incapacitated state signifies the illusory nature of any return to a protective maternal fold.

While Laura took a wrong turn in the road by marrying the rich man, the film's sympathetic portrait of this abused woman depends heavily on her unchanging goodness and a pervasive innocence that is unmarred by her encounters with her evil husband. We feel for the distressed heroine because her uncorrupted nature makes her deserving of such sympathies, retaining as she does the hallmark signs of virtuous bourgeois womanhood.

While we may suspect that she made her own pact with the devil—wanting to marry a rich man and not looking too closely at the man behind the wealth—the audience is enlisted in the repressive work of the film. The absence of any trace of destructive or selfish motives on the part of the protagonist grants her some status as a woman entitled to fight back. And fight back she does, as she kills her husband in self-defense at the film's conclusion while her would-be male protector lies prostrate on the floor. The pleasures offered to women by this Hollywood film lie in its legitimizing of female aggression and resistance to male domination, while preserving the dual ideals of bourgeois femininity and the harmonious heterosexual couple.

In the course of carrying out field research in Pine Ridge, discussion of violence in indigenous communities turned to another film—*Once were warriors*, based on a novel by Allan Duff (1995). Cangleska advocates introduced the film to illustrate common terrain with Aboriginal groups in New Zealand who were also working on the issue of domestic violence. I make use of the film here to draw out the dynamic tensions that emerge in storytelling about race, class, gender, and violence. It is a story of female deliverance but one that maps a rougher road ahead for the valiant heroine than those represented in most Hollywood films.

Once were warriors opens with the skyline of a New Zealand city, with freeways looming over wreckage below. Rusted-out shells of cars shelter the homeless, while street rappers and local food vendors suggest a restive human spirit at work. Much of the rough vibrancy of this urban scene is palpably masculine. It is a world where unemployed men idle away time pumping iron and hanging out at the local drinking spot, ironically called the Royal Bar. The men are tough, but no tougher than the world they occupy on the economic margins. The film lingers fondly on the bodies of these descendants of warriors, tracing the outlines of their hard, muscular edges and exquisite tattoo markings. The camera follows these men as they take the party home at the end of the day—men who let women in at closing time and sing to them of enduring devotion.

Juxtaposed to this masculine world of bars and empty parking lots is the more feminine world of the yards surrounding the government projects, a domestic space inhabited by women and children. Clotheslines crisscross the landscape, marking the borders of feminine identity and registering the endless toil and binding ties of women's lives. Yet the women are tough and defiant, easy companions for the rough men. And much like their men, the women insistently hold onto moments of pleasure, sucking deep and hard from life's meager offerings.

Directed and performed by Maoris, *Once were warriors* sets family violence against a backdrop of cultural devastation and frustrated desires. The film tells the story of a Maori couple, Beth and Jake, and their five children. While the ties that bind Beth and Jake grow out of a shared legacy of racism and poverty, this legacy is engraved with the complex markings of class and gender. The labile intensity of their relationship is suggested early on in the film, as Jake initiates sex with Beth on the kitchen table. The heat between them suddenly dissipates, as Jake cavalierly announces that he has lost his job. Beth stiffens with worry, and Jake storms out of the house, heading for the Royal Bar. Craving sympathy from his drinking mates, he complains about the ingratitude of women. When his mates ask for more of the story, Jake expresses his outrage. "I just told her I got laid off. You'd think my prick dropped off."

Beth and her daughter, Grace, are the shock absorbers on the domestic front, grounding the episodic storms of Jake's rage. But as the film progresses, the gender divide widens to reveal a more ancient source of enmity between husband and wife. Moments of warmth and tenderness are perpetually invaded by a deep resentment that wells up in Jake, an insurgent echo of past claims on him, claims that refuse to relinquish their hold. While picnicking on a hillside with three of their children, Jake and Beth reminisce over how they met. The beloved daughter of Maori royalty, Beth had defied her elders in marrying a man far beneath her in social station. As Beth looks back wistfully, Jake overrides her story with his own bitter account of the rejection he suffered at the hands of her kinfolk. "This black ass comes along and steals her away—her royal highness . . . Do you know where I come from kids? A long line of slaves." This long line extends into the pre-colonial past and into Maori rulers' subjugation of Jake's ancestral tribe. As Jake and Beth recollect widely divergent images of the Maori past, the distance between them widens into an unbridgeable gulf. The mood of the day sours, as Jake sabotages the family outing by stopping at the bar for "just one drink."

We can understand how a man such as Jake might come to destroy the things he loves most, and how the source of his love is so closely bound to the source of his bitter hatred. He loves his wife but is unable to give himself over too fully to her without threatening precarious psychic borders. On one front, there is a threatened loss of masculine potency—the defensive armor that binds things together and forms the very structure of his inner world. When Jake is threatened by the demands of Beth, or by her defiance of him, he finds comfort in the companionship of his mates. This restoration of a phallic world wards off the threat of psychic disintegration. On a second front, yielding to his wife threatens submission to the master. At moments when Beth rises up in response to his dictatorial demands, Jake's deep reservoir of class resentment erupts into class warfare. Jake enacts a historically dislocated struggle, placing Beth in the position of oppressor. His assaults on her revitalize his hatred and temporarily establish him as the victor.

Jake's explosive rage reverberates in after-shocks of trauma for the family. While the younger son and daughter are frozen in terror, the adolescent sons and daughter diverge along predictable gender lines in their modes of coping. The sons flee, seeking sanctuary in a code of manhood that operates alongside the bar culture of the father and his "mates." But the daughter stays home to restore order amidst chaos. Grace is the prototypical good daughter, the bearer of abandoned adult responsibilities.

Beth repents her defiance of the elders, journeying back to her native village with her children at the film's end. While the two adolescent sons accompany her as proud descendants of warriors, the teenage daughter, Grace, returns in a casket for a traditional burial. The tragic fate of the daughter, who kills herself after being sexually abused by an uncle, foregrounds the costs born by women of a brutally injured masculinity. There are no women's shelters on the scene, no places of refuge for Maori women and children in white society.[4] The guiding message of the film is that true salvation lies in a return to native practices. All other paths of liberation are illusory. Jake's drunken disparagement of native practices, his accusation that Beth is living in the past, lacks moral authority. Jake, too, is living in the past, but his past blocks any sustaining connection to the present. Beth charges back that "you are still a slave, Jake—to your fists, to your drink, to your self." In turning away from Jake, Beth repudiates the slave mentality.

Ultimately, the sons take the side of the mother against the father, just as the film does itself. At its denouement, it is a triumph of the life-sustaining mother over the life-destroying father. But our judgment of Jake depends on the degrees of freedom we grant him in the story. From one vantage point, the manly bar culture offers a mere illusion of freedom. It provides sanctuary to Jake but prevents him from suffering the state of conflict that might prompt a search for another way out. Yet we sense that his injuries go beyond any restorative possibilities at hand, blocking any path of deliverance. He is not able to love anything enough to make restorative use of it.

Beth, on the other hand, is able to idealize the warrior past because it evokes a proud legacy that continues to protect her from the ravaging effects of neo-colonial domination.[5] As a descendant of royalty, she is conferred a superior status that transcends the poverty and racism that grips husband and wife. Women's liberation is implicitly enlisted in staging the overthrow of brutish patriarchs. Yet class and kinship ultimately trump gender in this tragic display of competing powers, with the fate of woman tied to the status of her tribe.

In its final celebration of the warrior past and the return home, the film represses the destructive side of these same traditions. As Beth and her son turn their back on Jake, who is left howling pathetically at the Royal Bar, we recognize the vital importance of severing ties with this petty tyrant. But in its triumphant conclusion, the film seems to forget that the royal Maori clan that reclaims its beloved daughter is also implicated in the demoralization and destruction of the bastard son.[6]

Stories of struggle and reparation

Second-wave feminism created sites of refuge for women and introduced a more subversive denouement to the story as women came together to share their experiences in consciousness-raising groups and to support each other in emancipating from the control of abusive men (Davis, 1988; Peltoniemi, 1981; Schechter, 1982). In talking about everything from housework and childrearing to sex and violence, women pieced together a shared portrait of their lives and began to place it in a political context. And in forming a sisterhood of support and advocacy, women were able to resist collectively rather relying on individual coping strategies.

In reviewing transcripts of interviews with advocates in the various geographical settings, I was struck by how much of the storytelling centered on the drama of domestic confinement and strategies for escaping abusive situations. Dilemmas revolved around developing a safety plan and barriers to securing refuge more often than on the dilemmas women encountered once beyond the reach of their abusive partners. Sandra Horley, with Refuge in London, summarily assessed the situation: "We need to address structural issues. But we don't live in an ideal world and first and foremost this is a place of safety for women." Safety does take priority in a state of crisis but this aim may also be deployed defensively.

Women of color, however, more often discussed the rocky terrain ahead for abused women who took flight. Women's advocates at Pine Ridge Reservation, for example, spoke of their ambivalence over sending women to neighboring cities because the racism women encountered was often worse than the abuse they suffered at home. Women often returned to the harsh life of the reservation because there were aspects of tribal culture that were vitally sustaining.[7]

Domestic violence is a recurrent motif in the writings of many women of color, writings that center on the alloy of pain and pleasure, heartbreak and joy, binding family members in oppressed communities. But these same writings provide insights into the complexity of the anti-violence struggle, and the importance of a broader transformation of society in freeing women from the grip of violence. Set against a landscape of culture violence, stories of family violence in oppressed communities often undermine the stability of our moral categories. In the lights and shadows, figure and ground of this landscape, it is more difficult to discern a singular or primary evil that sets in motion the suffering that unfolds. Yet this wider landscape opens ground for narrating the net of social bonds required for sustained struggle.

Social movements require some understanding that freedom depends on mobilizing and organizing within the context of group life. You can't get there by going it alone. In the previous section, I noted that the history of abolitionism figured prominently in early histories of the battered women's movement, and many feminists continue to invoke the idiom of the *Underground Railroad*—a theme I discuss in more detail in Chapter 4. In this last section on stories of struggle and reparation, I offer a reading of *Incidents in the life of a slave girl, written by herself* (Jacobs, 1987)—a work that became the focus of lively discussion in several of the shelter trainings that I attended, particularly as an example of how wealthy white women have historically overlooked sexual abuse of domestic servants. I follow this reading with themes from Janet Campbell Hale's (1998) *Bloodlines: Odyssey of a native daughter*—a novel that invites reflection on what is at stake psychologically in making reparations in the aftermath of family violence.

Recognized for its historical authenticity as well as its literary merits, *Incidents in the life of a slave girl*, written by Harriet Jacobs (1987) and originally published in 1861, chronicles Jacobs' own journey from slavery to emancipation in 19th-century America, told through a first-person narrator, Linda Brent. This work registers some of the conventional narrative strategies of the domestic violence movement, even as it introduces a more complex terrain of gender identifications and moral conflicts than contemporary domestic violence scripts generally permit. Like other mid-19th-century slave narratives, *Incidents in the life of a slave girl* was published as part of the abolitionist struggle, intended to arouse sympathies among white audiences for the anti-slavery cause. With the passage of the Fugitive Slave Law in Congress in 1950, which made assistance of escaped slaves punishable by law, including fines and prison terms, slave narratives took on a more important role in mobilizing support. John Sekora (Sekora & Turner, 1982: 75) describes how both male and female slave narratives made "accommodations to white Christian piety and economic individualism." Frederick Douglass was pressured by white abolitionists to tell his story in a prescribed way—one that cast him as a heroic Moses character leading believers out of the Wilderness, omitting details of his escape that might offend white sensibilities. The slave narratives of black women were shaped by these same conventions, but audience sympathies depended more on the female protagonist's capacity to project devotion to maternal duties. Annette Niemtzow (1982: 104) notes distinctions between male slave narratives, whose tales centered on "triumph in a public sphere," and female narratives, where the drama is located within a private or interior space. Mary Ellen Doyle (1982) similarly traces these motifs, suggesting how the female Gothic novel shaped the narrative conventions available in telling stories of women escaping despotic husbands, as well as those escaping slave-holders.

Incidents begins with a confession to the reader: "I ask nothing—I have placed myself before you to be judged as woman whether I deserve your pity or contempt." In this supplicant address, Jacobs speaks from the position of a mother whose primary motivation is to seek the freedom of her children and for the "thousands of Slave Mothers that are still in bondage" (Jacobs, 1987: xiii). Published as a memoir with the editorial assistance of her friend, L. Maria Child, *Incidents* continues to generate controversy, particularly in assessing the role of white editors or "translators" in shaping this and other slave narratives—an issue easier to recognize from some historical distance than in current reform campaigns (Gates, 1987; McBride, 2001; Sekora & Turner, 1982).

Incidents establishes the strength of the protagonist's character through fleeting memories of a happy and vital girl in childhood, prior to her full entry into the harsh realities of the slave household. Through the voice of her first-person female narrator, Linda Brent, Jacobs draws on the story-telling trope of childhood innocence and the loss of an idyllic past. But Jacobs also subverts narrative conventions of the 19th century by casting her story of domestic tyranny within a wider web of oppressive relational ties beyond the matrix of the patriarchal nuclear family.

Jacobs invokes her "dear reader" throughout the narrative, simultaneously appeasing and admonishing white women who were her primary audience. She shields her readers from the depths of her actual fall from virtue, plaintively suggesting that her moral lapses should not be judged so harshly. "I have promised to tell you the truth, and I will do it honestly, lest it cost me what it may. I will try not to screen myself behind the plea of compulsion from a master, for it was not so" (1987: 53–54). This refusal to "screen" herself operates as a double-edged metaphor, implicitly confronting her readers with their own veils of innocence while alluding to her superior knowledge in sexual matters. Narrator Linda Brent makes a sexual bargain with a white man she loves and gives birth to two children by him. Sparing her readers the sexual details and alluding to what they can scarcely imagine, Jacobs invites respect as well as sympathy for the horrors that she has endured.[8]

In conformity to prevailing standards of middle-class decency, Jacobs casts female sexual desire as solely in the service of maternal responsibility. In order to gain leverage in negotiating the sale of her children to sympathetic whites, Linda Brent seeks a lover before her sadistic master can seize her for himself. She finally escapes and goes into hiding, suffering a torturous seven-year ordeal of crippling immobility, saved only by fleeting glimpses of her children playing in the yard outside the dirt basement where she hides under the protective watch of her grandmother. The protagonist nonetheless triumphs over her master by outwitting him, eluding his every calculated move.

Jacobs enlists her readers in her plight while also confronting white women with their own history of active collaboration in the institution of slavery. Jacobs locates the problem of slavery in the South, allowing some distance for her northern white readers from the shocking portraits of domestic abuse in southern families. But the white mistress in the narrative is no mere bystander to the cruelty.

> Mrs. Flint, like many southern women, was totally deficient in energy. She had not strength to supervise her household affairs; but her nerves were so strong, that she could sit on her easy chair and see a woman whipped, till the blood trickled from every stroke of the lash. She was a member of the church; but partaking of the Lord's Supper did not seem to put her in a Christian frame of mind . . . The slaves would get nothing to eat except what she chose to give them. Provisions were weighed out by the pound and ounce . . . She knew how many biscuits a quart of flour would make, and exactly what size they ought to be.
>
> (Jacobs, 1987: 12)

Jacobs testifies to the jealousy and cruelty of white women and of the cunning of Mrs. Flint, her mistress, who "possessed the key to her husband's character before I was born" (1987: 31). The oppressed—whether white women or blacks—learn to read the subtexts of countless encounters, perpetually on alert for both dangers and opportune moments. Elaborate unspoken codes of mutual understanding keep in place the precarious illusion of Christian piety and the fantasy of racial purity. For Jacobs, domestic violence unfolds as a racial drama, with the white woman holding the whip as confidently as the patriarch.

Linda Brent (as did the author herself) joins the anti-slavery movement when she arrives in Philadelphia and later New York, moving beyond the maternal fold of obligations granted her by sympathetic white readers. Still searching for her children, Jacobs positions Brent within a larger historical drama. As she finds her footing in the North as a freed slave, she confronts new obstacles. In the same breath that she inhales the fresh breeze of freedom, the weary Brent is overtaken with the stench of unanticipated prejudices. Traveling by train through the state of New York, the narrator recounts the racism of Jim Crow laws. She had arrived at a hotel with a white woman who had hired her to care for her daughter and she was barred from eating with the other household servants. Instructed to eat in the kitchen rather than in the parlor, and later sequestered in her room, Brent becomes outraged and refuses to comply. She exhorts others subjected to racist treatment to resist: "Let every colored man and woman do this, and eventually we shall cease to be trampled on by our oppressors" (1987: 177). As her journey continues, however, the protagonist finds that her survival depends on her capacity to sustain the tension between accommodation and resistance.

Jacobs never blurs distinctions between slavery and wage work. The institution of slavery dehumanizes everyone on a vast scale, from the slaveholders and their children to the blacks who are exploited, transported, and disposed as property. The triumph in legally abolishing slavery is unequivocally celebrated, as are the cross-race alliances and heroic resistances that brought it about. But this slave narrative offers a less cheerful destination at the end of the Freedom Road than many readers would hope for, even as she insists that continuing the journey is worth the effort.

In *Bloodlines: Odyssey of a native daughter*, Janet Campbell Hale (1998) enters into this same history of struggle from the vantage point of a century of uneven advances for women, particularly for minority women. Less known than the previous works discussed here, this memoir strains the bounds of many feminist analyses in that the protagonist declares early on her identification with her father and her contempt for her abused mother. Yet the memoir is itself a working through of multiple gender, race, and class identifications and feelings of rage, guilt, and grief in the aftermath of family violence. And it situates this process of working through in the context of an unfolding political consciousness.

As her mother's youngest and most defiant daughter, Hale seeks, through her writing, a connection with the mother who perpetually eluded her in childhood. Hale traces her own course of development within a family perpetually in flight, a family whose migratory movements across the American landscape are in the wake of the soul-shattering displacements of her people. Her childhood is punctuated by frantic departures from town on a Greyhound bus. In their furtive escapes from the father during his periodic "benders," mother and daughter form the emotional center of a kinship tornado, with the other children tossed about in the periphery. There is a chilly silence between this mother and daughter, a silence that is only relieved through the daughter's passionate writing, her only reliable means of resuscitating a positive maternal imago within her.

At the vortex of the mother/daughter conflict lie competing memories of the father. While the mother bitterly complains of the brutality of her husband, who regularly beat her in a state of drunken rage in the early years of their marriage, the daughter holds no such direct memories of him. In her own efforts to monitor the border between her mother and herself, she keeps such knowledge at a distance. When her mother displays her scars, insisting that her children bear witness to the cruelty she has endured, the daughter looks the other way. Closer at hand than the abusiveness of the husband/father, whom the daughter remembers more kindly, is the harsh side of the mother.

Early on in the novel, Hale instructs a schoolroom of children in her tribal homeland about her own hard-won successes in life. "Some families will, if they can, tear you down, reject you, tell you you are a defective person." This emotional abuse justifies, even requires, a counter-aggressive insistence on independence: "If you come from such a family and you have no one else to turn to, then you must, for the sake of your own sanity and self-respect, break free, venture out on your own and go far away" (Hale, 1998: xvi). But this journey out of bondage is a lonely one, even as the daughter makes strategic use of kinship resources: "Then you will have to rely on yourself and what you've managed to internalize regarding strength, stamina, identity and belonging . . . being courageous is part of our heritage. The most admired quality of the old Coeur d'Alene was courage. Courage has been bred into you. It's in your blood" (1998: xvi).

A professional writer and a college teacher, Hale marks the distance traveled in relation to her mother, her internal tormentor. Reaching back into the bloodlines of the past, into a richly dense web of kinship ties, Hale is more able to idealize distant, mythologized memories, including a largely absent father, than those in closer proximity. In many social movements, the progenitors, whether Earth Mothers or the Original People, are heir to such idealization. It may be that acts of rebellion against authority require some invoked sanctioning from a prior, more sacred ancestor.

In this Odyssey, the mother comes to embody for the novel's young protagonist the pathology of the Indian past—the most malevolent spirit in the daughter's burial ground of memory. Much like Odysseus (and Freud's Oedipus), Hale charts a journey of individuation, beset by forces that threaten to overwhelm and defeat the protagonist. The forces that beckon a return home compete with an equally strong urge away from the original source of life. The modern story of identity formation constructs self-development as a project, one that goes beyond assigned social roles (Bhabha, 1994; Sprengnether, 1995).

One of the more gripping stories in Hale's memoir, introduced to dramatize the rocky course of mother/daughter relationships, centers on a struggle over her hair. For Hale, a formative memory—a story told over and over by her mother to illustrate the obstinate nature of her daughter—vivifies her mother's pernicious attempts to crush her spirit. Her mother would repeat, over and over to anyone who would listen, her maternal plight:

> I worked so hard curling her hair, trying to make her look decent for school. Then I happened to look out the window one morning right after she left, and there she was, hiding in the alley, messing

> up her hair with both hands, trying to pull out the curls I'd worked so hard to make. I vowed then and there I'd never lift a finger to do anything for her again.
>
> (Hale, 1998: 69)

The author takes up this harsh story to convey her own sense of combative strength, vivifying the obstacles to independence she faced in the rigid persona of her mother. It is a valiant tale of her own defiance, and of how, even at six years of age, she was "not bending to her will," determinedly "undoing what my mother had done to me before stepping out into the world" (Hale, 1998: 70). She recalls her mother's punishment for this act of defiance: she cut off her hair, shearing it "so short she used my father's electric clippers." In looking back on this symbolic castration, on the mother's act of stripping her daughter of her female strength, Hale seems to be searching for a memory that crystallizes the event that set in motion this unceasing mother/daughter combat.

Hale does not fully escape, however, the fate of women like her mother. She comes to be battered by her own husband. Furtively leaving the house with her child, as her mother had done before her, Hale recalls deciding to return home. But she never does arrive at her mother's house, instead seeking refuge at a women's shelter in the city.

Much later, as her mother lay dying, Hale leans over her mother to hear her tell one last story. In a delirious state and confined within a critical care unit of a hospital, the mother greets her daughter as though she were returning home that night so many years ago. "'Go to bed. Get some rest. You must be exhausted after your long bus trip from California, you and the boy.' She thinks I'm an eighteen-year-old battered wife again," Hale adds. The mother continues, "'I've been waiting for such a long time . . . I was about to give up on you. If you're hungry . . . I cooked a big pot of chili.' She smiles at me. She knows her chili was my favorite" (1998: 81).

How do we make sense of this memory of a tender maternal moment, intruding into the narrative portrait of the cold rejecting mother? Is the story itself a means by which the guilty daughter makes reparation with the mother, perhaps as a means of dealing with the mother's impending death? Or in anticipating death, is the mother (delirious, perhaps drugged) making reparation with the daughter, finally able to express the affection toward her that she had so determinedly guarded against?

Other tender memories now come to the daughter, memories of her mother confronting her own abusive husband and defending her. As the daughter leaves the hospital room, her mother calls out, "Good night, Dear." This affectionate term arouses a dim recollection of her mother calling her "dear" as a child. "I'd forgotten, but now it sounds familiar." The daughter now confesses her own failings: "I didn't show up . . . And I didn't even care enough to pick up the phone and let her know I wasn't coming" (1998: 80).

The story continues with Hale putting the fragments of such memories together, and we may imagine a therapist or friend assisting her in this process of producing a coherent narrative. On a deeper level, Hale understands that she is morally implicated in her own story and she wrestles with how to integrate the positions of guilty daughter and defiant daughter. She was confused and desperate, Hale reasons to herself, and going home was a one-way road to nowhere. Not calling her mother was a means of punishing her first tormentor, the one she holds responsible for her subsequent misery.

It is only much later in the story, as the daughter discovers and makes use of a wider vista of cultural knowledge, that Hale is able to enlist her mother as an internal source of strength and make reparation with her. From this enlarged vantage point, which includes a Native history of proud endurance in the face of devastating cultural violence, the daughter finds some holding ground for the sadistic domestic dramas of her childhood. From a psychoanalytic perspective, this story foregrounds the process of moving toward ethical capacities based on enlisting the "good objects" in childhood. Making reparations with the mother grew from recognition of common identifications, but also finding the good objects in the collective past that provide the necessary holding to weather the destructive forces that threaten to overtake both mother and daughter, even as their paths diverge.

CONCLUSIONS

This chapter began with contradictory claims concerning wife abuse and the sanctions against it in Western history. By approaching this question more dialectically, however, we can distill contradictory motifs in this same history and identify broader dilemmas concerning how women give narrative force to experiences of abuse. The battered woman story, like any narrative that acquires social symbolic power in cultural life, has multiple functions. Patriarchal cultures have generated a vast folklore narrating the quandaries of damsels in distress, overtaken by merciless villains. Villains are necessary storytelling conventions under patriarchy, for they set in bold relief the beneficence and redemptive powers of the good male protectors.

The subversive storytelling that circulates in the domestic violence field, as well as in popular culture, continues to produce protagonists measured against an extreme standard of virtue. Those active female protagonists who take center stage in popular culture often remain moral virgins, forced into exile through the sheer malevolence of their abusive husbands. Women of color have generated a rich literature resisting this stereotypical plot.

Some of the research literature on family violence suggests that gender sets different wheels in motion as cycles of violence are reproduced. Boys typically identify with the batterer, whereas girls identify with the victim, setting the stage for the girl's later vulnerability to violence and the boy's later tendency to embrace violence as a right of manhood. While such dynamics are pervasive, gender identifications are not as monolithic as this. In *Bloodlines*, as one example, Hale confesses that her own defense against the depressive misery of her mother's life took the form of identifying with her father. Her mother must have invented such stories, or brought the abuse upon herself, Hale recalls reasoning as a young girl. While she later became a battered wife herself, she nonetheless fared better than does her mother. She was able to emancipate herself from the "cycle of abuse" because she had far more options in sight and avenues of deliverance than did her mother.

Returning to the myth and counter-myth at the beginning of the chapter, we may conclude that both claims carry some truth. On the one hand, there is a long history of sanctions against wife beating in Europe and America—even as this same practice was tolerated. In the early American colonies, beatings were one of the few grounds on which women could divorce husbands. So, too, Native American women invoke ancient stories of how woman abuse violates traditional belief systems. The ideal of the companionate marriage—where the good husband inspires devotion in his wife through his capacities as a provider rather than in beating her into submission—gained legitimacy throughout the 20th century. At the same time, feminists have exposed the façade of the harmonious modern family, with a man at the helm and a woman maintaining domestic harmony. The ideal of the nuclear family also creates a hothouse of expectations, pain, and disappointment—combustible forces that men more readily escape than do women.

The three genres presented here—stories of bondage, deliverance, and struggle and reparation—may be enlisted to describe the narrative trajectory of emancipatory movements. Stories at the beginning of a social movement—stories that bring recognition to the marginalized—may not serve the movement as well during later stages. As the oppressed become active agents in history, stories that sustain these efforts inevitably bring moral conflict into tales of suffering and deliverance. In moving through these stages, women in the anti-violence movement must continue to generate narratives that foreground the sheer pervasiveness of violence against women. But if these are the modal stories that circulate, relying as they often do on the stock script of virtuous (white) maidens and smarmy villains, too many plots and subplots are left behind.

NOTES

1 For a discussion of shifting historical discourses on victimization, see Lamb (1999).

2 For a more detailed exposition of Restuccia's work, see Haaken (2008b).

3 Goldner (1998) describes this dynamic of defensive splitting where abusive men separate the violence from personhood. I am suggesting here that women may also enlist this same defense in protecting the good representation of the partner from the bad. Framing the bad within the context of an illness discourse also opens up the possibility for a cure.
4 Since the 1990s, domestic violence organizing has emerged as an active area of Maori political culture, including the establishment of a number of shelters for abused women and their children.
5 For discussion of neo-colonialism and indigenous women, see Alexander and Mohanty (1997).
6 Indigenous women have led many of the campaigns around domestic violence in New Zealand/Aotearoa (see Te Kupenga Whakaoti Mahi Patunga (National Network of Stopping Violence Services NZ); www.svsw.org.nz/resources.html).
7 Many Native American/First Nations scholars have cautioned against romanticized and stereotypical images of indigeneous peoples, stressing the diversity of tribal practices, languages, and traditions with respect to gender and family violence (see, for example, Hamby, 2000; Norton & Manson, 1997).
8 For analysis of gender motifs in slave narratives, see Doyle (1982); Smith (1974).

Part 2

DILEMMAS OF PRACTICE

4

GOING UNDERGROUND: FEMINISM AND SHELTER PRACTICES

Myth: The home is a woman's sanctuary.
Counter-myth: Confidentially located shelters are the only places of refuge for women seeking protection from violent men.

In beginning this second section of the book, Dilemmas of Practice, I start with a story about one of the oldest surviving shelters in the world—Bradley Angle House—located in Portland, Oregon where I have lived and worked for the past 30 years. The history of Bradley Angle House, the most politically active of the shelters in Portland, illustrates how stories that circulate at a grassroots level often fail to find their way into the formal domestic violence literature. In discovering the subversive tale of the origins of Bradley Angle House, I was struck by how this history remained in local feminist lore much like an *alien introject*—the psychoanalytic term for an image or idea that has been taken in but not integrated into consciousness.

Bradley Angle House staff members begin volunteer trainings on Tuesday nights each month by distributing mimeographed materials on the history of their organization. This background includes the narratives of founders, including a story authored by "Bonnie," who recounts the story of how she and other women established the house in 1971 for women in crisis (Bradley Angle, 1978). Bonnie recalls the chaos and creativity of those early days and of falling in love with Sandra, a tough woman and prime force behind Prescott House, the forerunner of Bradley Angle. The house provided housing for women just out of prison, as well as for prostitutes and lesbians who lived on the streets. This place of sanctuary was no convent, Bonnie intimates, and the women were as rough as the places they were escaping.

Growing up in a Quaker pacifist household with parents who were liberal academics, Bonnie gravitated to this rough asylum for women on the margins, as well as to her take-charge lover. In a voice familiar to readers of domestic fiction and self-help literature, Bonnie explains the gravitational appeal of a wounded lover: "She touched me very deeply with the kinds of pain she felt," Bonnie offers in maternal tones, "for having been so long on the streets" (Bradley Angle, 1978: 36). With little in the way of skills or wages, the women pooled their resources. Scenes in the narrative shift from the convivial chaos of the shelter to the challenges of running a communal farm outside of town. As jabs between the two lovers escalated into bloody fistfights, with jealous rages fueled by alcohol, Bonnie, Sandra, and the other women at Bradley Angle finally turn to feminist theory to sober up. The violence that erupted in lesbian relationships, they learned, grew from the same forces that kept wives in check: economic marginalization, isolation, and feelings of insecurity. But their effort to find common ground with battered women also was strategic. Bonnie recollects how difficult it was to mobilize concern for women on the streets or just out of prison, or for lesbians who failed to conform to middle-class standards of womanhood: "We were not Mom and apple pie . . . A few of us were mothers, but we were prostitutes, we were lesbians. We were drug addicts. We were alcoholics" (1978: 45). The women who formed Bradley Angle developed a deep empathy for and identification with battered wives, Bonnie adds. But the image of a desperate wife fleeing her brutal husband in the middle of the night with toddlers in tow was a more winsome picture than their own combined portraits of suffering. "It was possible that America could be made to care about mothers who were being beaten," Bonnie notes pragmatically, "or children who were being beaten" (1978: 44).

Battered women's shelters have come to occupy a social symbolic place within feminism, in part because the need for shelter vivifies so palpably the brutal side of the patriarchal family. When students in my classes speak of their work in the shelters, they often assume a sacral tone. This service has become a rite of passage for many young women who demonstrate their commitment to the cause. Shelter work also is powerful because it breaks from the feminine position of nursemaid to an injured manhood, turning instead to the care of women.

This chapter constructs a dialogue on the role of shelters in the broader anti-violence movement. Just as "*home*" and "*family*" evoke multiple meanings for women, depending on how cultures and kinship systems structure households, so too do terms such as "*refuge*" and "*shelter*" carry a range of symbolic loadings (Cohen, 1992; Davis, 1988; Loseke, 1992). In interviews carried out in the various geographical locations, shelters emerged as a site of intense emotional investments. This was no less true for me as it was for other feminists. The findings reported in this chapter began with the premise that this strategy has been costly for abused women and for the larger feminist movement. My early feminist identity drew on the idea that patriarchal power depended on isolating women from one another. Whatever phallic threats men could muster would wither when confronted with the combined powers of women. So the strategy of spiriting women away into hiding to escape abuse ran counter to some of my earliest and most basic feminist principles. Yet my research also sensitized me to the complexity of this issue.

At the group interviews carried out Germany, England, New York, Pine Ridge, and Portland, Oregon, I presented findings from a study my colleague Nan Yragui and I (Haaken & Yragui, 2003) completed on shelter practices in the United States—a study that focused primarily on the mandate adopted at the federal level through the Violence Against Women Act of keeping the location of shelters secret. Our study grew out of concerns raised by women of color about the costs of spiriting women away to secret locations (Crenshaw, 1994; Davis, 2000). We also began to hear through the grapevine about open shelters throughout the United States, as well as in other countries (Peltoniemi, 1981). These open shelters were not discussed or acknowledged in the published literature, so the question of the extent of variation in practices emerged as an interesting empirical question worthy of study.

The standard rationale for the practice of maintaining the confidential location centers on the risk of violent men coming to the shelters and wreaking havoc. Overwhelmingly, the response to the question of the advantages of the safe location is "to keep women safe." Yet as Diana Rempe (2001) concludes from her research on practices in Arizona, Minnesota, and Oregon, shelters with published addresses were no more likely to experience threats from perpetrators than were those with unpublished addresses. Even though most advocates defended the policy of the secret location, they also offered examples that emphasized their capacities to cope with the men who came to the door. Every shelter reported that abusers had come to the property from time to time or made threatening phone calls, regardless of whether the address was hidden or not. Shelter workers reported that the abuser would flee when told the police were on the way, if an alarm were set off, or when simply confronted by staff members. Rempe also reviews media coverage of incidents at shelters, citing one example of a man in Indiana who had held a shelter worker at knifepoint and raped her as she left the building. The *New York Times* reported the incident under the headline "Shelters Disclosing Location in Spite of Risk," implicitly blaming the open address policy of the shelter for the violence (Rempe, 2001: 73). Rempe notes that this framing of the rape and assault reproduces the very victim-blaming that the movement has sought to overcome. Rather than focus on the man's violence and the importance of summoning the community to protect shelters, the message was to stay out of sight.

One director with whom I spoke in the course of my field research, who asked not to be identified, told of how the decision at her shelter to have a published address stirred bitter criticism from other feminists in her state. When a violent incident did occur at the shelter several years later, advocates from outside the area assumed that a male batterer was responsible for the damage. But a subsequent investigation revealed that an angry former employee—a woman—had carried out the criminal mischief. This same shelter director was cautious not to downplay the threat of male violence in women's lives. But she suggested that the practice of confidential locations may serve other boundary functions in the feminist community beyond the expressed aim of protecting women from their abusers.

HAVEN OR HELL: THE CONFIDENTIAL LOCATION

At a community meeting in my neighborhood in Portland, Oregon in winter 2000, a young black woman rose to tell her story. She described the hurdles she faced in getting into shelter and of her sense of isolation once inside. In testifying to the difficulties African American women face in escaping male violence, she cast the shelter as an alien world rather than a place of refuge. Cut off from friends and community, she found that her fears and despair mounted. The speakers who followed acknowledged the vital work of shelters in providing a safe haven, social programs, and outreach services for women and children. But many of the women at this event called for reform, and for the creation of neighborhood-based places of refuge and support for abused women.

The romantic conception of hidden shelters, sequestered from the harsh realities of women's lives, is more likely to be cast as an illusion by women in poor communities (Crenshaw, 2000; Davis, 1989; Haaken, 2002a; 2003). As Erica Burman and her colleagues (Burman *et al.*, 2004: 101) note, based on research carried out in Manchester on domestic services for minoritized women, the "climate of secrecy produces very intense relationships within refuges." The intensity of the relationships is exacerbated by the distressed state of women entering refuge, compounded further by lack of resources beyond immediate crisis services. The authors suggest that the feminist fantasy of the "'safety' of women's groups" may be enlisted defensively to protect staff from the anger of residents.

In her study of shelters in minority areas of Los Angeles, Kimberlé Williams Crenshaw (1994) concludes that women of color are less apt to conceptualize shelters as sacral places of protection, removed from the wider web of threats to women's wellbeing.

> In most cases, the physical assault that leads women to these shelters is merely the most immediate manifestation of the subordination they experience. Many women who seek protection are unemployed, and a good number of them are poor. Shelters serving these women cannot afford to address only the violence inflicted by the batterer; they must also confront the multilayered and routinized forms of domination that often converge in these women's

> lives, hindering their ability to create alternatives to the abusive relationships that brought them to shelters in the first place.
> (Crenshaw, 1994: 95)

Following from many observations such as these, our national study sought to determine the extent of variation in the actual practice of confidential locations, and also to find out more about how state coalitions—the umbrella organizations for domestic violence services in each state—were mapping the boundary between the shelter and the broader community. The practice of confidentiality typically includes having an unpublished address and the requirement that shelter residents not disclose the location to family or friends. Entering the shelter is much like going "underground" (Ferraro & Johnson, 1985). Women are dropped off at a discrete distance from the building and must maintain strict rules of secrecy about the location.

Although historical accounts of the battered women's movement do include mention of divergent strategies, debates over the secrecy of shelter locations seem to have "gone underground" as well. In presenting papers on this topic at domestic violence conferences, we found that audiences often responded with surprise and alarm that there should be any questioning of the practice. At these same conferences, however, there were activists and workers who spoke, sometimes conspiratorially in hallways or in small workshops, about their own doubts about the strict rule of secret locations.

Having worked in a feminist abortion clinic in Los Angeles and continued with abortion rights organizing when I moved to Portland, Oregon in the 1980s, I was very cognizant of the threats women face in accessing services from feminist organizations. But even after a wave of bombings and other terrorist threats to abortion clinics, feminists did not take the clinics "underground." The strategy was to defend these public spaces for women to access abortion services—whether through signing up groups to volunteer as escorts or forming human fire lines at the entrance to the clinics to protect women from the harassment of right-to-lifers.

In carrying out our study of shelter practices, we conducted telephone interviews with executive directors or staff at domestic violence coalitions in all 50 states of the United States and the District of Columbia (Haaken & Yragui, 2003). Of the 51 women interviewed, some had been involved in the domestic violence movement for over 20 years while others were relatively new to the field, having only one or two years of experience. Respondents were asked about the number of confidential and published shelters in their state, the advantages and disadvantages of each type of location, and whether there was any discussion of the issue of shelter location in their state. Coalitions reported a total of 1,558 domestic violence shelters in the United States, with a total of 135 having published addresses. The Alaska coalition reported that all shelters in the state had published addresses—a finding that was associated with trends in rural communities. More puzzling was the finding that there were twice as many (40) published shelter addresses as unpublished ones (20) in the state of Illinois.

Almost all respondents in our shelter study could identify drawbacks to the secrecy rule, even though most also defended the practice. One issue centered on whether it was of benefit for women to *feel* safer, even if this was illusory. As Noel Busch, with the South Carolina coalition describes it,

> "Women feel safer. The primary advantage, well, the disadvantage is this sense of safety may not be real, especially when she is inaccessible. He may be more motivated to find her and may be more unpredictable. It's not difficult to find where shelters are, especially if you are a savvy person—call the police, follow her, or call other social service agencies."

The question of how advocates participate in constructing the experience of a "safe house" is a complex one. One aim of shelters is to create a reassuring environment and to assist women in overcoming their fear and the after-effects of trauma. But another aim is to educate abused women about the danger signs—indicators of escalating threats. Creating a false sense of security would be counter to this last aim.

Many of the women we interviewed noted that shelters are often confidential in theory but public in actual practice, particularly in communities where they have been in a stable location for many years. Several respondents observed that children who have been residents in the shelter sometimes grow up to be batterers who know the location. Concealing the shelter location is particularly difficult in rural areas, where the gap between theory and practice is the widest. Verlaine Gullickson, with the South Dakota coalition, explains this phenomenon:

> "You can't do it in a rural state. There is no way that everyone in town doesn't know where the shelter is. They just do. Most of our communities are 15,000 or smaller. They don't publish their addresses. They use post office boxes. The fact remains that everyone knows where they are."

It was not surprising that respondents from Alaska and Illinois, where open shelters are common, advocated for the open practice. However, women from states with little or no variation in the practice of keeping sites confidential also expressed some ambivalence. The dominant argument for the published location was that it invites community support and protection of the residents and staff. Linda Isaacson, with the North Dakota coalition, discusses this issue of community support:

"It [the published location] allows the community to buy into supporting that particular shelter. Scout groups can plant flowers. Another group can paint. That is an advantage, especially in these days when resources are so tight. That support also tells women that they are not alone in the community. But, you really have to look at what the community will support."

For many respondents, the question of whether to publish the location was associated with women being forced into "hiding," as well as the broader issue of political invisibility. As collective responses to male violence, some respondents saw public shelters as an important step in moving beyond the cloistered, private spaces that mark the boundaries of a prototypically female world. Tess Sakolsky, with the Illinois coalition, warns about keeping the problem of domestic abuse "behind closed doors," suggesting that shelters may reproduce some aspects of the battered woman's experience of isolation:

"When locations are published, we know that this issue needs to be dealt with. We need to quit hiding behind closed doors and windows. We have been in private for too long; family secrets need to be pulled out."

In discussing these findings with advocates in Germany, England, New York City, Pine Ridge Reservation, and Portland Oregon, a key issue centered on the gap between the ideal behind the secret location policy and the complex dilemmas that arise in carrying it out. As women stay longer in shelters, the secrecy rule—the requirement that women do not disclose the location, including to friends or relatives—becomes more restrictive. One New York advocate describes the dilemma:

"It's one thing for a woman to not be able to tell her friends where she is, to not get phone calls, for her kids not to have friends over for six weeks when you're recovering from just having been battered and your whole life changed. It's a very different thing to live like that for a year and a half. What happens is that shelters are really like jailers. And then they've got to enforce these really unenforceable regulations. And then, women try to subvert it. Sometimes after a year they're dating and then they want to do what they want. They want to have a life. Or the kids tell their friends where they are because it's been a year. Then they're kicked out and some of our members have talked about how that affects them and how awful they feel. One woman was very articulate in saying when somebody else breaks curfew then we all suffer and I don't get to go out because now the shelter's clamped down."

Advocates in New York acknowledge that the secrecy rule, while codified in some of the state regulations governing VAWA funding, may no longer be in women's interests. Further, the practice may have been overdetermined by anxieties advocates experienced in the early organization of shelters—some of which were rational and some heightened by the experience of venturing into unknown territory. The question of safety for battered women was infused with more diffuse fears concerning the safety of working in the shelter movement. Several advocates suggested that the policy of secrecy grew out of their early identity as an "underground movement," which involved honing one's radar for danger signs. Sue Loeb, director of Voices of Women, describes the scene:

> "When I started this program in Staten Island back in 1980 . . . we had a whole discussion around safety and they said things like 'When you go to court . . . First of all, you should have a very confidential location. When you go to court wear a wig and don't park outside,' like they were really concerned about stalking. At that time there had been a very horrible case at one of the shelters outside of New York. I can't remember what state it was or where but some shelters workers were attacked and something was thrown at them, some acid or something like that. There was a whole horrible story. Everybody in the movement around the country was in a panic about our own safety."

Throughout history and throughout the world, women have developed secret societies to transmit female skills and knowledge. My research on women's perspectives on the Sierra Leonean Civil War, for example, included considerable discussion of the role of female secret societies in resisting male power—including colonial control throughout the 19th century—as well as in maintaining forms of female subservience (Haaken *et al.*, 2005). During the early 1970s, I was part of a feminist collective in Los Angeles that had operated underground, carrying out abortions during a time when they were illegal. The group sought to preserve these skills because the right of abortion felt precarious after *Roe v. Wade* in 1973, as it still does for many. From indigents and refugees to soldiers and revolutionaries, the capacity to cross borders and transmit information without detection can be vital to political survival.

At the same time, secret practices may take on considerable emotional freight over time. Identities forged through the romance of the political underground may become paranoid, particularly as they are isolated from those "above ground." Controlling behavior on the part of leaders of such cadres may intensify, as trust comes to depend on keeping secrets and demonstrating loyalty to the group.

With the labyrinthine system of apartment set-asides for battered women throughout the borough system, an advocate in New York City describes how the task of maintaining the secrecy policy becomes obsessively demanding. There also may be an element of paranoia that overtakes the process of implementation. She goes on to explain:

> "There is this whole feeling now in New York when shelters do screening . . . they really talk about subway lines. The Asian Women's Center doesn't mark their shelters on the same subway line as the Chinatown did because that's the line that everybody in the community uses. And if you come from a small community like that where everybody knows everybody, people just won't be safe. Your batterer will find out that she's on the N train everyday."

As the shelters have expanded in number and as gateways narrow for triaging women in crisis, the initial spirit of an "underground movement" may take less progressive forms. As discussed in Chapter 1, advocates hold differing assessments of the early shelter movement and different identifications with this legacy. In the following section, I present the specific lessons drawn by advocates in reflecting on that history, and how those lessons might inform current practices within their various locales.

UNDERGROUND AND ABOVE GROUND

In the course of discussing the issue of confidential locations, the romantic imagery of going underground increasingly intrigued me—as did the frequently cited parallels between the shelter and abolitionist movements, taken up in the last chapter. In 1984, Lenore Walker invoked the abolitionist legacy in describing shelters as a worldwide "underground railroad" (1984: 119). This metaphor underscores the connection—which early feminists sought to advance—between slavery and the domestic bondage suffered by abused wives, intersections pursued in earlier chapters. And, indeed, something akin to an underground railroad worldwide was created through the shelter movement.

Much of the early work of this movement was very much above ground, however. The early formation of shelters or refuges for women was part of a broader radical period of social experimentation, as was the formation of Bradley Angle House described at the beginning of this chapter. During the 1970s, many young people lived collectively and created alternatives to the nuclear family. The practice of taking in other women grew out of this ethic of care—the emphasis on collective responsibility for others, whether in the form of sharing childcare and distributing chores more equitably or challenging the bourgeois ideal of the home as a self-sufficient unit of consumption.

Socialist ideals also shaped the early refuge movement. Rather than viewing men as consciously exerting power and control over their wives, socialist politics tend to focus on the dynamics of class oppression, and on the role of the welfare state in regulating the lives of the poor (Gordon, 2007; Josephson, 2005). Working-class and poor men are more apt to be cast as caught in a cycle of despair and rage, often directed toward those closest to them rather than against their true oppressors, i.e., the bosses. British sociologists Evan Stark and Anne Flitcraft (1996) argue that class politics tends to be forgotten as a factor shaping the early shelter movement.

> The demand for shelter must be framed by the chronic housing shortage in postwar London, the increasingly marginal status of immigrant families thrown aside by massive disinvestments in jobs, and by the subjective expression of these conditions, the fact that more than 100,000 persons were already squatting in London when Chiswick opened.
>
> (Stark & Flitcraft, 1996: 336)

In Chapter 1 I described the legendary role of Erin Pizzey in the early shelter movement and some of the conflicts that arose over safe houses for women. Pizzey directed much of her outrage against the social welfare state and its failure to provide for women and children. Many British feminists criticized her, however, for aligning herself with professionals—with the growing ranks of social workers, psychologists, and psychiatrists who approached family violence as a form of psychopathology that required treatment rather than political action. In 1975, Pizzey came into conflict with feminists when she fought against the formation of the National Women's Aid Federation (Schechter, 1982). The organization was formed without her support and went on to establish many shelters in Britain based on what came to be known as the "feminist model."

In contrast to the Chiswick model, the *feminist model* excluded men from working at the refuge. Separatist politics were at the epicenter of many radical feminist debates in the 1970s (Donovan, 1996). In shelters, these politics were grounded in efforts to emancipate women from dependency on men as well as protect them from overt abuse. Indeed, helping women to stay in these safe houses may have may have been as important as keeping men out (Davis, 1988; Loseke, 1992). Concealing the published address required a commitment on the part of residents to uphold this policy and to break contact with abusive men. Much like the tradition of convents, which sometimes provided asylum for women escaping husbands or fathers, creating a female social order through a network of safe houses opened possibilities for self-development through disciplinary practices (Cohen, 1992).

As shelters or refuges were organized throughout Europe, Britain, and North America in the late 1970s, they were envisioned as exclusively female spaces, created by and for women. As early activists describe it, "There are only three rules at the house: no liquor, no drugs, no men" (Ridington, 1977: 569). Many experienced for the first time a sense of sisterhood and unity with other women, and of no longer feeling isolated. Thus, the power of shelter was in the form of sisterhood it created—one that displaced the patriarchal family as the legitimate protector of women (Davis *et al.*, 1994).

While shelters throughout Europe and in the United States generally followed the British feminist model, other models developed as well, with the role of men in the organization emerging as a primary site of difference between feminist and non-feminist shelter practices (Davis, 1988; Walker, 1995). Further, the practice of the secret location emerged as the *terra firma* of a movement that had expanded its borders to include recognizing the need to work with the police, the courts, and social service agencies, as well as securing funding from governmental agencies and the private sector.

Indeed, as coordinated services operated as the new mandate in the 1990s, the secrecy rule increasingly seemed disjointed from the realities of refuge work. Investments in the policy could be interpreted as a group defensive reaction—one that, much like a neurotic symptom, originates as a means of coping but loses its adaptive value over time. For groups as well as individuals, internal anxieties may overtake external threats as the prime motivators in maintaining security measures. And for both groups and individuals, rigid defenses often limit creative engagement in real-world problems.

One area where creative engagement languishes is in working through conflicts between shelter staff and residents. Indeed, the focus on the magnitude of the external threat of male violence may at times serve as a defense against attending to internal sources of conflict. Carol Hagemann-White, with the Berlin group, reflects on the early shelter movement, and how providing sanctuary for abused women involved the creation of sisterly solidarity among women. But this aim often produced bitter disappointments.

> "Some of the shelter workers started feeling cynical about this since some of the women went back to the men, saying 'they're not going through this painful process, they are just using us, then going back to the more comfortable life. They aren't joining the struggle against patriarchy.'"

The consistent lament expressed by advocates in Berlin centers on the shift from the early political vision of feminist solidarity and collectivity to a vision of shelters as primarily social service agencies. Some contrasted the idealism of early feminists with their own more pragmatic (realistic) approach. The younger advocates were more apt to view the earlier vision as too utopian. As one describes it, "The original demands were unrealistic to some extent. What still happens—and is much more realistic—is that these women [who enter the shelter] don't become feminists but they do become part of networks, which are mutually supportive."

Barbara Kaveman, also with the Berlin group, suggests that the early ideal of a sisterly collectivity downplayed the many differences among women and the barriers to achieving female solidarity. The fantasy of the shelter as an island of sisterly serenity was as illusory as that of the home as a safe haven, in part because it did not prepare women for the difficulties ahead. Kaveman and other German advocates emphasize how advocates have always attempted to be sensitive to conflict for abused women as they moved beyond their private tyranny to take up the challenges of political organizing. As Kaveman explains it,

> "You know, you see how different all these women are who suffer violence. This was a very important step in this discussion of domestic violence—to accept that most women who suffer violence are not equal, and that they do not like each other. It is not easy to live together in a shelter—and being so different. The only thing connecting the women is that they have suffered violence and they need a safe place. And this is a very poor, very small thing to keep them together in shelter life. So it is very important to recognize these differences."

This narrowing of expectations may be one way of coping with feelings of anger and disappointment that advocates experience—feelings that are not readily incorporated into a feminist theory of woman battering. As I noted in Chapter 2, aggressive feelings and impulses can feel alien to some forms of feminine identity, particularly when the object of those feelings is a vulnerable woman. To acknowledge these impulses in crisis work can feel tantamount to "beating up" on a woman who has already taken too many hard knocks.

At many of the domestic violence workshops I have attended, as well as in interviews, advocates look back nostalgically on the early shelter movement—on a time when women took other women into their homes. Yet as advocates at the South Asian Women's Empowerment and Resource Alliance (SAWERA), in Portland, Oregon lamented, this practice of taking in abused women became exhausting over time. More than the threats of violent husbands in pursuit of their fleeing wives, the issue of workload emerged as a concern for SAWERA advocates. Shelters with paid staff and volunteers grew from the recognition that women needed to form organizations to deal with the problem, as well as informal networks of mutual aid.

As shelters became institutionalized, advocacy work was absorbed into the grid of service and housing agencies. In most contemporary settings, shelter workers are required to "triage" women, deciding whether their story meets the criteria for domestic violence. Much like other gatekeepers in social service provision, shelter workers apply criteria in a range of ways, depending on availability of beds and other resources (Davis, 1988). Since shelters do not require police reports, admission depends on the course of the conversation between a distressed and often desperate woman on the crisis line and the advocate taking the call. Sometimes girls flee from home, whether asserting their independence or escaping abuse. Other girls and women are running for their lives.

At the shelter at Pine Ridge, the problem of enforcing criteria for what counts as domestic violence means drawing firm boundaries, in spite of the trend toward expanding definitions to include emotional abuse.[1] Flexible definitions make it difficult to draw the line, however, particularly in communities where abuse and bad treatment come in many forms. Depending on how domestic violence is defined, large numbers of women offer stories that would qualify for admission. Inez No Neck reflects on this dilemma:

> "Sometimes we don't know how to say no . . . A woman may say, my mom kicked me out and she may call later and say, well he did try to beat me up . . . But we say, but we are here for DV. If they are not in a DV situation, but just treated badly by family members, we say there is a mission in Rapid City we can call for you . . . We have to set priorities, because there are women who are running for their lives."

Women are running for their lives in many places in the world, confronting a series of punishing roadblocks along the way beyond the threat posed by husbands. In Germany, since unification, migrant women, primarily from Turkey, must get legal papers before entering a shelter, and they must establish that they have been with the man for three years. Some shelters take migrant women in, however, even when they do not meet the criteria. But funds are only provided by the state for legal residents, placing tremendous pressure on the refuge houses to not accept migrant women. As one German advocate explains, "The duration is three months with options to continue. But for illegal aliens it can go up to three years. Everything functions from one day to three years. One of the complications is that there are more apartments available now [so women do not depend so much on shelters]." The women in German shelters are more apt to be migrants than in earlier times, advocates suggest, and this shift requires more complex analyses of links between gender, national politics, and domestic violence. Once again, shelter workers find themselves in a difficult position as they coordinate their services with the policing arm of the state.

In addressing the problem of triaging crisis services for women, the Berlin group notes the vast divide between social welfare in the United States and in Europe. And they worry about intensified pressures in Germany to adopt American policies in cutting back on social services. With the opening up of borders between East and West Germany, women's shelters became key sites of refuge for migrant women seeking work. While above ground and regulated by the state, women's shelters have assumed a new role in Germany in providing sanctuary for migrants. As alliances with the state are strengthened, feminists walk a fine line between policing and protection as they offer refuge to migrant women escaping the various forces unraveling their lives. One Berlin advocate describes the situation:

> "The biggest problem that is comparable [to problems of minority women in the United States] here is the migrants. They have no legal status and they are staying longer and longer, there is no place for them to go. They can't get housing or a doctor for their kids . . . There are a number of women who were sold into prostitution . . . They [the shelters] gave refuge to the women but at the same time realized they were being exploited. This was not their issue so they had to refuse."

Sharma recounts similar dilemmas in refugee and immigrant communities in the UK, and how immigration politics has very much become "their issue." Although activists have won ground in establishing violence against women as a basis for securing asylum in the UK, the process of establishing this status is grueling. Refuges are not legally permitted to accept undocumented women, although many do in spite of the laws prohibiting it. Sharma offers a story of one undocumented woman seeking asylum who had lived in a refuge for a year, financially supported through the largesse of a local woman lawyer:

> "If you leave [your husband] you are able to say, 'there was DV and if I go back it will be horrible for me.' If the officers believe your story then you get your stay. Which means you can stay in the UK as long as you like. She has not gotten that yet. Her in-laws checked her out and they were going to take the child away. But she ran with the child. She found the legal woman's place, there was nowhere for her to go that night so she stayed. Then she went to social services the next day, and they said, 'no, we will take your child into care, but we will not give you money. Our duty is to the child, not to you.' The absolute hypocrisy, the way people approach social service in this country!"

Even with a much stronger social welfare state than the frayed system in the United States, activists in the UK do battle with social welfare agencies daily, particularly in securing support for migrant women. In London, housing officials police the provision of refuge services, but some advocates stress that working in the domestic violence field brings a wider view of the needs of women. Rather than casting the refuge as a step toward "self-sufficiency," advocates critique crisis models that minimize the needs of minority women. As one advocate who previously worked in the homeless movement explains,

> "Everyone is coming at it with their own views and language about what is needed and who is responsible. Housing people might think the woman doesn't have a house, we can get her a house. They don't think that a woman might not be ready to live in a self-contained situation, to be left alone. Ten years ago I would have thought that all anyone needs who is homeless is a house. I have learned that that is not the case. So, what we are aiming to do is more complex, which requires people with a wide range of backgrounds. But I think the housing movement has not accepted that."

In resisting the compartmentalizing and minimizing of women's needs, advocates in England also are thrown into turf battles with activists and workers in other social problem areas. There has been little in the way of coalition-building between advocates for the homeless, the housing movement, and women's advocates in the domestic violence field. In struggling to defend services for women, staff in the various settings find themselves monitoring the boundaries separating battered women and other vulnerable groups seeking shelter.

Although the history of the shelter movement can be traced to the housing crisis in London in the 1970s, the two problems—domestic violence and lack of affordable housing—are intertwined lines of what Colman describes as the "gridlock" in New York services for women as well. Several New York advocates who have worked in the movement for 20 or more years remember a time when there were more resources available for housing. Sue Loeb notes that the crisis has become more acute over time: "In New York City, full back to 1983, 84 and 85, you could still find affordable housing in a reasonable amount of time. So the women in our shelter stayed for about six weeks . . . Now in New York City women stay six months, nine months, 18 months."

One of the New York advocates describes the scene: "If you just look at the shelters alone, we have about 1,400 shelter beds run by 13 different programs." Another advocate concludes that a more basic problem involves how state funds are distributed for temporary housing. Before the Violence Against Women Act was passed in 1994, funding for domestic violence shelters in New York City was based entirely on welfare funds. In order to access these services, Warrior explains, "you [the woman] had to apply for public assistance. If you are denied, you had to pay a certain amount of money to the shelter. So the shelter becomes a landlord." If a woman was earning wages, she was expected to pay rent for the use of shelter.

> "So what happens is that it became up to the shelter to collect the money. If they don't pay it, that puts pressure on the shelter, especially the smaller programs. Overwhelmingly, the women can't pay. So a few things are done: (a) you don't take women who are working; (b) you tell women who are working to quit their job and to get on assistance; (c) you kick out women who are working when they don't pay; or (d) you pick up the cost."

Another advocate nods in agreement, commenting that "none of them are good choices." The women go on to describe the acute conflicts that these situations pose for women who think of themselves as part of a social movement that is "partly underground." In addition to conceding power to the state over the shelter system, there is pressure to fill the available beds. As one New York advocate assesses the situation,

> "One of the things that happened was that people got a per diem rate, which means you don't get money for empty beds, which makes shelters want to take in large families. So a family with five kids is the same as five single women, which is easier to do. It is much harder for single women and small families to get shelter [in New York City]. It is harder if you have large boys, this has been a problem. We have seen things where shelters feel uncomfortable with boys as young as 10."

Advocates in all four sites commented that women were staying in shelters far longer than in previous years—primarily because they have no place to go. Policies for shelters include "supporting women to leave when they are ready," and moving women into transitional or permanent housing. Yet in some cities, governmental agencies have supported crisis services over permanent housing subsidies. By approaching homelessness as a short-term crisis and granting women "refugee" status, the scope of the problem may be minimized. And crisis workers become active participants in a crisis model of violence, one that all too readily reproduces the crisis-oriented modes of coping common to poor and abused women.

Many advocates struggle with the conflict between the "good advocate"—the nurturing and supportive role that is a vital aspect of feminist ideals—and the "bad advocate"—the quasi-landlord who periodically denies women access to shelter, depending on whether her income matches funding guidelines, or evicts women who have not followed the rules. In the Berlin group, one advocate describes the early feminist model:

> "The idea is in theory that people made rules, certain instructions of how the houses would be run, but the houses established themselves with real flexibility in deciding what each individual woman needs who seeks help. They determined how to approach her and how to interact with her, how government agencies can interact with her and the shelter on her behalf."

The issue of how shelters handle children emerged as another site of border tension—one that often pits staff against women residents. One of the most consistent conflicts between staff and women seeking refuge, advocates suggest, centers on the rule restricting males over age 12 (and age 10, in some settings) from going with their mothers to the shelter. With the exception of the Pine Ridge shelter, this rule was in place at all of the shelters where advocates worked. An advocate with the New York group offers what she describes as a typical story: "What happens is, when you call the hotline and you are told that your son is 11 years old, you're angry at the hotline and you feel that the hotline failed you. Which it did because it didn't give you any options."

While women from a range of ethnic backgrounds register distress over this rule, African American women have been the most vocal in my own community. At a domestic violence conference in Portland, Oregon in 2001, Berje Barrow, an African American activist, began her workshop by posing the question, "Who makes the decisions in the shelters?" She went on to explain that young white women have power and control over the residents of the shelters. "It's like I'm back in school or being punished because my life hasn't worked well," she stated sardonically. "Do I get an allowance if I do my chores?" Barrow suggested that women's refuge should encourage "peerness," rather than authority, and that addressing issues of poverty, unemployment, and lack of education need to be at the center of the movement against domestic violence. Barrow continues: "The minute I get loud, what happens? I get blackballed. Sorry for the word, but that's how it is. I get written up."

Discussion of diversity in Barrow's workshop extended into the wide continuum of meanings and behaviors subsumed under terms such as "*violence*" and "*aggression*." In bourgeois society, many forms of aggressively charged behavior, particularly those of people of color, are interpreted as violent. Talking loud, swearing, moving fast, arguing—all of these behaviors may be viewed through a racist, paranoid lens as disturbing indicators of a threatening proneness to aggression. The movement against domestic violence is not immune from this readiness on the part of whites to perceive people of color, particularly black people, as threatening.

Bridgette Fahnbulleh, director of the African American Providers Network, an organization that provides information and referral on domestic violence services in the Portland metro area, and a staff member at Bradley Angle House, also addresses the issue of race. She claims that black women are more apt to leave for behavior that is perceived by white staff and residents as violent. While this sometimes includes hitting children, it also includes more subtle forms of expressive behaviors, for example, talking loud or yelling. The exclusion rule preventing puberty-aged and adolescent males from entering shelter, out of the assumption that males are prone to violence, painfully evokes racist stereotypes in America society, where black males are viewed as "suspect." This practice of separating older male children from their mothers further fragments families that have been ravaged by poverty.

Fahnbulleh also suggests that the case management of women in the shelters can be quite controlling, offering little room for women to develop relationships with each other or to heal emotionally. "Women are kept too busy," she states emphatically, "and they have to do too much work to really heal . . . In finding resources for the shelter, it should include hiring people or having volunteers to help with the cleaning and childcare."

Many women of color associate the process of entering shelter with "going into hiding," and with the loss of more primary cultural alliances (Crenshaw, 1994; Perilla *et al.*, 1994; Rivera, 1994; Sorenson, 1996). In discussing this issue, Fahnbulleh insists that "secret shelters don't work for women of color . . . They are too isolating, and they cut you off from your community." She also stresses the importance of having the community involved in making safe space for women, and of demanding more involvement on the part of men. The isolation of the shelters from the communities in which women live, and the secrecy surrounding the shelters, also may intensify the burdensomeness of crisis work. Power struggles arise over the monitoring of women and the maintenance of the confidential location, and staff, as well as residents, may feel adrift.

At the Pine Ridge Reservation, the shelter does allow adolescent males into shelter, although staff determine whether a particular youth can be managed in the setting. An area of conflict that it shares with other settings, however, concerns disciplinary practices. Most shelters have a no-spanking rule, although there is more latitude in the area of physical discipline of children than with partner violence. Yet shelters differ considerably in how they confront women who hit their children. In describing the Cangleska approach to childrearing practices, Inez No Neck emphasizes gentle appeals to both the woman's empathy with her children and her Native identity. "Women feel guilty when they spank their children, because we believe that your children are a gift and they choose their parents. So we emphasize that hitting children is not the native way of doing it."

DIVERSE VISIONS OF REFUGE

Terms that convey the movement's ideals for some feminists may elicit in others a more wary response. Indeed, one woman's sanctuary may become another woman's prison. In "The fantasy of the perfect mother," Susan Contratto and Nancy Chodorow (1982) explore the unconscious demands that accompany such idealization, and the dilemmas that arise as women create new forms of solidarity. Second-wave feminists deployed the more egalitarian kinship category of *sisterhood*, rather than motherhood, just as male workers enlisted the idiom of *brotherhood* in the labor movement. Yet as Contratto and Chodorow observe, childhood disappointments are readily revived in striving for new relational possibilities. Siblings do fight, but sisterhood offers the hope of a community free of such squabbles. However, feminist places of refuge for women inevitably suffer, as do mothers and wives, under the burdens of such expectations, particularly when there are so few spaces in the broader society to offer sisterly comfort.

Describing a transitional house for battered women in New Jersey, a house created exclusively for South Asian women, Sujata Warrior recounts the complex cultural boundaries that divide women. In regions of the world where hostilities between neighboring countries run high and divisions between castes or classes run deep, women struggle to find common ground (Abraham, 2000; Preisser, 1999; Sorenson, 1996). Yet she draws inspiration and hope from the transition house established in New Jersey:

> "Women come together as Hindus, Muslims, upper and lower castes, but there are lots of conflicts. They want separate places for garbage, different food, and to not use the same bathrooms. But the women also want to go to shelters run by Asians, and they are discussing these issues at house meetings."

Minority women seeking shelter face a range of obstacles, depending on their history and cultural identifications, just as they vary in their access to resources. In areas where advocates invoke a common set of traditions, creating more open shelters holds less of a threat. Karen Artechoker describes the conception of community behind a new shelter being constructed at Pine Ridge. Like the present one, the new space will be open, with an entry area where women may receive guests. Artechoker continues that "We have a vision of a housing community, communal living, shared cars, and tasks that are shared." Laughing, she adds, "But I don't want to be there while people are healing, because it is going to be very messy." Artichoker expands on the vision behind the new shelter: "There would be innovative people, counseling, dispute resolution help, to guide people as they grow and learn. Like in the shelter, they say, 'she is mad as hell' and that is part of the healing process . . . It's important to channel that energy into making things happen."

Some Latina advocates interviewed in Portland, Oregon prefer the term "time out" rather than shelter to describe refuge space for women and children. This distinction has some strategic value, particularly in allaying anxiety among Latino men over the prospect of women abandoning them. Pressure to hold the family together is often more intense for women of color than it is for many white women (Espin, 1999; Rivera, 1994; White, 1985). But it would be a mistake to view the softening of the shelter boundary as simply a response to community pressures, just as it would be reductive to interpret a woman's decision to return to an abusive situation as an expression of ethnic solidarity. Any assessment of these dilemmas must take into account the various cross-currents of women's lives, and the contradictory nature of women's social obligations. Community and kinship ties inevitably impose constraints and repressive demands, just as they offer sustenance and protection. The mix varies from society to society, of course, as does the distribution of freedoms and constraints within the society.

In the fall of 2000, Casa Esperanza (House of Hope) was established by a group of Latina women in Portland, Oregon, with the support of several local churches. The aim was to provide a place of refuge where Latinas would be able to communicate easily in Spanish, prepare meals together, and live free from the stereotyped expectations they sometimes experienced at shelters. After many debates, the group chose to organize Casa Esperanza as an open shelter with a published address. At the dedication of the shelter, those present—an ethnically mixed group of women's advocates, clergy, and neighborhood supporters—were collectively enlisted in the protection of women residents and staff of Casa Esperanza.

In describing the process of deciding on shelter practices, Linda Jaramillo, one of the organizers of the shelter, emphasizes the importance of community involvement:

> "There was lots of discussion around whether secrecy was even feasible because of the strong community tie. We saw the confidential location as further isolating ourselves and that would be falling into the same trap. There is risk involved either way. We got on the Internet and looked at research and found that there are no greater amount of incidences at known shelters . . . Basically [with the open shelter], the need and evidence of the problem is apparent to everyone."

CONCLUSIONS

Just as *home* elicits associations of protection and nurture, *shelter* evokes similarly maternal associations. Through the lens of a feminist analysis, the appropriation of maternal imagery is a means of reclaiming the value of female protectors. Further, feminism shifts the object of female nurture from the exclusive claims of the nuclear family—specifically, children and male partners—to a broader nexus of social relations and sustaining bonds of sisterhood. But this same imagery may enclose the movement in a protective membrane that closes off possibilities for critique and self-reflection.

In working through the multiple meanings of shelter, it is important to distinguish between the need for female-only spaces in the women's movement—whether in the form of shelters or other sites of feminist organizing—and the question of whether or not such spaces should be hidden from public view. All movements of oppressed people require some degree of separation in order to develop collective sources of strength and solidarity, even as they must be able to challenge the dominant social order and establish political alliances with other oppressed groups (Incite!, 2005).

While the creation of female-only spaces is vital to the women's movement, drawing the boundary too rigidly between "good women" and "bad men," between safe places of female sanctuary and rampant male violence, may obscure other social boundaries. Feminists who work with multiple axes of oppression are more apt to recognize the illusory nature of many sites of refuge for women, however, and to challenge the fantasy of an all-good space of female nurture (Crenshaw, 1994). While such forms of idealization are vital to developing a sense of collective strength and hope, idealization may also have the effect of suppressing conflict. Claire Renzetti (1999) makes a similar argument in suggesting that the romanticizing of women and the denial of power dynamics within feminist organizations have inhibited direct discussion of group conflicts. If "power and control" motives are located entirely within men and outside the protective fold of the shelter, it is more difficult to confront sources of aggression within the organization.

The state of emergency created by spiriting women away to an undisclosed location may magnify women's fears by making men seem boundless in their powers. Sequestered away, women are not able to find a strong enough holding space to keep the threats men pose at bay. Shelter workers also experience anxiety by identifying with the experiences of residents, and may become overly sensitized to violence. While they offer procedures for screening calls and for maintaining the operations of safe houses, shelter policies that require constant vigilance create a siege mentality (Stout & Thomas, 1991).

As volatile economic forces displace people throughout the globe, many women's refuges have become quasi-asylums, much like the asylums of the 19th century that sheltered not only the "mad" but also the poor—people who were displaced by the massive dislocations that accompanied the industrial revolution. Waves of dislocation continue in the present era. The rightward political drift of the United States in the late 20th century, which ushered in the systematic dismantling of social welfare programs for the poor, led to a patchwork quilt of raggedy safety nets for women. In the context of global capitalism, the American model places pressure on other countries as well to create a more lean and mean social welfare state (Kelly *et al.*, 2001). And refugees from the patriarchal family join refugees from war-torn and economically devastated regions throughout the globe in finding safe harbors. Like national borders, the boundary between domestic violence and other social problems is, in part, an artifact of history.

Women-only spaces remain vital sites for experimenting with forms of democratic self-organization and for developing a sense of female solidarity apart from the influence of men. But these same spaces of refuge may operate more as fantasy than reality, not simply because abusive men can still find their female partners, or because so many women return to violent households. Rather, the problem lies in the isolation of shelters from a larger feminist strategy to claim public space and to make the larger social world—as well as the domestic sphere—safer and more hospitable for women.

NOTE

1 The expansion of the definition of battering to include emotional abuse began with Lenore Walker's early work on the battered woman syndrome but gained currency as a feature of domestic violence and as a stage in the escalation of violence with the adoption of the Duluth model in many settings during the 1990s.

5

BETWEEN THE DEVIL AND THE DEEP: INTERVENING WITH BATTERERS

Myth: Men who batter are mentally ill.
Counter-myth: Men who batter are different from other men only in their choice to use violence.

In *The third life of Grange Copeland*, Alice Walker (1970) gives narrative force to the theme of domestic violence by casting the protagonist's assaults on his wife as an expression of his social disintegration. While the novel vividly portrays the brutality of Brownfield, the main character in the novel, his violence emerges out of the dehumanizing conditions that trap him as a southern sharecropper, compounded by an early history of neglect. As his father and relatives head north, Brownfield's world as an infant narrows to the presence of his mother, who is forced to leave him alone on the porch as she goes to work gutting fish for making bait. "His mother left him each morning with a hasty hug and a sugartit, on which he sucked through wet weather and dry, across the dusty clearing or miry, until she returned" (Walker, 1970: 6). Brownfield grows up to suck on women as the one source of sustenance in a barren world. As this deprivation is elaborated through the codes of manhood, his emotional life becomes increasingly split between his wife, who is the displaced maternal object and focus of his bitter resentment, and his lover, Josie, heir to the split-off "pleasurable" mother.

> His crushed pride, his battered ego, made him drag Mem away from schoolteaching. Her knowledge reflected badly on a husband who could scarcely read and write . . . It was his rage at himself, and his life and world that made him beat her for an imaginary attraction she aroused in other men, crackers, although she was no party to any of it. His rage and his anger and his frustration ruled. His rage could and did blame everything, *everything* on her.
>
> (Walker, 1970: 55)

Much of the work of the women's movement has been to interrupt this deathly romance, and to warn women about the seductions of such emotionally injured men (Horley, 1991). Ann Jones and Susan Schechter (1992) conclude their domestic violence manual on the litany of excuses women make for abusive men in a pronouncedly patronizing tone. Pointing out what women presumably should have learned in kindergarten but failed to remember, the authors instruct: "Let's review again the simple explanation we offered at the beginning of this chapter. Why does he treat you this way? Because he *chooses* to" (1992: 65).

Once the moral victory has been won and woman battering delegitimized, the question arises as to what to do with men who "choose" to persist in their abusive behavior. Further, there are quandaries over how to draw boundaries between acceptable and unacceptable forms of aggression, between normal fighting and patriarchal terrorism, and the role of female aggression in family violence. For feminist activists, the challenge has been to re-label many normative male behaviors—whether "blowing off steam," forcing sex on women, or "putting her in her place"—as forms of violence. As Jones and Schechter (1992) point out, working in the domestic violence movement came to mean recognizing more subtle forms of "force" men employ to keep women under control.

This chapter addresses dilemmas in programmatic efforts to intervene in male violence and offers insights on how advocates are responding to them. As the interviews in various group settings warmed up, advocates discussed the question of why allowing greater room for the humanity of men was so agonizing. The concern that abusive men held Svengali-like power over women was important to explore, in part because such beliefs risk perpetuating the idea that the powers of men are boundless. But there are moral and political considerations in framing stories about abusive men, and particularly in portraying men who share with the women in their lives a history of oppression. This chapter looks at conditions under which women are able both to intervene in male violence, holding men accountable for their behavior, and to provide a group context for reparation and reintegration into their communities. This group strategy extends beyond direct intervention with violent men to include alliances across social justice movements.

INTERVENING WITH MEN WHO ABUSE

There is controversy among feminists over family courts and other dispute mediation practices, even though the early movement was able to build considerable consensus to criminalize battering (Schneider, 1994). The term "*woman battering*" replaced "*wife beating*" because it foregrounds the status of the victim—as a woman—and forged a linguistic connection with the felony crime of battery. Criminalizing woman abuse within the household was part of a larger strategy of de-privatizing the family and framing domestic violence as a violation of women's civil rights. Mandatory arrest of batterers is now standard law enforcement practice in the United States, as are stricter enforcement of restraining orders (Gondolf, 1999a; Gross *et al.*, 2000).

At first glance, groups for batterers would seem to be consistent with a programmatic feminist response to male violence. Rather than focusing on women as the source of the problem, societal resources should be directed toward changing men. Advocates interviewed in all four sites commented on the pressure they experience from abused women to provide such services. Pat Ing, with the Berlin group, explains the dilemma:

> "Most of the women came with the perspective that they didn't want to leave. They just wanted the batterer to stop. They didn't want to get in the system or to send them to jail. So they might want us to talk to him and we really didn't have a model for that. The most the battered women's movement had to offer was to lock batterers up or to take women and children away. That really wasn't helpful to the immigrant families. These community-based programs figured out that those models weren't working for these communities."

This account echoes concerns registered in other regions where I carried out interviews. Advocates were particularly aware of the limits of policing strategies in minority and poor communities. However, once advocates embraced the Duluth model of coordinated community response (CCR), questions over how to intervene with batterers were guided by new mandates. In the introduction to *Education groups for men who batter*, Pence and Paymar (1993) describe the acute need for batterer programs after changes in the law led to a wave of mandatory arrests. "The courts refused to impose jail sentences on first offenders without first giving them an opportunity to rehabilitate themselves" (1993: xiii).

Of the feminists remaining at the Roundtable in Germany, once the Berlin Domestic Violence Intervention Group was established and radical feminists had pulled out, there was no real quarrel over CCR, including the plan to integrate women's crisis services with governmental agencies and the police. The emergent arena of feminist conflict centered on batterer intervention groups, also called "*perpetrator groups*." Feminists from the east and the west were united in their wariness toward groups for men. As Inis Meyer explains, "There was a split between the administration personnel who were excited about the perpetrator program and the women (staff) who were more taken by the aspect of community involvement and had reservations about the perpetrator program." She goes on to add that resources focused on helping perpetrators would inevitably take resources away from "making sure women are safe."

The development of the Duluth curriculum for batterers emerged out of converging forces—both pressure to do something with men incarcerated under the new mandatory arrest laws and the desire of many abused women to find ways of changing the behavior of their partners. The Power and Control Wheel—which lists controlling behaviors associated with violence—was derived from the experiences of battered women, but it also was intended to teach women to be better observers of their own experiences. Ellen Pence (1989) notes a struggle from the very beginning, however, between feminists and many battered women themselves over how to view abusive men. While the feminist strategy centered on severing ties with abusive men, many battered women sought reparation, even as they came to understand that they were not the source of the problem. Pence (1989: 65) describes this tension in women's crisis services:

> The women we work with want their partners to have feelings. "Put him in the abuser's group and teach him how to talk," they tell us. It makes sense from their perspective, but it's wrong. The problem is that if we teach him how to express his feelings and he still believes that he has the right to control her, he will use his new skills at self-expression to control her even more.

In consciousness-raising groups, feminists challenged conventional ways in which women were socialized to relate to men. But feminism also required an attitude of respectfulness regarding women's choices. Batterers' programs could be viewed as a compromise—a means of distancing feminist interventions from therapeutic approaches, associated with "coddling men," while still offering some path for male "re-education." Many feminists maintained a hardline, however, insisting that men only change under the threat of law and that the problem of changing men should not be the project of women's organizations.

Bringing diversity into the movement requires attending to the multiple relational ties of women's lives, and the co-existence of oppressive and supportive dimensions of many forms of relationship, including relationships among women. An advocate in the New York group describes differences in the stories of women of color and white women who seek services.

> "Where the differences come out in their communities is in issues around men. There is much more like 'these guys are our brothers, they're our fathers, and they are part of our families. And if you want to change things, you need to change them, and putting money, resources, and effort into changing them.' That is where the conflict happens, a lot of leadership in New York State thinks that energy shouldn't go into men."

Although they recognize the pressures women are under to stay in abusive situations and note the limits of mandatory arrests, many advocates find it more difficult to work with the conflicting feelings and loyalties of abused women themselves. With the exception of the Cangleska program at Pine Ridge, advocates interviewed in all geographical sites expressed feelings ranging from wariness to outright hostility toward batterer/perpetrator programs. The most common response to my probing the basis of this antipathy was that "groups with men don't really work." In responding, I suggested that the criminal justice system also "does not really work," and yet feminists—particularly white feminists—have near-universally supported mandatory arrest laws and other criminal justice interventions. It seemed that the intensity of feeling was overdetermined by other factors, beyond assessing "what really works."

Before exploring the basis of feminist resistance to batterer programs and group dynamics that shape such responses, the next section offers an analysis of the Pence and Paymar (1993) approach to men who batter. Even though the Duluth curriculum was a compromise between punitive and therapeutic approaches, the Duluth-based groups emerged as a site of intense conflict within the domestic violence field (Babcock & Steiner, 1999; Bennett & Williams, 2000/2001; Davis *et al.*, 2000; Feder & Forde, 2000; Gondolf, 1997). Some of the conflict surfaces in turf battles between women's advocates and men who work with batterers. But groups for men also remain an area of tension between battered women themselves and their advocates.

PEDAGOGY FOR PERPETRATORS

The Duluth educational approach to batterers gained authority in the domestic violence field in part because it was positioned outside of the mental health system. In the 1990s, feminist activists became increasingly vocal in their critique of therapeutic approaches to batterers—an issue taken up in Part 1 of this book (Goldner, 1999; Shamai, 1996). As a corrective, the Duluth model frames male battering as a component of patriarchy in that men develop a sense of entitlement to control and dominate their female partners. In addition to physical violence, emotional, economic, sexual, and verbal abuse are tactics used to subjugate women. The stated goal of the educational groups is to hold men completely accountable for their violence (Pence & Paymar, 1993).

In addition to the men's groups, the Duluth model is associated with the movement toward disallowing the testimony of the victim in adjudicating cases. The most consistent effect of this change in procedures was that the batterer's fate was no longer in the woman's hands: "The prosecutor would [now] not interpret a woman's request to drop charges as a sign that she was safe but as a sign of her vulnerability" (Pence & Paymar, 1993: 17–18). Pressing for stricter state intervention, the authors call for "increasingly harsh penalties and sanctions on men who continue to abuse their partners" (1993: 18). Men who enter the batterer groups must sign a release of information to allow contact with his partner, who is regularly notified and asked about incidents of abuse.

As early as 1984, the Duluth Domestic Abuse Intervention Program (DAIP) had moved away from Batterers Anonymous and anger management groups to an approach focused on challenging beliefs that support patterns of male violence. Men are required to establish specific behavioral objectives and to identify rationalizations for abusive behavior. This cognitive-behavioral approach emphasizes beliefs, rather than emotions, as the primary motivational impetus behind human behavior. In the Duluth model of group intervention, discussion of emotional stress or childhood trauma is considered a form of avoidance. Men must develop "action plans," including "changes I am making" and "steps to take."

Education groups for men who batter begins with a quote from Paulo Freire, the Brazilian educator who produced one of the founding texts of the critical education movement. Citing Freire, who states that "education is never neutral," Pence and Paymar (1993) cast the issue of family violence as a political problem rather than a clinical issue. In rejecting Walker's battered woman syndrome, the authors assert that this and other "cycle of abuse" theories obscure the immediate interests served by men in their exercise of violence and other controlling behaviors.

Although they note the histories of hardship in the lives of many violent men, Pence and Paymar (1993: 15) insist that violence must be understood as an individual choice.

> Many of the men who walk into the group have serious emotional problems . . . Their collective history is filled with violence. These factors are contributors to or modifiers of a man's behavior but they do not cause his violence. They are extensions of his violence and obstacles to meaningful change.

It is true that many abusive men externalize responsibility for their behavior, often blaming the women in their lives for their difficulties. But identifying external (societal) and internal (individual motivational) factors need not be an either/or proposition. Indeed, the consciousness-raising groups of the 1960s and 1970s combined political and personal insights. Acknowledging a history of oppression was part of the struggle, but this history did not grant the oppressed the right to act out against others. In combining a feminist and psychodynamic approaches to couples therapy, Virginia Goldner (1998), for example, confronts men with their tendency to externalize responsibility for violence while identifying points in their responses where infantile conflicts are revived.[1] Goldner emphasizes the convergence of emotional deprivations and trauma in the lives of abusive men and their sense of entitlement to act out those deprivations in their relationships with women. The Emerge Collective in Boston developed a similar model in combining a feminist analysis and psychodynamic principles in groups for abusive men (Adams & McCormick, 1982).

Whether interventions are oriented toward mandatory arrest, jail time, or educational groups for batterers, the question of how people change is central to social movements. Feminists have long argued, however, that the question of how to get men to change is a vast drain of female psychic energy. Nonetheless, any intervention presupposes some theory of behavior change (Mankowski *et al.*, 2002). In confronting abusive men with their power and control motives, it is not entirely clear how such confrontations might alter the hearts and minds of men.

The curriculum designed by Pence and Paymar does include an alternative model of interpersonal relationships, one based on principles of equality. A pyramid in the text illustrates social hierarchies and serves as a basis for orienting the groups to a series of questions:

> What would happen if the workplace had a more democratic system for decision-making? Would it create more motivation among the workers? How were the families the men grew up in structured? Where were each man's father, mother, older brother, and younger sisters on the pyramid? What was the impact of these hierarchical relationships on individuals in the family?
>
> (Pence & Paymar, 1993: 43)

Facilitators then explain how people at the bottom of the hierarchy are forced to give up their identity to support people at the top. "Using slavery, a colonial relationship, or an oppressively structured workplace as an example, the facilitator can draw a picture of the consciousness of domination" (1993: 49).

Yet in locating the cause of violence within the individual, as a conscious choice to dominate, Pence and Paymar (1993) depart from the work of Paulo Freire, who combines a political analysis and psychodynamic insights in his *Pedagogy of the oppressed.* As noted in the Introduction to this book, Freire's pedagogy includes recognition of how the oppressed often displace rage from their real oppressors—the colonial powers and bosses—onto others among the oppressed. Pence and Paymar make no use of this aspect of Freire's work, instead emphasizing that "we must each be accountable for the choices we make" (1993: 4).

Some facilitators describe the importance of the groups as settings where men are able to help one another, rather than looking to women to meet their emotional needs. "Ironically," Chris Huffine, facilitator of groups in

Portland, Oregon, comments, "batterer groups are among the few places where men really look critically at masculinity, both in terms of the pain and the privileges it brings." Yet in the literature on batterer intervention, as well as in my own discussions with facilitators, there seems to be deep reticence in addressing the infantile dependencies of many abusive men (Wexler, 1999).

The Duluth curriculum does create space for consciousness-raising beyond the immediate "choice to batter" and could serve as a context for discussing displaced hostility, along with the responsibility men hold for how they handle their own emotional pain. Therapeutic use of Freire's *pedagogy of the oppressed* might direct men to consider how they take out their disappointments and deprivations on the women in their lives. Women serve as the buffer zone in systems of oppression, with women in the position of carrying the pain and dependency men refuse to acknowledge as their own—a dynamic discussed in Chapter 2.

Even as anger is recognized as an effect of oppression, the Duluth curriculum focuses on how men make use of their anger to justify violence against women. Men are confronted with their sense of entitlement, and their refusal to grant legitimacy to female anger, but not with their displaced rage.

> The anger of people who are dominated by another is always powerful. Whites are afraid of the anger of people of color, parents are afraid of their teenagers' anger, management is afraid of labor's anger and men are afraid of women's anger. Women's anger reveals to men their outrage, resentment, resistance, and defiance. Anger is also a feeling that women are discouraged from showing, whereas it is often the only feeling men are encouraged to express.
>
> (Pence & Paymar, 1993: 62)

While this discourse addresses sources of anger in men's lives, facilitators are instructed to not "get tangled up in all of the issues men bring up in the groups" (1993: 69). If facilitators respond to the pain of these men, the fear is that they will lose their bearings. The capacity of men to seduce others with stories of personal suffering is a palpable source of anxiety in the text. A woman facilitator, Linda, is cited to illustrate this caveat:

> I find myself getting drawn into men's stories about their wives if they tell the story in an interesting way. Sometimes the meetings can start dragging or get depressing because of the nature of the discussion. So this one guy, Hal used to go on and on when he did his log, and I finally realized I was letting him do that because he was funny and interesting. He'd brighten up the meeting, but he

> was getting away with trivializing his behavior until I finally confronted him on his storytelling methods.
>
> (Pence & Paymar, 1993: 83)

Pence and Paymar (1993) conclude with descriptions of some of the men in the groups—men smoking outside before the meeting starts, wearing baseball caps and raggedy jeans. These affectionate portraits of batterers seem to be a siren song, however—one brought to an abrupt close at the end of the book. In summarizing, the authors reiterate the central message: "The use of this curriculum challenges men to see their use of violence as a choice—not an uncontrolled reaction to their past, their anger, or their lack of skills—but a choice" (1993: 181).

The curriculum includes further caveats, raising questions about the effectiveness of any program aimed at altering the behavior of abusive men. "About three years after the program started we noticed a big increase in court rulings in disputed custody cases favoring men who had completed our program." The batterer could also use "his participation in the DAIP as evidence that he has worked through his problems while claiming she has not" (1993: 175).

TURF BATTLES

Reconciling the therapeutic and the disciplinary aims of batterer intervention groups can be daunting and leaders emphasize how holding batterers accountable—the disciplinary side—must take top priority. Programs sometimes develop creative ways of navigating between these rocky shoals. Similar to early models developed in Finland (Peltoniemi, 1981), the Alternative to Violence (ATV) program in Norway works between the two poles of the problem by combining elements of the Duluth model with psychodynamic principles. Marius Råkil (2006) describes the four phases of the program, beginning with having men tell the story about why they are there—"reconstructed in a very detailed way, in terms of what happened, where did it happen, how did it happen, and to whom" (2006: 196). Phase two involves taking responsibility for the violence. Through the reconstruction of what happened, "it becomes clear that the violent acts are rational and controlled, indicating that violence is actually a chosen act among other alternative acts" (2006: 196). Defenses such as minimization, externalization, and denial are confronted in getting men to take responsibility. While phase three opens the process to exploring childhood experiences and personal history, phase four—the final phase—invites discussion of how "violence is about himself . . . rooted in the lack of recognition of his own feelings of powerlessness" (2006: 196–197).

The process of telling the story—of reconstructing in detail what happened—is a principle of many therapeutic approaches, although the aim here is more disciplinary. The claim that "it becomes obvious that violence was a choice" suggests that the Duluth script intervenes in a forceful way in the progression of the narrative. There is only one story to tell at this juncture in the road. But for leaders and participants, this adoption of the official script also opens the door for other stories that might not otherwise be told. The last phase of the treatment, where men are encouraged to understand how they express feelings of powerlessness through violence, may represent a "return of the repressed" in the Duluth model. Opening this ground—where the pain of men threatens to take over the political project—requires confidence on the part of leaders and on strategies for addressing interpersonal violence on the part of the community.

The term "*community*" encompasses a wide range of meanings and forms of social affiliations, however, as well as practices that are both repressive and supportive. Communities may enforce gender hierarchies in rigid ways, even as they offer protection and forms of care. In one of the most comprehensive cross-cultural studies of family violence, David Levinson (1989) found that rates of wife beating were lowest in those societies where women organized their own work groups, whether in the form of working side by side in the fields, trading as a group in local markets, or establishing their own economic associations. He concludes that "the presence of exclusively female work groups, whether an indicator of female solidarity or of female economic power, or both, serves to control or prevent wife-beating" (1989: 58).

The importance of work groups, where conflicts are confronted through shared projects and common interests, remains a key principle of feminist politics. Yet fighting for change brings its own set of hard knocks. Advocates working in crisis services for women compete with other programs to demonstrate how their social problem category remains the most urgent one as state budgets are slashed. Although funding through the Justice Department protects women's crisis services from Draconian cutbacks in the United States,[2] this same source of protection may reproduce the dilemmas of battered women themselves: advocates become isolated and increasingly dependent on a patriarchal protection racket to secure their survival. As one advocate in the BIG program in Germany describes it,

> "We think we have a strangle-hold on this issue—we have this issue and we want to keep it. The thing that we're struggling against is that there's this men's movement out there, this, like, scary men's movement, and it's true, it's real. Now men are [thought to be] victims too. And pretty soon we're going to have some head to heads, which I don't think is that far away."

The image of a "strangle-hold" suggests the life-and-death struggle over resources, as well as the importance of honing one's fighting skills. The "men's movement" encompasses a range of campaigns, from "dads' rights" and other groups that target feminism in explaining the decline of male wages and other social problems to self-help groups for men that include a critique of masculinity.[3] While the threat of backlash against feminism is palpably real, feminist opposition to all organizing on the part of men in addressing violence may be overdetermined by rivalry, including among experts who compete to name and treat the problem of family violence (Gordon, 1988).

Women's advocates who are critical of the Duluth curriculum point out how women are seduced by the false hope of changing the hearts and minds of violent men. Women may view the groups as the path toward reconciliation, or men may simply use the groups to become more sophisticated in their techniques for controlling women. In response, Pence and Paymar (1993: 172) caution against programs carried out by mental health agencies, versus programs situated "in a political and historical context of the feminist anti-violence movement."

There are limits to what any intervention can provide, whether through psychotherapy, counseling groups, or feminist educational groups based on the Duluth model. The research literature in the United States on court-mandated groups for batterers raises doubts about their effectiveness (Bennett & Williams, 2000/2001; Feder & Forde, 2000), although criteria vary for evaluating effectiveness. Although researchers emphasize reports from female partners as the best indicator of effectiveness (Tolman & Edleson, 1995), many of these same researchers are wary of the reliability of women's reports. A man entering a counseling group, according to Edward Gondolf, researcher in the field, is the best predictor of a woman's return to her batterer after leaving shelter (Gondolf, 1987). Programs vary widely in structure and approach, even those drawing on the Duluth curriculum, making the job of assessing overall effects even more challenging (Edleson & Syers, 1990; La Violette, 2002). Yet criminal justice responses have been proven to be ineffective in reducing domestic violence as well, particularly in poor communities (Goodman & Epstein, 2008; Gross *et al.*, 2000; Incite!, 2005). In addressing this dilemma, the next section discusses programs where the Duluth model is integrated into a wider community response to male violence.

BRINGING DIVERSITY TO DULUTH

In her introduction to *Birth of a nationhood: Gaze, script, and spectacle in the O. J. Simpson case*, Toni Morrison (1997) describes the heat surrounding the O. J. Simpson trial in the mid-1990s and debates among feminists over what the trial was "really about." Although media coverage of the case initially focused on Simpson's history as a batterer, the legal focus of the trial turned to the Los Angeles Police Department (LAPD) and its flagrant tampering with evidence. Nicole Simpson's desperate calls to 911, replayed during the early months of the trial, anointed the victim with more authority in death than she had summoned in life. Yet the jury gave more weight to tampered evidence and racist practices of the LAPD in coming to their decision. After pronouncing the defendant "not guilty," members of the jury were embraced as heroes by some and resoundingly condemned by others, with a deep racial divide separating views on what this "trial of the century" was really about (Morrison, 1997).

While the simplest moral response among white observers was to declare that Simpson got away with murder, women standing at the intersections of group affiliations were more apt to recognize other scripts circulating in this media-saturated drama.[4] And they were more able to see how one story may serve as a defense against another. Going beyond the riveting issue of the guilt of Simpson, legal scholar Kimberlé Crenshaw (1997) offers an interpretation of what made the case so riveting for white audiences: uncovering the brutal ghetto nature of an American black hero who had "passed" for a nice (white) guy. In the transformation of the persona of O. J. throughout the trial, love turned to hate as the story of the fallen hero disrupted the "American redemptive fantasy of racial transcendence" (1997: 97).

Through the singular lens of a gender analysis, race and class motifs may recede from the picture. Yet in working with the concept of "intersectionality"—a term introduced by Crenshaw and discussed in the Introduction of this book—we can recognize how feminist critiques of male violence may carry unintended political freight. From a psychoanalytic perspective, we also may see how one storyline may serve as a defense against another. Take, for example, the typology introduced by John Gottman and Neil Jacbson (Gottman *et al.*, 1995) that divides abusers into "cobras" and "pit bulls." Cobras lash out in a methodical way, find violence calming, and are more likely to be sociopathic. Pit bulls, on the other hand, are more impulsive, hot-headed, and are more amenable to intervention. This typology is intended to break up the monothematic theorizing in the field and to acknowledge differences between sadistic violence and more anxiety-ridden forms. There is some basis to efforts to distinguish between different emotional states associated with aggression, even though this typology is dehumanizing. Many advocates point out that higher-status men conceal their abuses more effectively (and are more cobra-like) whereas the abuses of working-class and poor men are more apt to be detected (as pit bull-like), particularly in communities heavily controlled by the police. Correspondingly, affluent women beaten by their husbands are able to check into a hotel or see the family doctor, whereas poor women have fewer resources to mask bruises and broken bones.

Framing social class differences in this way—as a difference in capacities to *conceal* or *manage* the problem of domestic violence—preserves the idea of an underlying experience shared by all women. Feminists working in minority communities have been vocal in disrupting this notion of a unifying story, however (Crenshaw, 2000; Ho, 1990; Kanuha, 2005; Renzetti, 1999; Richie, 2005; West, 1999). Researchers from minority communities also have explored different conceptions of domestic violence as a social problem (Merry, 2001). Lea White Bear Claws, an advocate with the Cangleska program at Pine Ridge, situates the problem of family violence in a historical context, explaining how colonization both created and reinforced forms of patriarchal power in tribal communities:

> "When the cavalry came, they constantly put our men in a bad situation. They never assumed that the woman had power—that her job was as important as his . . . But they also constantly made him feel so low that he had to do these abusive things to make himself feel better . . . You get a lot of men now who can accept that his wife goes to work, but the young men, especially, have to prove something."

Minority women and white women share a strategic interest in deprivatizing family violence. Yet women in oppressed communities are more apt to go beyond the policing of individual batterers to include socially distributing responsibility for the reparation of damaged men. Sacred Circle, a national resource center addressing violence against Native women, emphasizes the role of internalized oppression in framing the problem of battering.

> As Native people we're taught, often through violence, to despise and fear our own cultural and spiritual ways . . . Even though many of our children have not experienced boarding school, we see them continue this attitude that being Indian or Native is not something good or something to feel proud of . . . We need to be able to speak openly about our experience as Native people. We need to know that even though what happened to us is not our fault, we're still 'buying into' oppression when we don't support each other and fight among ourselves.
>
> (Artichoker & Mousseau, 2003: 14–15)

In schematizing factors associated with the maintenance of violent behavior, Sacred Circle uses a triangle rather than the customary Power and Control Wheel that circulates in the domestic violence field (Cangleska, 2000). The triangle describes hierarchies of power, with colonization placed at the top as an external force determining the structure of social relationships. The European conquerors imposed forms of hierarchy onto colonized people that overturned more egalitarian traditions and relations between men and women. Sacred Circle explains these intersections of power and the forms of splitting that result.

> Many of our own People now believe that violence was a part of our way of life, when the reality is that violence threatens the survival of the People and goes against spiritual beliefs . . . All people contain within their spirit the masculine and feminine. Setting rigid boundaries of what is male and what is female limits all of us. We have the right to explore and know our total selves.
> (Artichoker & Mousseau, 2003: 27)

Although portraits of traditional Native cultures may be over-idealized, the process of reparation requires a capacity for recovering the good aspects of the collective past. By framing domestic violence as an effect of colonization, Sacred Circle charges that men collaborate with the oppressor when they are violent to women. It is an act of self-destruction as well as destructive to women. Rather than resist the terms of their own oppression, men displace their rage, either acting out destructively or self-destructively. White Bear Claws describes how her own history forged alliances with men around resisting violence:

> "In the first grade, when we lived in Nebraska, I was called a little Indian whore—people pulling my braids. When we came back to the reservation, it felt so much better, even though this is the poorest county in the US . . . I tell my kids, it is better to be here with your own people—where you won't be picked on . . . I introduce my kids to a lot of traditional things here . . . Even talking with the women, I say your husband isn't always like that . . . We go back for the good reasons, because we are partners and have good times together. But unless he starts to deal with his bad parts, it's going to be like this."

Many feminists are wary of cultural practices that redeem men, arguing that patriarchal societies are in the habit of enlisting women in perpetual programs of forgiveness, granting continual indulgences. Yet feminists in oppressed communities often hold a more complex understanding of the limits on human freedom, including the "choice" of battering. The process of confronting the legacy of colonial domination opens up space for reclaiming the "good" as well as confronting the "bad" in the history of violent men. While men are held responsible for their behavior, the community holds some responsibility to create alternatives to violence. On the other hand, there is agreement that men inherit forms of entitlement that contribute to violence against women, and that women must collectively resist those parts of Native traditions. As Jackie Randall, another Cangleska advocate notes, "For many women, loving can mean that they feel they can really change a man . . . My grandmother always told me, though, that you have to love yourself, no one else can do that for you."

Artichoker and I took up the question of whether the contemporary focus on domestic violence narrows understandings of the problems of Native peoples, still placing too much of the load on Indian men as the primary cause of hardships on reservations. The process of overcoming destructive behavior, Artichoker adds, is intertwined with confronting self-destructive behavior as well. "It's a thousand times harder for these guys when you factor that in . . . Our suicide rates, our violence rates, child abuse rates, are just way out there." Advocates emphasize the difficulties men have in acknowledging their own pain, and the stoicism that blunts their capacity for human connection. Whether rituals centered on tolerating pain were predominant in the pre-Conquest era is unclear. But the psychic pain generated by contemporary forms of racism and economic oppression powerfully reinforces such stoicism. It also creates a tendency to turn rage inward—either against intimates or against oneself—in the form of depressive withdrawal or substance abuse.

Rather than alcoholism or mental illness, previous ways of locating the source of myriad difficulties in Native communities, the United States government is now willing to subsidize this new social problem category. Artichoker responds:

> "There is some of that bandwagon effect. Some of that is happening. But for us, this is the first time we have had any real resources. When these other issues were in vogue, we did get assessments. They would contract with some psychologist to come down once a month to do assessments. But I think I could do that! How much value can this counseling be? This child, this woman, this man, needs something in their lives. We are from here. We are not going anywhere. People can call on us."

The dilemmas of indigenous women are similar to those of other minority women, but there also are key differences. The tribal police on reservations in the United States have some autonomy from the federal government, which allows more space for women to have a voice, particularly through the tribal councils. In Canada, women in First Nations organizations also emphasize that "there is 'good medicine' and 'bad medicine' in Aboriginal communities" (McGillivray & Comaskey, 1999: 51). While tribal councils sometimes intervene on women's behalf, they as readily rule in favor of abusive men. Even though Aboriginal women tend to favor mediation and alternative remedies to the criminal justice system, researchers Anne McGillivray and Brenda Comaskey (1999) found that some women preferred outside police intervention to the local councils. This position hinges in part on the extent to which indigenous women have been able to mobilize around their own interests in tribal communities and gain representation and leadership through the tribal governance.

In addressing cultural dimensions of domestic violence, Evelyn White (1994) emphasizes the acute conflicts that arise for black women in extricating themselves from the pain of men. While this is a consistent refrain in popular literature on the psychology of women, White keeps in sight the social forces impinging on women's conflicts over leaving abusive situations. She makes a distinction between empathizing with the oppression black men face and taking responsibility for their pain.

> You don't have to become your partner's target because the bank didn't give him a loan. You do not have to become the scapegoat when the landlord raises the rent. And you do not have to become the punching bag because he can't afford to take the children to Disneyland. Physical and emotional abuse are not acceptable demonstrations of Black manhood . . . Black men will not heal their wounded pride or regain a sense of dignity by abusing Black women.
>
> (White, 1994: 26)

In her presentation on the dynamics of family violence, an educational workshop for probation officers that I attended on my first day at Pine Ridge, Rosa Lee places a graphic on the blackboard, a spiral beginning with "self" and circling through successive spheres of relationships. In Lakota culture, "men are not 'king of the castle,'" she explains, nor do they "own their wives." In her circular model of abuse, Lee emphasizes how abuse is embedded in wider contexts, and how a vulnerable sense of self is partial cause and partial effect of domestic violence. She also offers her "tea-pot theory" of the spiraling effects of family violence—the ways in which violence erupts when other pressures overtake families, particularly in cramped quarters. In a hopeful tone, Lee introduces examples of how men can find ways of enjoying their children—for example, planting a garden—even when the ground of their lives feels pretty hard and barren.

CONCLUSIONS

Women historically have held some authority in Western capitalist societies to reign in male vices, particularly when those vices depart from socially acceptable norms for men as providers. Even the 19th-century "rule of thumb," the chastisement law that allowed men to discipline their wives with an instrument no wider than their thumb, suggests that there were limits to the operations of male power (Pleck, 1979; Siegel, 1996).

Feminists confronting male violence are often caught on the horns of a dilemma: they must make visible the power of men in women's lives and simultaneously expose the illusory aspects of this power—the ways that images of masculine omnipotence operates as a cultural fantasy. Intervention strategies that focus exclusively on the power of men—their Svengali-like capacity to hypnotize women with their seductive stories of pain—risk reproducing the very god-like portraits of masculinity that feminism has sought to dispel.

The disavowed dependencies of men can be as important a part of the holding power of abusive relationships as are power and control tactics. While a woman may put up with her man's abusiveness at times, implicitly accepting his right to restore a sense of masculine potency, she also may make claims on her man during the "honeymoon" periods following outbreaks of violence. As one client of mine described the dynamic, "He goes off sometimes, and I put up with it. But then he comes around and helps me out when he is trying to make up. It's like he's had his tantrum and now he owes me."

When we tell stories of violence through the lens of social class and racism as the axes of injustice, areas of alliance are possible between men and women in addressing social forces that determine their common fate. Both men and women in oppressed communities experience hopelessness and despair. If the battered wife suffers from learned helplessness, so too does her batterer. The helplessness is born of blunted opportunities and bitter disappointments. Fighting also may be motivated by a desire for engagement. Where work involves self-monitoring and submission to hierarchical control, home is a place where controls may be safely suspended, although the home also becomes a site for acting out displaced aggression.

By establishing social distance from male suffering, the Duluth model encourages women to abandon the futile feminine project of resuscitating a wounded masculinity. But the power and control model may also reinforce women's anxieties that men are omnipotent in their powers—that any space allowed for male suffering automatically collapses the space available for women to assert their own needs. Stronger forms of community and sisterhood are as vital in managing this anxiety, however, as they are in confronting the combustible mix of emotional deprivation, trauma, and masculine entitlement that underlie so many expressions of violence.

NOTES

1 Post-traumatic stress disorder, for example, is a condition associated with violent reactions and exaggerated perceptions of threats. Repressed or dissociated

disturbing feelings and images from events in the past are revived in a contemporary encounter. Judith Herman (1993) describes this as a reaction to war that may contribute to family violence and patterns of abuse.

2 For a discussion on the politics of the Violence Against Women Act, see Crenshaw (1994) and Goldfarb (2000).

3 Erin Pizzey, founder of Chiswick House in London, became a champion of "dads' rights" after leaving England and coming into opposition with feminist groups (see Dugan, 2008).

4 Shoshana Felman, who has written extensively on trauma, similarly focuses on how the trial served as a cultural screen memory for earlier injustices. She describes how the Rodney King trial, with its videotaped evidence of police brutality and officers ultimately acquitted, formed one of many unresolved traumatic contexts for spectators of the O. J. Simpson trial (see Felman, 1997).

6

RUNNING ON EMPTY: WOMEN, CHILDREN, AND STRATEGIES OF SURVIVAL

Myth: Woman battering and child abuse are symptoms of dysfunctional family systems.
Counter-myth: Child abuse and woman abuse are effects of the patriarchal family.

In *Terrifying love*, Lenore Walker (1989) recounts the highly publicized case of Hedda Nussbaum—a case that ignited heated controversy in the late 1980s. Nussbaum was arrested in 1987 along with her companion, Joel Steinberg, for the death of their illegally adopted daughter, six-year-old Lisa Steinberg. The police were sent to their Greenwich Village apartment early in the morning after a call from Nussbaum, reporting that her daughter was having trouble breathing after choking on her food. When the police arrived, they found Nussbaum badly bruised with a broken nose. Lisa lay comatose on the floor while her younger brother sat soaked in urine and tied by a cord to his playpen. Lisa died several days later when doctors took her off life support, and the boy, also illegally adopted, was returned to his biological mother during the legal proceedings that followed. While neighbors claimed to have frequently called the police after violent arguments and other red-alert signs of abuse, records of 911 calls failed to support this claim. Nussbaum was charged as an accomplice in the death of their daughter, although charges were later dropped when she agreed to cooperate with the prosecution. Joel Steinberg—the indisputable monster in the case—was sentenced to 11 years in prison. Hedda Nussbaum—the more morally ambiguous figure in the drama—spent several months at a psyhiatric hospital, after which she went on a speaking tour.

There are many ways of telling this story, depending on the political sympathies of the storyteller. Most participants and observers agreed on the essential facts of the case, with the exception that Joel Steinberg steadfastly maintained his innocence. There was little question, however, that the young girl had been brutally beaten for at least a year, that Hedda Nussbaum had also been routinely beaten by Steinberg, and that the couple's 18-month-old son suffered from severe neglect. Yet news reports differed in their assignment of moral responsibility for the death of the girl. Grisly details gleaned from court testimony and interviews with neighbors and teachers were woven into varying tales of the horror (Span, 1989; Stephens, 1988; Volk, 2009).

Women's advocates interviewed by reporters shortly after the case foregrounded the nightmarish plight of Nussbaum who, like many battered women, steadily disintegrated with each blow delivered by her sadistic partner (Span, 1989). As her world collapsed, so, too, did Nussbaum's capacity to protect her children or even to recognize the gravity of the situation. Lenore Walker (1989), who serves as expert witness in such cases, passionately concurs with this perspective on the story, insisting that Nussbaum was not accountable. Walker confesses to identifying with this beautiful woman disfigured from years of abuse—a Jewish girl from New York who, much like herself, searched as a young woman for a successful man with whom she might create a happy family. In cautioning against blaming Nussbaum for not protecting her child, Walker (1989: 148) insists, "Joel had taken over her mind." Walker and other advocates made use of the case to draw public attention to the pervasiveness of domestic violence and how the battered woman syndrome that results from chronic abuse may strike even the most successful of women. Nussbaum, a bright and up-and-coming editor of children's books at Random House before she was fired for absenteeism, could be Any Woman.

Those who approached the story from a child advocate perspective brought into bold relief the horrific cruelty endured by the young girl, as well as the severe neglect and abuse of her younger brother. Reporting on the monstrosity of Steinberg, a criminal lawyer who traded cocaine for legal services, media accounts fixed on child protection workers as the anointed experts of the moment (Brownmiller, 1989). They chronicled how Nussbaum had allowed her crazed obsession with her husband to blind her to his lethal sadism—and how she sat passively by as Steinberg brutally beat their daughter over a period of a year.

In the line-up of socially responsible parties, Hedda Nussbaum remained the most elusive protagonist in the drama, standing Janus-faced before the spotlight of public opinion. While many feminists saw the broken spirit of a battered wife, others saw the grotesque image of a heartless mother. Yet for many Americans, the passive mother—the mother who *fails to protect* her child—arouses a mixture of pity and contempt. Unlike tormented women who kill their children—those women who fail to register at all on the meter of public sympathies—mothers who fail to protect their children stir a more complicated set of emotions. Although she did not directly inflict the injuries, Nussbaum was implicated in the abuse as a passive observer. Having also been abused by Steinberg, Nussbaum exhibited the psychic numbness and emotional detachment that had become, by the late 1980s, widely recognized as hallmark signs of trauma. Because she cooperated with the prosecution in the case against her husband, formal charges against Nussbaum were never filed. But this case also riveted attention on the responsibilities of bystanders, ushering in a wave of legislation throughout the United States making *child witnessing* of domestic violence, specifically *failure to protect* a child who is affected by domestic violence, prosecutable under the Child Protection Act of the 1980s.

In pointing out, rightfully, the disproportionate outrage directed toward women who fail to protect their children, Lenore Walker (1989) leaves no space for degrees of responsibility. Whereas Nussbaum had no control, Steinberg had complete control in deciding "not to control his violence" (1989: 150). Yet as Susan Brownmiller (1989) points out in her discussion of this controversial case, feminist efforts to completely absolve Nussbaum are costly. Such efforts preserve the status of women as permanent minors under patriarchy. The Nussbaum case dramatizes how the engines of child protection and women's crisis services—areas where female social service professionals and activists have advanced in influence—were on a collision course.

This chapter takes up the conflict between children's advocates and women's advocates and their competing positions in framing how stories of family violence get told. In responding to this dilemma, psychologist Erica Burman (2008: 178) cautions that we (as feminists) "have to resist getting caught into this competition and refuse its terms." The competition Burman references centers on pitting "child-centered concerns" against "anti-child feminists." Even as she points out the tendency on the part of conservatives to blame feminists, along with mothers, for various social crises, Burman warns that feminists get caught in the competition because they do often experience the conflicting forces that impinge on the lives of women and children.

The past is crucial to understanding the present because we live the consequences of histories not of our own making. As Linda Gordon (1988) argues, woman battering and child abuse share a long history of perpetual rediscovery as social problems. One effect of this form of cultural amnesia is that interventions operate without awareness of their historical contexts. Without some understanding of the history of child protection and domestic violence intervention campaigns, we are less in a position to work through the tensions that emerge. As a result, efforts to coordinate services run the perpetual risk of institutional splitting, as each group accuses the other of blindness and views itself as the true protector of women and/or children. The following sections draw on the insights of advocates to identify sources of the conflict that are less readily articulated and thus less available to group consciousness in working through border tensions in the field.

CONFLICTING MANDATES

Feminists were part of the movement to de-privatize family violence and to demand the state intervene to protect women and children (Goldfarb, 2000; Marcus, 1994; Schneider, 1994). By the late 1980s, most of the United States had passed mandatory reporting laws, requiring professionals to report suspected child abuse. Similar child protection legislation was passed in Canada, Europe, Britain, New Zealand, and Australia (Morgaine, 2007; Mullender, 1996). Feminists intervened in this expanded state mandate by bringing child sexual abuse to the forefront of the political agenda—a form of abuse that overwhelmingly implicated men as abusers (Haaken, 1998). But the expansion of child protection legislation to include *child witnessing* of domestic violence represented a deeper challenge for feminists in buffering the effects of punitive state interventions.

After operating semi-autonomously for decades, workers in the fields of domestic violence and child protection were increasingly required by the state during the 1980s and 1990s to coordinate their efforts. This new era of cooperation manifested itself in federally funded programs in a number of countries that brought non-profit organizations (the voluntary sector), where domestic violence services had been largely located, into greater contact with governmental agencies involved with child and family services. The advocate role was reconfigured to be more responsive to the new reporting guidelines and state-funded mandates (Breckenridge & Ralfs, 2006; Humphreys, 2006).

The coordinated community response (CCR) movement, discussed in the last chapter, brought with it various realignments of worldviews as well as institutional practices. As one of the Berlin advocates comments, "It is important to have these confrontations because there isn't an easy solution. It's really a hostile encounter between the different groups, even within the shelters themselves." She goes on to explain:

> "The problem is in the definition of violence. Is it only if the child gets hit or whether the child should get protected from observing violence in the family? The institutions that are trying to create these new restrictions are having a difficult time and there is not much trust. The biggest work right now is to take a step-by-step approach to open up more contacts and try to communicate what the issues are before they can be formalized."

Coordinated community response initiatives, based on variations of the Duluth model, emerged as the terrain where attempts to communicate more openly also gave rise to heightened border tensions. Women's advocates and children's advocates found common ground in calling on the state to intervene in situations of family violence. But the question of how victim and perpetrator positions are cast remained highly contested—as was the issue of how the positions of women as both victims and perpetrators of violence are reconciled.

Advocates in the field of domestic violence tend to view family abuse through a political lens, with victim/perpetrator relations configured through a critique of the patriarchal family. Whether in the role of wife or mother, women's actions are circumscribed by male domination over the private and public spheres. Many advocates stress the unequal burdens women carry as primary caregivers and the failure of the state to protect women from male violence. These factors combined have the effect of undermining the capacity of mothers to protect their children.[1] For feminists working with the Duluth power and control model, however, with its unwavering emphasis on violence as an "individual choice" and its focus on disciplinary measures, the question of how to extend the model to women who abuse their children represented a deep quandary.

CYCLES AND SYNDROMES: CHILD ABUSE AND WIFE ABUSE

Part of the animosity toward psychologists in the area of women's advocacy revolves around the tendency within the mental health community to focus on "the interests of the child," and to adopt punitive attitudes toward mothers. As Tawa Witko, a psychologist with the Cangleska program points out,

> "It was psychologists who came in and insisted on safeguarding the children, but they didn't generally talk with advocates . . . It's been hard to find points of compromise . . . People tend to be on one side or the other. It's been hard to recognize both . . . courts tend to be biased toward taking kids away."

In looking back on the history of psychological interventions in the family, it is easier to understand the deep resistances to psychologists on the part of many women's advocates. The emergence of competing syndromes in framing the problem of family violence registered broader contests over power and the shifting boundaries of authority in both the family and social service delivery systems. With the expanded entry of women into social service positions during the 1970s and 1980s, debates over family protection measures were overdetermined by broader social anxieties over the shifting boundaries of female authority in public life as well as in the private sphere.

The *battered woman syndrome* articulated by Walker in 1979 had developed in reaction to the *battered child syndrome*—a condition identified by

Henry Kempe and colleagues in the early 1960s (Kempe & Helfer, 1968; Kempe *et al.*, 1962). While the battered child syndrome focused near-exclusively on mothers as the "hidden pathogen," Walker (1979b) enlisted the same trope to defend women. Turning the paranoid clinical gaze away from its habitual focus on mothers, Walker implored physicians to look more carefully at what was happening "behind closed doors."

By framing violence as a predictable cycle with clear antecedents and consequences, both the children's rights and women's rights movements were able to enlist medical authority to advance their claims. A key area of divergence, however, concerned the configuration of power relationships within the family and how the culpability of non-abusing parents was morally adjudicated. Whereas Kempe had focused on the mother as the primary abuser, Walker argued that the battered woman suffered from a syndrome induced by the patriarchal family. In enlisting this medical discourse, Walker was able to make visible the hidden problem of wife abuse and to reframe it as a public health concern.

The term "*syndrome*" also suggests an identifiable constellation of symptoms of an unknown cause. Whether it is the failure to thrive syndrome, sudden infant death syndrome, abuse accommodation syndrome, or, more recently, false memory syndrome, the concept of a syndrome inevitably invites a story (Haaken, 1998). Syndromes are merely descriptive, correlational rather than causal accounts of findings that go together. Identifying a group of symptoms as a syndrome successfully brings the problem into medical discourse without establishing specific causes.

Media and scholarly reports alike expressed urgency over the "hidden epidemic" of child battering and woman battering—a rhetorical strategy that ushered in legions of professionals whose job it was to manage the crisis. And both syndromes implicated the medical and mental health professions for their historical blindness, for their refusal to see the warning signs. Doctors engaged in an implicit privacy pact with their patients—a kind of "don't ask" policy—concerning injuries sustained at home. While adopting a stance of clinical discretion concerning private family matters was upheld as a virtue throughout the history of professional medicine, by the late 1970s such practices were widely denounced as an ethical failure.[2] Further, feminists pointed out that it was largely men who dominated both the institutions of medicine and the family, and these same men formed allegiances at the expense of abused women and children (Herman, 1993).

The child abuse syndrome also could be framed as a "*bystander effect*"—a concept taken up in Chapter 2—in that Kempe and his colleagues (1968) placed *failure to recognize* the pattern behind the injuries at the apex of the clinical condition. The syndrome was more a malady of practitioners than it was of the child. Blinded by traditions extolling the sanctity of the family, practitioners were unable to see the cause of the broken bones and bruises of children under their care. While advanced x-ray techniques facilitated more precise diagnosis of fractures associated with abuse, the youth movements of the 1960s were pivotal in making visual the disturbing etiology of injuries that eluded clinical detection in the previous generation.

As women increasingly entered positions where they administered the power of the state, they found that talking about child abuse required more than a mere willingness to listen. As Jan Breckenridge and Claire Ralfs (2006: 112–113) note, frontline service workers face sobering dilemmas as they assist children in constructing a "narrative that is coherent, undistorted, and does not pathologize or blame non-offending others." This important aim confronts daunting obstacles, however, over how to best produce an "undistorted" story. Children and protection workers may not be in alignment over who is cast as the offending parent. Further, professional listeners bring their own anxieties into the process of making sense of the story, even as they may channel these anxieties through the voices of children.[3]

In identifying dilemmas for feminists in responding to family violence mandates in the UK, researchers Cathy Humphreys and Nicky Stanley (2006: 9) note the "profound separation in the discourses of child abuse and woman abuse which underpins structural and organization barriers to an integrated response to the issue." These structural and organizational underpinnings include assignment of domestic violence to the voluntary sector and responsibility for child protection to the statutory sector—distinctions grounded in different political priorities. Women's Aid, which has been at the forefront of the shelter movement in England, focuses on keeping the voices of abused women at the forefront of public intervention. But as progress is increasingly articulated through the Duluth model of multi-agency intervention, survivors and women's advocates are finding it difficult to "have their voices heard" (2006: 10).

Child protection issues have served as a portal of entry for psychologists and psychological discourses into domestic violence advocacy work as well. Networks of institutions in the United States and Britain now track the mental health impacts on children of exposure to domestic violence. Psychologists and counselors increasingly are recognized as having a legitimate role in shelter/refuge work, even though there is reluctance to extend these same services to women survivors. Conflict emerges in shelters over how to integrate recognition of clinical conditions related to domestic violence, on the one hand, and feminist claims that psychology distracts from the political nature of the problem, on the other. Erica Burman (2008) offers an example from her field research of how this conflict may be enacted in refuges. As child victims of domestic violence are referred for therapy or counseling, Burman explains how mothers feel "blamed" in ways that resonate with feminist critiques. "For some mothers it seems that giving permission for their children to see the therapist somehow compounds their sense of guilt and responsibility. They sometimes oppose such proposals, and experience recommendations from staff as disempowering" (2008: 189).

Beginning with the point that women are "overwhelmingly the primary victims" in couple violence, Humphreys (2006: 13) cautions that "acknowledging this dominant, gendered pattern of violence can give rise to problems in identifying minority patterns of abuse." She adds that "failure to acknowledge the diverse forms of violence in the family may limit professionals' capacity to safeguard children" (2006: 13). Yet professional procedures for safeguarding children have also produced new risks. Modern computer technology provides the technical infrastructure for inter-agency coordination and databases for tracking cases of family violence. These systems undoubtedly benefit many abused women, for example, in alerting the courts if men have not completed group sessions or if they reoffend. But these same systems reproduce some of the very social problems they purportedly have the task of managing. Humphreys and Stanley (2006: 40) address this critical issue: with the "widening of data collection and monitoring systems, a vital cornerstone of the coordinated agency response, the aim of confidentially for women escaping violence is compromised or at risk."

Preoccupation with data-gathering may serve as an institutional defense against the anxiety generated by these same practices. Reports produced by feminists on multi-agency monitoring emphasize that the primary aim of tracking systems is still to "preserve the voices of survivors" and "to keep women safe" (Humphreys, 2006; Pence & McDonnell, 1999). But the aim of "keeping women safe" may be used in the service of professional interests as much as it is in the interest of abused women and children (Allen, 2003). On the other hand, feminists bring political and ethical commitments to social service work that keeps them potentially accountable in ways that other professionals may feel less bound.

TOWARD A RAPPROCHEMENT

Advocates in all sites where interviews were carried out emphasize that child protection and women's advocates in their regions are beginning to speak to one another. They share the view that reconciling these two perspectives remains vital. Yet in working with these dual lenses, advocates in both fields are confronted with the complexity of the problem of family violence. In Chapter 4, conflict between shelter/refuge staff and women residents over childrearing practices was discussed. Advocates at Refuge in London offer that the focus on children in situations of domestic violence has created an opening for psychologists and counseling services in refuges, which has gradually extended in some settings to "skills training" for women who are mothers. Even with these steps toward cooperative working relationships, tensions remain over how to reconcile child welfare and domestic violence services. As one advocate in Berlin explains in describing the shift toward incorporating children's programs, "There are lots of attempts to educate and change the focus from the women alone."

In recovering historical contexts for contemporary border tensions, Linda Gordon (2007: 314) notes that "the very concept of family violence is a product of conflict and negotiation between people troubled by domestic violence and social control agents attempting to change their supposedly unruly and deviant behavior." Many social service workers have sought alternatives to the paternalistic interventions of professionals in the past—and particularly interventions that have been disempowering to women (Humphreys & Stanley, 2006). As Gordon cautions, however, the border between social control and social support—between oppressive authority and responsive care—remains a tense one.

The dissonance between social support and social control that Gordon describes may be as acute for social service workers as it is for clients. A case manager in a shelter in Portland, Oregon describes this dilemma: "We're supposed to stick to one thing, right, which is to have one storyline. This is what is going on. But what if it's not exactly or what if it's both or neither?" Another advocate working at a Portland shelter told a story to illustrate the double-binds produced by conflicting mandates:

> "The women in the child welfare system and in all the systems get told that if you just be the 'good victim' or the 'good survivor,' you will make it and the reality is two things. One is that even for women who fit this extremely—almost fit, because nobody really can fit it—stereotype of what a 'good victim' or 'good survivor' is—it's very difficult, even for them. Some of them don't get the support they need to be safe, so it's a set-up . . . The second thing is . . . women involved in child welfare . . . If this woman goes to family court, she gets mandated to have her kids see the batterer; the woman in child welfare gets told if she even lets them see the batterer, she will lose her kids. These are not very different families and sometimes it's the same family."

The role of the battered woman's advocate emerged out of recognition that abused women needed allies in doing battle with the state, whether in securing crisis services, obtaining protection orders, or fighting to retain custody of their children, as well as in escaping abusive partners. As CCR became the new mandate in the United States and other countries during the 1980s and 1990s, anxieties over how to "preserve the voices of abused women" were managed by turning to advocates as the gravitational center of the system. In situating the CCR model in a feminist analysis, Melanie Shepard and Ellen Pence (1999: 115) describe their vision of the role of advocate:

> Creating and maintaining a supportive infrastructure requires collaborative efforts among many community agencies that share mutual goals. Advocates for battered women are the stewards of this infrastructure as they direct, guide and support battered women while confronting and challenging obstacles to their safety.

Brian Littlechild and Caroline Bourke (2006: 208) describe how frontline case workers experience unsettling dissonance in their "positions as both powerful agent of control and source of support, working in 'partnership' with parents." For those working in the domestic violence field, reconciling feminist ideals of empowering women and carrying out the various mandates of the state inevitably heightens this state of dissonance (Burman, 2008; Humphreys & Stanley, 2006).

A key conflict between child advocates and women's advocates centers on how to address women's differing experiences with the state. Sue Loeb, with Voices of Women (VOW) in New York City, describes how tensions arise around state interventions with regard to child protection services. She recalls one such episode when she and other VOW women attended an annual conference entitled "Women fighting poverty."

> "And so two of our members spoke. These two women have had very bad experiences with the child welfare system. They've removed their children and they were both women of color and poor . . . But there were four other women from the organization in the audience supporting them. Two of them were white women and one of them comes from California and is a pretty middle-class woman and has had a horrendous experience and got screwed by the courts. The other woman is a very working-class woman from Brooklyn. There was a woman in the audience who was African American, and because the child welfare system in New York is so racist that it's overwhelmingly the children of women of color that are removed . . . Anyway, I guess the white middle-class woman from California said something about the systems. And the African American woman said, 'You have no idea because you're not a woman of color.'"

In titling the conference "Women fighting poverty," VOW advocates opened the ground for addressing tensions that inevitably arise in working at the intersections of race, class, and gender. Forms of collective counter-transference inevitably emerge as women bring their histories into the group and relive earlier traumatic engagements with the state as well as with abusers. Yet in seeking shared ground through activism, VOW is able to create a "safe space" where conflict among women can be acknowledged without overwhelming the group.

Sujata Warrior, an advocate from New York City, describes the tensions that arise for frontline workers in reconciling the *authorized accounts* of women—accounts that depend heavily on establishing the virtue and non-culpability of women as mothers—and the complex realities of women's lives:

> "You talk to women and you get them to talk about a 10-year relationship. They did some really weird stuff. I mean they may be, in my mind, someone who is absolutely what I would define as a victim of oppression, of power and control in a gendered way. Right? But if you're a cop or a child welfare worker, or a judge hearing a divorce (or whatever you are) and someone tells you some of the stuff she did during the time that she was struggling, they may not see it that way."

Warrior grants some credibility to competing interpretations of women's culpability in situations of abuse and emphasizes how feminist organizations must make room for competing perspectives, rather than falling into all-good mother/all-bad mother categories. Part of the dilemma, Warrior explains, centers on the ambivalence on the part of advocates and finding little support for acknowledging such conflicting feelings.

The skills involved in the emotional labor carried out by women are often made invisible or devalued in capitalist societies, even as such labor becomes more complex and demanding over time (Hochschild, 1983). In Berlin, advocates who have worked in shelters for many years claim that the problems women bring into the shelters are more complex than in prior periods. So, too, are the problems of shelter staff. The shelters are now required to report suspected child abuse and most shelters have a no-spanking rule—a source of tension as discussed in Chapter 5. One of the Berlin advocates elaborates on the dilemma: "It's a difficult problem that we're facing, not necessarily approving of the methods that battered women use to deal with their children and yet wanting to find a compromise."

Women and children often depend on the same lifeline of social services. As a result, advocates emphasize the failure of this lifeline rather than the failures of women as mothers. Sue Loeb offers a depressing assessment of the situation in New York City, particularly for women with children who are seeking domestic violence services:

> "In some cases the system backfired on them, like the welfare issue. Because the culture [of New York City] is really child removal oriented, women don't want to call the police—because coming to their home might be the trigger for the child welfare office to come and remove their children. So their ability to use the system is theoretical and for them doesn't exist in their mind."

Advocates in New York City express further concern that child witnessing laws "backfire" on women. In the United States, women may be charged with child abuse—and may lose custody of a child—if they permit an abusive partner to remain in the home. For some women, the threat of losing their children motivates them to sever ties with their abusers. But for other women, the threat binds them more tightly to an abusive situation and undermines their capacities to seek help.

As domestic violence gains legitimacy as an area where women can "reasonably" expect protection from the state, advocates for the poor find that framing poverty as an effect of domestic violence has greater political currency than does addressing structural sources of poverty. Indeed, as the ink was drying on the Violence Against Women Act of 1994, welfare reform, the Personal Responsibility and Work Opportunity Act, one of the most devastating assaults on poor women, was being drafted in the United States Congress. Activists struggling to ameliorate the harsh impact of welfare reform rushed to insist that domestic violence was a leading cause of women seeking public assistance. Congress finally passed a ruling allowing states to adopt waivers that stopped the clock on time limits for public assistance if women could demonstrate that they were victims of domestic violence (Riger & Krieglstein, 2000).

The joining of domestic violence and poverty did open up political space for talking about the vulnerabilities of poor women (Josephson, 2005). However, discussion centered on domestic violence as the primary cause of female poverty, rather than on poverty as a cause of family violence. Stories began to appear regularly in the press featuring women who were desperate to get off welfare, but whose male partners defeated them at every turn.

> Doris Roberston can tell you all about how black eyes, uncontrollable crying fits and fear of embarrassment can keep a woman on welfare. She says that's what her husband wanted. "He wanted me to be too down and out of control to go out and get a job," said Robertson, who claims her husband's abuse caused her to lose two jobs during their 14 years together. "He wanted me to live on public aid forever."
>
> (*Chicago Daily Herald*, 1999)

In both poor and affluent communities, women are routinely undermined by the men in their lives. But the line of argument adopted by many welfare activists lays responsibility for female poverty at the feet of poor men. Further, the subtext centers on fortifying the boundary between "deserving" and "undeserving" poor women. If getting help from the state to overcome poverty requires a redemptive banner of moral justification, women who can display their broken bones and bruises make more compelling victims than do "ordinary" poor women.

In the 1980s and 1990s, shelters become an avenue for access to public housing and other forms of public assistance, and screening for domestic violence part of the triaging of poor women. It is not surprising then that poor women increasingly came to frame their experiences through a discourse of domestic violence. This is not to suggest that poor women invent stories of abuse. Rather, it is to suggest that if there is only one exit door from a burning building, it will get a great deal of traffic.

CONCLUSIONS

In one of the trainings I attended at a shelter in Portland, Oregon, two women came to speak one evening and offered testimonies of abuse that deviated markedly from the standard scripts. After a series of valorized accounts of battered women, these hard-living women spoke of how they had stayed with abusive men to get the next fix, looking the other way when their children were crushed under the boot of their soul-less companions. The women spoke of turning their lives around, and feeling painful guilt over the choices they had made even as they recognized that addiction was not really a choice. The addiction model permitted some protective moral distance between the woman—as a mother—and the behavior that placed her in a position of social damnation.

Women and children have shared a common fate throughout much of human history, joined at the hip through their subjugation to the Law of the Father. Since the 19th century, women and advocates for children have periodically staged rebellions against the patriarchal fathers, seeking sanctuary and freedom beyond their reach. For some women, leaving means facing the harsh stigma of the Bad Mother—the accusation of "maternal abandonment," a term for which there is no paternal equivalent. Stories of men hitting the road are legendary, occupying a central place in American folk literature. Although male protagonists often require "domestication" after a youthful sojourn of wildness, the moral loads they carry are far lighter than those born by women who similarly flee from their familial duties.

In framing the problem of family violence, the broader ideological and social structural contexts of family life may easily get lost—particularly as energy is channeled toward tracking information through systems that break up the coherence of the stories told. Early feminists' organizing emphasized links between family violence and systems of hierarchy and domination. The religious parent who regularly dispenses whippings to "break the will" of the child exists within a hierarchical cosmos extending from the heavens to the fiery pits of hell. Earthly authority operates as agent of a wrathful god, intent on ferreting out vestiges of resistance in the human soul. Within this belief system and the dramas generated by it, beatings of children, and sometimes wives, are readily integrated into a morally justified script. But the parent who occasionally "loses it," feeling a loss of self-esteem in the process, requires a different response.

There are clinical issues here in terms of motivations for getting help and capacities for change. But there also are broader political issues concerning how we intervene in the cultural scaffolding of violence. An important contribution of feminism, including the Duluth model, is its focus on beliefs that support patterns of violence. But exporting the model has carried a heavy toll in softening the critique and enlisting rhetoric about "individual accountability" that resonates well with conservatives.

Conflict between children's and women's advocates is in part symptomatic of this dilemma: the latent (unconscious) aggressive elements of the model become manifestly conscious as it turns its full force onto mothers who are violent. Declaring a man a perpetrator morally condemns his actions and calls for public interventions that relieve women of private responsibility. In cases against women, however, feminists have understood the work of the movement as shifting from the position of prosecutor to defense counsel. While feminist psychology remains aligned with the defense position, the work has been too heavily constrained by individualistic and legalistic discourses that seek decisive verdicts to questions of guilt or innocence.

Advocates have pointed out how romanticized portraits of the good victim are repressive for many women who don't conform to the prototype, but they also are repressive for advocates. Crisis and other forms of social service work are immensely difficult and often downplayed in appealing to feminist principles of solidarity. Contests between child advocates and women's advocates over who represents the true interests of victims may be another form of institutional splitting with each side projecting onto the other some portion of the hostility and resentment generated by very stressful jobs.

The erosion of social welfare services in the United States, as well as in other parts of the world, means that case workers are carrying increasingly heavy loads, even as they are situated as the shock absorbers in societies where women who come for services are feeling these same effects. In reframing the conflict between advocates over who is the better protector of vulnerable family members, and whether mothers who abuse their children are all-good or all-bad, this broader oppressive frame may easily recede from view.

NOTES

1 Linda Gordon (1988) suggests that stories of family violence in American history must be understood in the context of the shifting economic basis of kinship ties. Her portraits of turn-of-the-century immigrants in Boston capture poignantly the

cultural dilemmas of working-class parents who struggled to maintain some control over their children amidst earth-moving changes in their lives.

2 The American Psychological Association's ethical guidelines were expanded during the 1980s to include social responsibilities to address injustices.

3 For an analysis of the debates over child testimony and recovered memory of sexual abuse, see Haaken and Reavey (2009).

CONCLUSIONS: BEYOND SURVIVAL

> We are volcanoes. When we women offer our experience as our truth, as human truth, all the maps change. There are new mountains.
>
> (Le Guin, 1989: 160)[1]

This book began by identifying four areas of acute border tensions in the history of the battered women's movement and sought to understand how advocates in different regions with long histories of activism had managed those tensions over time. The conversations that took place produced important insights, some of which were bound to the specific locale and others more generalizable to the wider anti-violence movement. Throughout the book, I have tried to show how broader historical and cultural contexts shape how stories about family violence get told and the social symbolic loadings they acquire as they gravitate across the political landscape. Through the dual lenses of psychoanalytic social theory and feminist theory, I have explained how reading the subtexts of various scripts, including those transmitted through the "underground" of the movement itself, makes us less vulnerable to their hypnotic influence. Further, reflecting on the stories we tell reveals a great deal about the multiple identifications and dramatic conflicts that arise in the process of fighting for social change. In closing the book, I summarize key insights that emerged in unpacking the four recurring zones of conflict in the field—areas where battle fatigue has been most evident.

FEMINIST ALLIANCES WITH THE STATE

The most divisive area of controversy concerning feminist engagement with the state centered on working with the police and the courts. Whereas the critique of therapeutic authority centered on a seductive alliance between female patients and male doctors, many of the early feminist critiques of the police stressed the passivity of the state in legally intervening and punishing abusers. The seductiveness of police powers tended to be overlooked in feminist discussions of the controversy, even as advocates generally recognized how different experiences with the police shaped strategic responses.

Yet as support for mandatory arrest policies collided with mounting evidence of the ineffectiveness of such policies, it became clearer that there was more at stake than simply the rational effectiveness of particular policies. The power of the state through its judicial and legal system could be enlisted in the name of justice but also as a force for acting on punitive and paranoid anxieties. Forms of mutual recognition—where advocates and officers have worked together to bring abusive men under control—represent an area where the gains and losses of this advance in the movement have been difficult to untangle. As one advocate reflects back ambivalently,

> "I think it is hard to say whether it was a mistake to focus on the legal system. Twenty years ago, we started out with nothing. We basically started putting women up in our homes. And then the shelters and hotlines evolved. We wanted the police to arrest and they were saying, 'Okay, we'll give you this, but you give a little bit too.' It didn't seem like a lot. They're things that maybe we shouldn't have given up, and things that maybe we shouldn't have done."[2]

Part of the appeal of the battered women's movement for many advocates interviewed was that it opened ground for taking on men—for a fight—where women could claim the issue as their own and assert moral authority. As one German advocate recalled, left groups were often sexist, but also increasingly isolated and splintered by the 1970s. The battered women's movement created places of refuge for advocates, as well as for abused women, but there also was a pull to break out of the enclosure of the shelters and to take a more public role—to "make a real difference." In this sense, the tensions over whether to keep the shelters hidden and secret were symptomatic of this very ambivalence over how to reconcile private and public forms of female authority.

Advocates both consciously and unconsciously recognized that woman battering was an issue where feminists could more effectively take on the state and win ground. Unlike issues where sexuality has been central, such as the abortion rights, anti-rape, and anti-sexual harassment campaigns, the prototypical battered woman story did not arouse the same uneasiness among conservatives. Sujata Warrior, an advocate from New York City, offers an important insight in explaining social dynamics that contributed to the separation of domestic violence from the sexual assault movement: "Rape, because of the way it occurs, happens in a context where it is easier to blame the victim. The subtext is that she invited it. In the DV arena, because of the way the injuries appear, you are able to shift blame to the perpetrator in a way that you are not able to do in the rape movement." Warrior goes on to explain that the splitting of the two areas of the domestic violence movement—downplaying marital rape and focusing more on battering—allowed women themselves to talk more openly about their oppression.

In reflecting on the early history and the gains that have been made, Ellen Pence, a founder of the Duluth Model, remembers how inter-agency tracking systems in the 1980s initially confronted a wall of resistance among women's advocates (Shepard & Pence, 1999). She describes the shift in the 1990s from being seen as "pushy, single-issue, and inherently biased outsiders" (1999: 45) to partners where their expertise as advocates was valued. Yet as advocates achieve forms of recognition by the state, forms of recognition that would have been unimaginable several decades ago, the costs of such alliances must be assessed as well. As Hagemann-White recalls, reflecting back to the early form of radical feminism that guided the movement, "it was a notion of women being complicit in a patriarchal tradition." Extending this line of thought, we might interpret quarrels over the absolute innocence or guilt of mothers as a displaced appeal to be absolved of our own guilt.

In assessing the elaborate system created through the Duluth Domestic Abuse Intervention Project (DAIP), Dennis Falk and Nancy Helgeson (1999) describe the expansion of computerized platforms and databases and the challenges in getting buy-ins for transmitting data from one agency to another. "We think that maybe one or two people fully comprehend the tracking system and how to use it," the authors concede, even as they offer flow charts to explain how researchers at Duluth are tackling the problem. Among other recommendations, the authors stress control at the top:

> A strong individual must be available to make connections with all the agencies involved in the tracking and monitoring system . . . This individual must articulate the "big picture" of what the tracking system is about and encourage key individuals and organizations to buy into the tracking system concept.
>
> (Falk & Helgeson, 1999: 108–109)

Powerful tracking systems administered by the state may generate paranoia—an excess of anxiety over modern technologies that penetrates into personal life. Such paranoia often fuels right-wing anti-government populism in the United States. But hysterical blindness to such effects is yet another condition. Just as the bystander effect was enlisted in bringing a more social framework for understanding wife abuse and child abuse, the operations of the state may similarly occlude the vision of observers.

Further, authority figures who claim the mantle of "protection of women and children," much like physicians and politicians in the past, may know the scripts that have been effective in seducing observers.

Since the late 1990s, women of color in the movement have built on their early critiques of the criminal justice response by reclaiming some of the radical roots of the movement. The statement issued by Incite!—supported by groups such as Sista II Sista and Critical Resistance—situate violence against women in the context of a broader social justice agenda, including calls for abolition of the prison system in the United States (Incite!, 2005). They point out that criminalization has not reduced partner violence in poor communities and that mandatory arrest policies have resulted in growing incarceration rates for black women. And they call for restorative justice programs on the community level even as they caution against initiatives that put pressure on women to reunite with abusive partners (Smith, 2005; Strang & Braithwaite, 2002).[3]

Another way of managing feminist ambivalence in relation to the state has been to separate it into "good" and "bad" parts and to align with the maternal side, the social welfare state, over against the patriarchal criminal justice system.[4] In the contested terrain where child protective services and women's crisis services meet, anxiety over the legitimacy of interventions may also take the form of split images between the good and the bad maternal agent of the state. Just as women in situations of family violence may be cast as either good mothers or bad mothers, depending on the sympathies of bystanders, so, too, are workers whose job it is to intervene in family violence. The muddy ground where women's and children's advocates meet becomes even muddier with the passage of child witnessing statutes in many countries in recent years.

My interest throughout this book has been in attending to those aspects of crisis work that are more apt to be cast to the margins of group consciousness. The interviews carried out and presented here suggest that crisis work evokes a far more complex range of feelings and identifications than is generally recognized, including in the forms of battle fatigue described. And as unauthorized feelings slip through organizational censors, such as anger toward clients, feminists may be particularly vulnerable to feelings of shame, guilt, or betrayal. Further, recognition that women working in the field—even as feminists—may be simultaneously agents of oppression and agents of social change can be difficult to reconcile with feminist principles. Such disturbing states of awareness may motivate a search for external enemies—places to locate the disturbing feelings that give rise to a guilty conscience.

While separating the state into its patriarchal policing functions and its maternal social welfare functions has some basis in reality, the repressive aspects of much of the state apparatus in capitalist societies may be overlooked. The problem of what to *demand* of the state on behalf of women is complicated by the differing political conditions that women confront in various countries and locales of the world, even as the reign of neoliberalism throughout the globe tightens the space for meeting basic human needs, from healthcare, housing, jobs, clean air, and water, as well as to other conditions vital for building thriving communities (Kelly *et al.*, 2001). The social welfare system in the United States is weaker than in most other Western countries, and the "safety net" increasingly frayed. The ideology of individualism—the collective fantasy of a society bound together by self-reliant and self-determining individuals—has a deeper hold in the United States, even as this ideology increasingly confronts contrary realities.

Working in the refuge/shelter movement, advocates may feel less implicated in the repressive apparatus of the state, either in their hard or soft versions. Yet here, too, secure boundaries between good and bad forms of authority are as elusive as are boundaries between safe houses for women and the threats they are fleeing. The over-idealizing of refuge spaces—as womb-like sites of protection—may reproduce another cultural fantasy that circulates widely in bourgeois societies: that crisis services, refuges, or "transitional housing" are temporary stations on a trajectory toward independence and self-reliance. Good people may rely on the "safety net" of social welfare services if they demonstrate the requisite capacities to get up and back onto their feet.

DOMESTICATING VIOLENCE

A second area of border tension where psychology is enlisted to explore group defenses in the battered women's movement centers on the question of whether domestic violence is a special case that differs from other violent behaviors. One source of conflict centers on the trade-offs in the historical movement to extend civil rights protection to the household where women carry out much of their social labor. In making a special case for the unique risks women face as potential victims of male assaults within the household, feminists were able to make demands on the state for protection in the private sphere. But this strategy ran the risk of splitting off the issue of domestic violence from a broader critical and social analysis of violence. Progressive positions that contextualize violent crime, emphasizing how poverty, unemployment, militarism, and other social factors contribute to or exacerbate violence, run afoul with feminist demands that men "choose violence"—that it is an individual volitional act.

Limiting discussion of violence to the domestic sphere also may reproduce the very domestication of the problem that feminists initially sought to overcome. With the problem fenced in by the borders of the household, the complex links between gender, violence, and broader social structures continue to be mystified. On a social psychological level, the cordoning off of domestic violence from a broader social justice analysis registers a form of collective splitting. It also binds too tightly the political commitments of women to the domestic sphere—the one area where women have traditionally held authority to reign men in.

In Chapter 6 of this book, debates in the child welfare field were taken up, focused on conflicts over how to tell the story of child abuse. Beyond feminist investments in defending women and protecting them from the punitive actions of the state, women's advocates struggle with conflicting aspects of their own social identity. Prohibitions against "mother-blaming" operate as an important principle in women's advocacy work, but these prohibitions may operate repressively in groups, with the anger acted out in staff conflicts. Many advocates described bitter conflicts between "old feminists" and the "young feminists," with fights enacted along generational lines. Political differences are real, but they also can be fuelled by disturbing feelings carried from one sphere to another.

COMMONALITIES AND DIFFERENCES

The experience at Refuge in London was among those that lingered longest in my memory, perhaps because there was such a disjuncture between the official history displayed on the conference room walls—the heroic tale of the origins of Chiswick House—and the grisly account of the origins of the house that unfolded in interviews with staff. The story that began with Pizzey gathering women and children into refuge houses in London offered two starkly different portraits[5]: one of a Brechtian Strong Mother and the other of the Dickensian Matron. Pizzey describes in heroic terms how she led women to take over many houses in the boroughs as squatters. Horley portrays her predecessor as recklessly irresponsible, setting the messy scene for her own big job of cleaning things up.[6]

The romantic history displayed on the walls of Refuge nonetheless pays tribute to Pizzey and to the importance of heroic stories in social movements, and particularly for the women's movement where so many heroines have been killed off in the official readings of history. But the two separate stories, one for public display and the other the privately held official story, register painful dilemmas in how to integrate the various narrative threads of the movement, stymied by the problem that each narrative may hold one pole of a difficult group conflict. The battered women's movement includes a proud legacy of street fighters, but it also has over time been domesticated by its own successes.

While refuges may be more in compliance with housing codes today than they were in the 1970s, the housing crisis remains an acute problem for women seeking shelter in most locales. As advocates in New York City pointed out, the length that women spend in shelter has steadily increased over time, exposing some of the illusory aspects of crisis services. With crises increasingly chronic, the myth of transitional housing—temporary aid for good women in bad situations—is strained by the realities that perpetually overtake it.

In claiming more space for the complexity of women's experiences, as well as those of men, the threads of female solidarity risk coming unraveled. The counter-myth discussed in Chapter 1—that all women everywhere are at risk of male violence—may be true in the absolute sense but not in the relative sense. As a unifying myth, it is costly both to abused women and to the feminist movement. And it defends against recognizing power differences among women. The boundary between batterer intervention groups and therapy also became invested with surplus emotional loadings as psycho-educational groups for batterers carry the additional political load of proving their effectiveness in bringing male violence under control. Yet just as therapy is not sufficient to transform society, neither are groups for batterers. But their failure to deliver on a culturally proscribed set of demands—to satisfy the redemptive fantasy carried over from therapeutic culture—does not mean that they are of no value. Indeed, the demands need to widen beyond such modest proposals.

Women and violence

A fourth and final key site of recurring conflict, generating the most heat, centered on the question of whether women can be violent in ways that are not purely defensive. In reflecting on what is at stake in taking a position on this question, I sometimes recall an incident in one of my Gender and Violence courses. One young female student raised her hand boldly during the first week of the term to assert that women could be as vicious and mean as men and that this proved that feminists were wrong. She glanced at her classmates, with gestures of nervous fidgeting returning from some students and reassuring nods from others. I conceded her point: "Of course women can be as mean as men. That is why we needed a women's movement. If we were good because of our natural tendencies, we would not have needed to create feminism, nor would we have much to claim as our achievements." My didactic response gave evidence of my own defensiveness, my reluctance to be tutored by this brash young woman.

My irritation with the question—and its implicit aim of educating me on feminist blindspots—was shaped by the over-burdened history of this very question. And my didactic response—like the myth–fact rhetorical strategy critiqued throughout this book—deployed one claim to trump another. The implicit accusation may also be read as a demand for a form of recognition—how being good for younger generations (where "bad" often means "good") may very well be different from earlier generations. T-shirts now celebrate girls who "kick butt." But this can be a superficial endorsement of female aggression, even disempowering in its implicit message that (white) girls cannot really do serious harm.

So how *do* we acknowledge the destructive capacities of women—a vital part of claiming a fuller humanity—while holding onto a gender analysis of domestic violence? If we begin with the premise that the regulation of aggression is part of human defensive systems, women as well as men must work through problems related to destructive impulses. Hierarchies structure the social and psychological terms of this working through, including groups implicitly or explicitly authorized as acceptable targets for aggression and various displaced grievances. From this vantage point, violence perpetrated against those with lesser status or power originates in a system of domination and the trauma and impoverishment it generates. The relational dynamic that often results, described throughout this book as projective identification, centers on externalizing disturbing emotions by making the more vulnerable person the receptacle of unwanted emotions, whether terror, dependency, or vulnerability. As Jessica Benjamin (1988) describes this same dynamic, the ones in the position of "master" experience terror at those moments where they must confront their dreadful dependency on the subjugated for forms of recognition. Much like the story of the battered woman told by Lenore Walker, the oppressed subject may discover forms of power over the master at moments in the cycle as well—both the power to serve as reassuring mirror and the power to refuse the role. But breaking from the dominant script requires the mediating force of groups and social movements that intervene in the drama.

Aggression and violence are charged with gendered meanings but assume variable forms as we move across political categories. Women, no less than men, are subject to defensive processes, including the transfer of rage directed against one object or person onto another. We do not need to insist that each and every aggressive response on the part of a woman is in direct proportion to a present threat to make the general case that women are victims of male violence. Further, it is important to recognize distinctions between the violent *actions* of women and societal *over-reaction* to women perceived as violent. Feminists may internalize social hysteria over incidents of female violence through a hysterical disavowal of any identification with the problem of destructive forms of female aggression. There also are areas where working-class men are more apt to be victimized by violence than are women, for example, in war, or through the violence of the criminal justice system. These arguments are still consistent with a feminist analysis in that patriarchy—the rule of powerful men—oppresses men and women, although it offers more private and public compensations for the injuries suffered by men at the hands of their rulers. Men are granted license to make enormous claims on women—to find consolation in the arms of women—and they are more apt to be cast as heroes in wars fought to pursue the interests of those in power.

Capitalist societies thrive on perpetual crises, as Naomi Klein (2007) so trenchantly argues, and feminist crisis work has been incorporated into this systematic tendency. One effect of living with chronic states of emergency is that the focus narrows to immediate survival, with diminished capacity for perspective-taking. Further, crisis modes of coping may perpetuate crises in that people learn to thrive in a chaotic environment. At the institutional, group, and individual levels, the result may be increased *investment* in crises. In most training manuals, advocates are encouraged to engage in self-care and warned about the risk of vicarious trauma. But they are less apt to be cautioned that a magnified fear of men may be an occupational hazard.

One of the real difficulties in feminist theorizing concerning abusive men is that any concession of the suffering and humanity of violent men seems to lead to lost ground for women. It does feel like a zero-sum game, where the larger the emotional space allowed men the more diminished the space for female grievances. As many advocates interviewed here suggest, however, this is not inevitably the case. The hope of feminist organizing rests on claiming this rough terrain where virtue and villainy are difficult to untangle. Collective forms of psychological splitting between the idealized and the demonized, between the innocent and the guilty, are costly because the oppressed ultimately come to depend on the oppressor for group identity (Haaken, 1998).

My aim in this book has been to show how these same dynamics operate in women's groups, even as they may take less extreme forms. In entering an adult arena of struggle, where social alliances and forms of solidarity permit new denouements, the stories of childhood work their way into the subtexts of adult encounters. Liberation movements mobilize anxieties and defenses on the part of oppressors, but so, too, do they arouse these same reactions on the part of the oppressed. In recognizing the place of unconscious dynamics in social movements, we may be more able to resist the shame that often accompanies their emergence in group life. Groups that recognize how the insults and injuries of childhood are bound up in destructive human tendencies may be better able to bring such tendencies under control.

Such forms of recognition may widen the space for addressing the emotional loadings of various axes of oppression beyond gender as well. Since social hierarchies rest on the oppressor's capacity to disavow unwanted states and feelings and to project them onto an Other, anti-violence practices that acknowledge such dynamics in their own groups may be better able to widen space for addressing the psychopolitics of intersectionality—for example, how homophobia rests on the same terrors of unauthorized desires as does fear of women and minorities.[7]

The concept of domestic violence—as male violence against women in the household—never mapped comfortably onto the habitats of poor and minority communities. Similarly, the boundary between the household and the community—the private and the public—may be less clearly demarcated. Sujata Warrior describes the work carried out by women activists in her home country of India, and how strategies of resistance differ from those adopted by many feminist organizations in the United States: "Community shaming is powerful. If men are abusing wives, the community mobilized to shame them. People camp out in front of the family's house. If he is caught, a garland of sandals is thrown at him—which represents something dirty and polluting." Warrior argues that the struggle against woman battering must be framed within a wider social justice movement. She adds that it has been easier to secure funding in the United States for special projects and single issues than for advancing an analysis that brings into question the broader organization of society.

Incite! (2005) brings many of these same critiques to the anti-violence movement. It argues that feminist responses that separate domestic violence from a broader social analysis of racism and institutional violence end up colluding with the state in ways that are oppressive to immigrant women, poor women, and communities of color. As an example, Incite! points out that the state and national coalitions on sexual and domestic violence have not taken a stand on anti-immigrant policies in the United States, even though immigrant women, particularly undocumented workers, are not able to secure protection from the police and are routinely abused by the police and immigration officers.[8] Allied with Critical Resistance, an activist group that calls for dismantling of the prison/industrial complex, Incite! revives the spirit of radical feminism that was a palpable force in the early battered women's movement.

Even as it calls for alternatives to incarceration, Incite! cautions against community-based responses that minimize the effects of violence or pressure women to reconcile with abusive men. The term "community"—while evoking warm associations of convivial social ties—encompasses a wide range of affiliations. Communities can be repressive as well as supportive, and often are both. As Levinson (1989) points out, group alliances among women and relative gender equality have been important in enforcing sanctions against woman battering throughout the world.

TOWARD A FEMINIST PSYCHOLOGY OF STORYTELLING

Storytelling practices in the domestic violence field are mapped throughout this book in a historical trajectory from narrating a state of bondage, to paths of deliverance, and, finally, to struggles to achieve aims that elude full realization. This trajectory moves from captivity and deliverance narratives to more complex tales that encompass a richer range of human capacities and moral dilemmas.

As women and men step beyond the threshold of the household and work to build more vital and sustaining forms of community, we can imagine new denouements to the quiet suffering of women in countless households, as well as more creative means of breaking out of the deadly trance of the Gothic romance. The three genres—stories of captivity, stories of deliverance, and stories of struggle and reparation—may be enlisted to claim the cultural legacy of the battered women's movement while interrupting the voyeurism and enchantments that accompany its passage into popular culture.

One place for intervening in the vicious cycle of group conflicts, of going beyond defensive stalemates, is to make political use of patriarchal anxieties over women's potential for violence. Rather than refusing to acknowledge offensive forms of female aggression, we may want to claim the capacity for destructive rage and insist on the same space accorded men in this area and directing it toward social transformation. The Sista II Sista organization in Brooklyn, New York, for example, creates a space where young women of color can "tap into their collective power to fight against injustice." The Loud Mouth Project, which includes workshops on the history of revolutionary women, deploys white anxieties over "big" or "loud" black women, taking these images up to talk back to power.

Throughout this book I have tried to show how movements for social justice can produce forms of battle fatigue over time, particularly as groups come to depend on the enemy for feelings of internal wellbeing. Progressive movements must be able to build on the "good objects"—sustaining representations of human connection—even as they resist the "bad objects" that inhabit the internal and external worlds of the oppressed. The early shelter movement centered as vitally on alternative visions of community as it did on combating abuse. Although the romanticizing of female-only spaces created a context for bitter disappointments, as did the over-idealization of abused women, the feminist anti-violence movement has enough history and experience to draw on to adopt more psychologically and politically integrated forms of idealization.

The ethical demands that accompany anti-violence work are implicit in a range of *restorative justice* programs around the world—a wide umbrella term for community-based alternatives to the criminal justice system. Restorative justice projects focused on intimate partner violence, where batterers must acknowledge their abusive behavior and make restitution, have generated intense controversy among feminists (see Krieger, 2002; Stubbs, 2002). In addition to pressuring women to reconcile with abusive partners, community-based responses may rely on the unpaid labor of women to bring justice about at the local level. An important aim behind the movement to criminalize domestic violence was to shift the burden of managing damaged men from the shoulders of women to the power of the state. At stake in this debate are different visions of the state and how to advance demands on the state to *support* experiments in community, from restorative justice programs, respite care for families in crisis, to alternative housing arrangements.

Cangleska practitioners have directed some of the resources that have come to the Pine Ridge Reservation through the Violence Against Women Act to building such places of reparation. On the last day of my visit at Pine Ridge, I was given an audiotape from the Canglaska weekly radio show. The taped program featured Marlin Mousseau and Russ Cournoyer, who began by telling their own stories of growing up with violence and how they had come to identify with the very fathers they had hated in childhood. Cournoyer reflected back on the blindspots in his Indian identity. "I was proud of being a sundancer and carrying a pipe," he explained, "but I overlooked the feminine powers of the universe."

Cournoyer then turned to the story of Sacred White Buffalo Calf Woman who brought the peace pipe to the Lakota people. "The Sweat Lodge that we enter into is a representation of the Mother Earth's Womb and our mother's womb." Rather than treating women as equals and respectfully, men use their masculine entitlement to act out against women in infantile ways. "When you see children throwing tantrums, that is appropriate for little children. But it carries into adulthood. If I didn't get my way, I would throw a tantrum, be abusive, to get my own way and maintain control. I was an adult exhibiting three- or four-year-old behavior."

Cournoyer and Mousseau move then to a discussion of jealousy and envy as key dynamics in violence. Although such feelings originate in real histories of deprivation, Cournoyer adds that "a lot of the jealousy was my projection of my own thoughts about other women onto my partners." The two men describe a dynamic described elsewhere in this book as projective identification. Mousseau describes the man's violent attempts to control his female partner, to make her feel the terror that he refuses to acknowledge as part of his own experience.

> "I came to understand the effects of being put on this reservation . . . I realized that I was no different than the very men who were sent out here to either assimilate us or kill us off. We were solely dependent on the Cavalry, government agents, for our survival. This made us vulnerable to their brainwashing . . . and we did the same to our partners—isolating them, making them feel worthless, begging for crumbs of love from us men."

Cournoyer concludes the radio program with a "tribute to the great-grandmothers who escaped the Massacre at Wounded Knee," and the lineage of female resistance to male violence that continues. In honor of those women, and in making reparation with them, the two men conclude with *Imagine*—the song by John Lennon that remains an anthem in the anti-violence movement.

Social science research is guided by intellectual curiosity, but also by emotional investments in what is at stake. My aim here has been to capture some of the passion of the anti-violence movement and to deepen our capacities to hold the "good objects" along with the "bad objects" in our collective past. To remain a vital force for social change, movements must make room for a wider range of storytelling practices and assess the hard ground that has been won in light of contemporary realities. We are no longer entirely outside the kingdom, no longer completely voiceless. Feminism has come of age and we now have a rich history to look back on, a vast landscape of experience to celebrate, and a proud legacy of foremothers to guide and inspire us. This book has been an effort to draw on that vast wealth of experience and to pass it on to the next generation. But it remains to younger generations of activists to create their own stories and to wage their own battles, even as we elders stand ready to watch their backs.

NOTES

1 Excerpt from *Dancing at the edge of the world*, copyright © 1989 by Ursula K. Le Guin. Used by permission of Grove/Atlantic.
2 Cited in Shepard (1999: 120–121).
3 For review of controversies associated with these initiatives in the domestic violence field, see Strang and Braithwaite (2002).
4 In his psychoanalytically informed history of the emergence of the social welfare state in England, Eli Zaretsky (2004) suggests that the idiom of the "mommy state," invoked by right-wing critics of social welfare, registers broader social anxieties over dependency—states of need that are routinely disavowed or pathologized in capitalist societies. He goes on to explain how the *maternalizing* of the social welfare state in Britain also opened ground for public assertions of female authority.
5 Pizzey continues to campaign around domestic violence but has aligned herself with the fathers' rights movement in arguing that women can be as violent as men, thereby challenging a cornerstone argument of the movement (see Dugan, 2008).
6 In *The politics of domesticity*, Barbara Epstein (1981) offers a historical analysis of how middle-class women made political advances in the 19th century by enlisted traditional roles and asserting their superior skills in "cleaning things up" in public life.
7 A number of radical psychologists and psychiatrists have enlisted the term "*psychopolitics*" in working at the boundary between social structures and psychodynamic processes. (See Greenblatt (1978) and Post (1999).
8 For the Incite! "Statement on Gender Violence and the Prison/Industrial Complex," as well as other materials on organizing projects, see www.incite-national.org

REFERENCES

Abraham, M. (2000). Isolation as a form of marital violence: The South Asian immigrant experience. *Journal of Social Distress and the Homeless*, *9*(3), 221–236.

Adams, D. C., & McCormick, A. J. (1982). Men unlearning violence: A group approach based on the collective model. In M. Roy (ed.), *The abusive partner* (pp. 170–197). New York, NY: Van Nostrand Reinhold Company.

Alexander, M. J., & Mohanty, C. T. (1997). *Feminist genealogies, colonial legacies, democratic futures*. New York, NY: Routledge.

Alford, C. F. (1989). *Melanie Klein and critical social theory: An account of politics, art, and reason based on her psychoanalytic theory*. New Haven, CT: Yale University Press.

Allard, S. A. (1991). Rethinking the battered woman syndrome: A black feminist perspective. *UCLA Women's Law Journal*, *1*(1), 191–208.

Althusser, L. (1969). *For Marx*. Trans. Ben Brewster. London: Allen Lane.

Artichoker, K., & Mousseau, M. (2003). *Violence against native women is not traditional: Handbook*. Rapid City, SD: Sacred Circle.

Ayyub, R. (2000). Domestic violence in the South Asian Muslim immigrant population in the United States. *Journal of Social Distress and the Homeless*, *9*(3), 237–248.

Babcock, J. C., & Steiner, R. (1999). The relationship between treatment, incarceration, and recidivism of battering: A program evaluation of Seattle's coordinated community response to domestic violence. *Journal of Family Psychology*, *13*(1), 46–59.

Barthes, R. (1972). *Mythologies* (A. Lavers, Trans.). New York, NY: Hill and Wang.

Baxter, A. K. (ed.) (1980). *The memoirs of Mrs. Abigail Bailey*. Manchester, NH: Ayer Publishing.

Benjamin, J. (1988). *The bonds of love: Psychoanalysis, feminism, and the problem of domination*. New York, NY: Pantheon Books.

Bennett, L. W., & Williams, O. J. (2000/2001). Controversies and recent studies of batterer intervention program effectiveness. Applied Research Paper Series, 1–18.

Bentzel, S. B., & York, R. O. (1988). Influence of feminism and professional status upon service options for the battered woman. *Community Mental Health Journal*, *24*(1), 52–64.

Bhabha, H. K. (1994). *The location of culture*. London: Routledge.

Bograd, M. (1984). Family systems approaches to wife battering: A feminist critique. *American Journal of Orthopsychiatry*, *54*(4), 558–568.
Bradley Angle, H. (1978). *Escape from violence: The women of Bradley Angle House*. Portland, OR: Bradley Angle House.
Breckenridge, J., & Ralfs, C. (2006). "Point of contact" front-line workers responding to children living with domestic violence. In C. Humphreys, & N. Stanley (eds), *Domestic violence and child protection: Directions for good practice* (pp. 110–123). Philadelphia, PA: Jessica Kingsley Publishers.
Brenner, J. (2000). *Women and the politics of class*. New York, NY: Monthly Review Press.
Browne, A. (1987). *When battered women kill*. New York, NY: The Free Press.
Brownmiller, S. (1989). *Waverly Place*. New York, NY: Grove Press.
Bruner, J. (1990). *Acts of meaning*. Cambridge, MA: Harvard University Press.
Burman, E. (2003). Childhood, sexual abuse, and new political subjectivities. In P. Reavey and S. Warner (eds), *New feminist stories of child sexual abuse* (pp. 34–51). London: Routledge.
Burman, E. (2004). Organising for change? Group-analytic perpectives on a feminist action research project. *Group Analysis*, *37*(1), 91–108.
Burman, E. (2008). Beyond "women vs. children" or "womenandchildren": Engendering childhood and reformulating motherhood. *International Journal of Children's Rights*, *16*, 177–194.
Burman, E., Smailes, S. L., & Chantler, K. (2004). "Culture" as a barrier to service provision and delivery: Domestic violence services for minoritized women. *Critical Social Policy*, *24*(3), 332–357.
Butler, J. (1990). *Gender trouble: Feminism and the subversion of identity*. New York, NY: Routledge.
Butler, J. (1997). *The psychic life of power: Theories in subjection*. Palo Alto, CA: Stanford University Press.
Campbell, A. (1993). Intimate rage: Violence in marriage. *Men, Women, and Aggression* (pp. 103–124). New York, NY: Basic Books.
Cangleska (2000). *Domestic violence: Information packet*. Rapid City, SD: Sacred Circle.
Carney, S. K. (2004). Transcendent stories and counternarratives in Holocaust survivor life histories: Searching for meaning in video-testimony archives. In C. L. C. Daiute (ed.), *Narrative analysis: Studying the development of individuals in society* (pp. 201–221). Thousand Oaks, CA: Sage Publications.
Center for Democratic Renewal (1992). *When hate groups come to town: A handbook for effective community resources*. Atlanta, GA: Center for Democratic Renewal.
Chicago Daily Herald (1999) State considering Welfare Waivers, 17 April, p. 6.
Chodorow, N. J. (1978). *The reproduction of mothering*. Berkeley, CA: University of California Press.
Cohen, S. (1992). *The evolution of women's asylums since 1500: From refuges for ex-prostitutes to shelters for battered women*. New York, NY: Oxford University Press.
Collins, P. H. (1998). *Fighting words: Black women and the search for justice* (vol. 7). Minneapolis, MN: University of Minnesota Press.
Contratto, S., & Chodorow, N. (1982). The fantasy of the perfect mother. In B.

Thorne (ed.), *Rethinking the family: Some feminist questions* (pp. 54–75). Boston, MA: Northeastern University Press.

Craig, D. (1996). Psychoanalytic sociology and the Holocaust. In C. Sumner (ed.), *Violence, culture and censure* (pp. 29–62). Bristol, PA: Taylor and Francis.

Crenshaw, D. A. (2000). The color of violence against women. *Color Lines: Race, Culture, Action, 3*(3), 4–10.

Crenshaw, K. W. (1994). Mapping the margins: Intersectionality, identity politics, and violence against women of color. In M. A. Fineman, & R. Mykitiuk (eds), *The public nature of private violence* (pp. 93–118). New York, NY: Routledge.

Crenshaw, K. W. (1997). Color-blind dreams and racial nightmares: Reconfiguring racism in the post-civil rights era. In T. Morrison, & C. B. Lacour (eds), *Birth of a nation'hood: Gaze, script, and spectacle in the O. J. Simpson case* (pp. 97–168). New York, NY: Pantheon Books.

Daiute, C. L. C. (ed.) (2004). *Narrative analysis: Studying the development of individuals in society*. Thousand Oaks, CA: Sage Publications.

Daly, J. E., & Pelowski, S. (2000). Predictors of dropout among men who batter: A review of studies with implications for research and practice. *Violence and Victims, 15*(2), 137–160.

Dasgupta, S. D. (2000). Charting the course: An overview of domestic violence in the South Asian community in the United States. *Journal of Social Distress and the Homeless, 9*(3), 173–185.

Davis, A. (2000). The color of violence against women. *Color Lines: Race, Culture, Action, 3*(3), 4–8.

Davis, L. V., Hagen, J. L., & Early, T. J. (1994). Social services for battered women: Are they adequate, accessible, appropriate? *Social Work, 39*(6), 695–704.

Davis, N. J. (1988). Shelters for battered women: Social policy response to interpersonal violence. *The Social Science Journal, 25*(4), 401–419.

Davis, R. C., Taylor, B. G., & Maxwell, C. D. (2000). *Does batterer treatment reduce violence? A randomized experiment in Brooklyn*. New York, NY: Victim Services Research.

DeKeseredy, W. S. (2006). Future directions. *Violence Against Women, 12*(11), 1078–1085.

DeKeseredy, W. S., & Dragiewicz, M. (2007). Understanding the complexities of feminist perspectives on woman abuse: A commentary on Donald G. Dutton's rethinking domestic violence. *Violence Against Women, 13*(8), 874–884.

DeKeseredy, W. S., & Schwartz, M. D. (1998). Measuring the extent of woman abuse in intimate heterosexual relationships: A critique of the conflict tactics scale. Retrieved March 3, 1998, from http://www.vaw.umn.edu/Vawnet/ctscrit.htm

Devisch, R. (2006). A psychoanalytic revisting of fieldwork and intercultural border linking. *Social Analysis, 50*, 121–147.

Dinnerstein, D. (1976). *The mermaid and the minotaur: Sexual arrangements and human malaise*. New York, NY: Harper & Row.

Dobash, E. R., & Dobash, R. P. (1979). *Violence against wives: A case against patriarchy*. New York, NY: Free Press.

Donovan, J. (1996). *Feminist theory: The intellectual traditions*. New York, NY: Continuum Publishing Company.

Douglas, A. (1977). *The feminization of American culture*. New York, NY: Avon Books.

Doyle, M. E. (1982). The slave narrative as rhetorical art. In J. Sekora, & D. T. Turner (eds), *The art of slave narrative: Original essays in criticism and theory* (pp. 83–95). Macomb, IL: Western Illinois University.

Duff, A. (1995). *Once were warriors*. New York, NY: Vintage International.

Dugan, E. (2008). Defender of abused women finds a new cause: Male victims. *The Independent UK*, January 17.

Dutton, D. G., & Corvo, K. (2007). The Duluth model: A data-impervious paradigm and a failed strategy. *Agression and Violent Behavior*, *12*, 658–667.

Dutton, D. G., & Nicholls, T. L. (2005). The gender paradigm in domestic violence research and theory: Part 1—The conflict of theory and data. *Aggression and Violent Behavior*, *10*(6), 680–714.

Dutton, D. G., & Starzomski, A. J. (1993). Borderline personality in perpetrators of psychological and physical abuse. *Violence and Victims*, *8*(4), 327–337.

Dutton, D. G., Bodnarchuck, M., Kropp, R., Hart, S. D., & Ogloff, J. P. (1997). Client personality disorders affecting wife assault post-treatment recidivism. *Violence & Victims*, *12*(1), 37–49.

Dutton, D. G., Corvo, K. N., & Hamel, J. (2009). The gender paradigm in domestic violence research and practice part II: The information website of the American Bar Association. *Aggression and Violent Behavior*, *14*(1), 30–38.

Eaton, M. (1994). Abuse by any other name: Feminism, difference, and intralesbian violence. In M. A. Fineman, & R. Mykitiuk (eds), *The public nature of private violence: The discovery of domestic abuse* (pp. 195–223). New York, NY: Routledge.

Edleson, J., & Tolman, R. M. (1992). Group intervention for men who batter. *Intervention for men who batter: An ecological approach* (pp. 52–87). Newbury Park, London & New Delhi: Sage Publications.

Edleson, J. L., & Syers, M. (1990). *Relative effectiveness of group treatments for men who batter*. Minneapolis, MN: School of Social Work, University of Minnesota.

Ehrenreich, B. (1989). *Fear of falling: The inner life of the middle class*. New York, NY: Pantheon Books.

Eisikovits, Z. C., & Buchbinder, E. (1996). *Toward a phenomenological intervention with violence in intimate relationships*. Thousand Oaks, CA: Sage Publications.

Eliade, M. (1967). *Myths, dreams and mysteries: The encounter between contemporary faiths and archaic realities*. New York, NY: Harper & Row.

Epstein, B. L. (1981). *The politics of domesticity: Women, evangelism, and temperance in nineteenth-century America*. Middletown, CT: Wesleyan University Press.

Espin, O. (1999). *Women crossing boundaries: A psychology of immigration and transformations of sexuality*. New York, NY: Routledge.

Falk, D. R., & Hegelson, N. (1999). Building monitoring and tracking systems. In M. F. Shepard, & E. Pence (eds), *Coordinating community responses to dometic violence: Lessons for Duluth and beyond* (pp. 89–113). Thousand Oaks, CA: Sage Publications.

Feder, L., & Dugan, L. (2002). A test of the efficacy of court-mandated counseling for domestic violence offenders: The Broward experiment. *Justice Quarterly*, *19*, 333–375.

Feder, L., & Forde, D. R. (2000). *A test of the efficacy of court-mandated counseling for domestic violence offenders: The Broward experiment* (Final Report, NIF 96-WT-NX-008). Washington, DC: National Institute of Justice.

Feder, L., & Wilson, D. B. (2005). A meta-analytic review of court-mandated batterer intervention: Can courts effect abusers' behavior? *Journal of Experimental Criminology*, *1*(2), 239–262.

Felman, S. (1997). Forms of judicial blindness, or the evidence of what cannot be seen: Traumatic narratives and legal repetitions in the O.J. Simpson case and in Tolstoy's The Kreutzer Sonata. *Critical Inquiry*, *23*(4), 738–788.

Felson, R. B., & Tedeschi, J. T. (1993). A social interactionist approach to violence: cross-cultural applications. *Violence & Victims*, *8*(3), 295–310.

Ferraro, K. J., & Johnson, J. M. (1985). The new underground railroad. *Studies in Symbolic Interaction*, *6*, 377–386.

Fine, M. (1998). Working the hyphens: Reinventing the self and other in qualitative research. In N. K. Denzin, & Y. S. Lincoln (eds), *The landscape of qualitative research* (pp. 130–155). Thousand Oaks, CA: Sage Publications.

Fine, M., & Vanderslice, V. (1992). Qualitative activist research: Reflections on methods and politics. In F. Bryant, & J. Edwards (eds), *Methodological issues in applied social psychology: Social psychological applications to social issues* (vol. 2, pp. 199–218). New York, NY: Plenum Press.

Foucault, M. (1995). *Discipline and punish: The birth of the prison*. New York, NY: Vintage Books.

Freeman, M. (2004). Data are everywhere: Narrative criticism in the literature of experience. In C. L. C. Daiute (ed.), *Narrative analysis. Studying the development of individuals in society* (pp. 63–81). Thousand Oaks, CA: Sage Publications.

Freire, P. (1999/1970). *Pedagogy of the oppressed*. New York, NY: Continuum.

Freud, A. (1936/1966). *The ego and the mechanisms of defence*. New York, NY: International Universities Press.

Freud, S. (1957/1914) On narcissism: An introduction (pp. 73–102). In *The standard edition of the complete works of Sigmund Freud: Vol 14* (p. 91). London: Hogarth Press and The Institute of Psychoanalysis.

Friedan, B. (1963). *The feminist mystique*. New York: W. W. Norton.

Frosh, S. (1995). Masculine mastery and fantasy, or the meaning of the phallus. In A. Elliot, & S. Frosh (eds), *Psychoanalysis in contexts: Paths between theory and modern culture* (pp. 89–105). New York, NY: Routledge.

Gates, H. L., Jr. (ed.) (1987). *The classic slave narratives*. New York, NY: Mentor.

Gergen, K. J., & Gergen, M. M. (1986). *Narrative psychology: The storied nature of human conduct*. New York, NY: Prager.

Gergen, K. J., & Gergen, M. M. (1988). Narrative and the self as relationship. In L. Berkowitz (ed.), *Advances in experimental social psychology, vol 1* (pp. 17–56). San Diego, CA: Academic Press.

Gergen, K. J., & Gergen, M. M. (1997). Narratives of the self. In L. P. Hinchman, & S. Hinchman (eds), *Memory, identity, community: The idea of narrative in the human sciences* (pp. 161–184). New York, NY: State University New York.

Gergen, M. M., & Davis, S. N. (eds) (1997). *Toward a new psychology of gender*. New York, NY: Routledge.

Goldfarb, S. F. (2000). Violence against women and the persistence of privacy. *Ohio State Law Journal*, *61*(1), 1–87.

Goldner, V. (1985). Warning: Family therapy may be hazardous to your health. *Family Therapy Networker*, (6), 19–23.
Goldner, V. (1998). The treatment of violence and victimization in intimate relationships. *Family Process*, *37*(3), 263–286.
Goldner, V. (1999). Morality and multiplicity: Perspectives on the treatment of violence in intimate life. *Journal of Marital & Family Therapy*, *25*(3), 325–336.
Goldner, V. (2002). "Private terrors" and public disclosure—how do we write about countertransference? Commentary on paper by Janine de Peyer. *Psychoanalytic Dialogues*, *12*(4), 537–543.
Goldner, V., & Dimen, M. (2002). Toward a critical relational theory of gender. In Anonymous (ed.), *Gender in psychoanalytic space: Between clinic and culture* (pp. 63–90). New York, NY: Other Press.
Goldner, V., Penn, P., Sheinberg, M., & Walker, G. (1998). Love and violence: Gender paradoxes in volatile attachments. In B. M. Clinchy, & J. K. Norem (eds), *The gender and psychology reader* (pp. 549–571). New York, NY: New York University Press.
Gondolf, E. W. (1985). Fighting for control: A clinical assessment of men who batter. *The Journal of Contemporary Social Work*, *66*(1), 48–54.
Gondolf, E. W. (1987). Seeing through smoke and mirrors: A guide to batterer program evaluation. *Response*, *10*(3), 16–19.
Gondolf, E. W. (1993). Treating the batterer. In M. Hansen, & M. Harway (eds), *Battering and family therapy: A feminist perspective* (pp. 105–118). London: Sage Publications.
Gondolf, E. W. (1997). Batterer program: What we know and need to know. *Journal of Interpersonal Violence*, *12*(1), 83–89.
Gondolf, E. W. (1999a). A comparison of four batterer intervention systems: Do court referral, program length, and services matter? *Journal of Interpersonal Violence*, *14*(1), 41–61.
Gondolf, E. W. (1999b). Characteristics of court-mandated batterers in four cities. *Violence Against Women*, *5*(11), 1277–1293.
Gondolf, E. W. (2001). Culturally focused batterer counseling for African American men. *Trauma, Violence, & Abuse*, *2*(4), 283–295.
Goodman, L. A., & Epstein, D. (2008). The justice system response. In L. A. Goodman, & D. Epstein (eds), *Listening to battered women: A survivor-centered approach to advocacy, mental health, and justice* (pp. 71–87). Washington, DC: American Psychological Association.
Gordon, L. (1988). *Heroes of their own lives: The politics and history of family violence*. New York, NY: Viking Press.
Gordon, L. (2007). Family violence, feminism, and social control. In L. L. O'Toole, & J. Schiffman (eds), *Gender violence: Interdisciplinary perspectives* (2nd ed.) (pp. 305–322). New York, NY: New York University Press.
Gottman, J. M., Jacobson, N. S., Rushe, R. H., Shortt, J. W., Babcock, J., La Taillade, J. J., *et al.* (1995). The relationship between heart rate reactivity, emotionally aggressive behavior, and general violence in batterers. *Journal of Family Psychology*, *9*(3), 227–248.
Greenblatt, M. (1978). *Psychopolitics*. New York, NY: Grune & Stratton.
Gross, M., Cramer, E. P., Forte, J., Gordon, J. A., Kunkel, T., & Moriarty, L. J.

(2000). The impact of sentencing options on recidivism among domestic violence offenders. *American Journal of Criminal Justice*, *24*(2), 301–312.

Gülerce, A. (2005). Anxiety and phantasy as psychopolitical agents in resistance: Converging Klein and Lacan on theorizing subjectivity and society. In A. Gülerce, A. Hofmeister, I. Staeuble, G. Saunders, & J. Kaye (eds), *Contemporary theorizing in psychology: Global perspectives* (pp. 306–316). Concord, Ontario, Canada: Captus University Publications.

Haaken, J. (1998). *Pillar of salt: Gender, memory, and the perils of looking back*. New Brunswick, NJ: Rutgers University Press.

Haaken, J. (1999). Women's refuge as social symbolic space. *Journal for the Psychoanalysis of Culture and Society*, *4*(2), 315–318.

Haaken, J. (2002a). Stories of survival: Class, race, and domestic violence. In N. Holmstrom (ed.), *The socialist feminist project: A contemporary reader in theory and politics* (pp. 102–120). New York, NY: Monthly Review Press.

Haaken, J. (2002b). Bitch and femme psychology: Women, aggression, and psychoanalytic theory. *Journal for the Psychoanalysis of Culture and Society*, *7*(2), 202–215.

Haaken, J. (2003). Traumatic revisions: Remembering sex abuse and the politics of forgiveness. In P. Reavey, & S. Warner (eds), *New feminist stories of child sex abuse* (pp. 77–93). New York, NY: Routledge.

Haaken, J. (2008a). Too close for comfort: Psychoanalytic cultural theory and domestic violence politics. *Psychoanalysis, Culture & Society*, *13*(1), 75–93.

Haaken, J. (2008b). When White Buffalo Calf Woman meets Oedipus on the road: Lakota psychology, feminist psychoanalysis, and male violence. *Theory Psychology*, *18*(2), 195–208.

Haaken, J., & Reavey, P. (Eds) (2009). *Memory matters: Contexts for understanding sexual abuse recollections*. London and New York, NY: Routledge.

Haaken, J., & Yragui, N. (2003). Going underground: Conflicting perspectives on domestic violence shelter practices. *Feminism and Psychology*, *13*(1), 49–71.

Haaken, J., Fussell, H., & Mankowski, E. (2007). Bringing the church to its knees: evangelical Christianity, feminism, and domestic violence discourse. *Psychotherapy and Politics International*, *5*(2), 103–115.

Haaken, J., Ladum, A., de Tarr, S., Zundel, K., & Heymann, C. (2005). *Speaking out: Women, war, and the global economy*. Portland, OR: Ooligan Press.

Haffner, S. (1979). Victimology interview: A refuge for battered women. *Victimology: An International Journal*, *4*(1), 100–112.

Hagemann-White, C. (1998). Violence without end? Some reflections on achievements, contradictions, and perspectives of the feminist movement in Germany. In R. C. A. Klein (ed.), *Multidisciplinary perspectives on family violence* (pp. 176–191). London: Routledge.

Hale, J. C. (1998). *Bloodlines: Odyssey of a native daughter*. Tucson, AZ: University of Arizona Press.

Hamberger, L. K., & Hastings, J. E. (1993). Court-mandated treatment of men who assault their partner: Issues, controversies, and outcomes. In Z. N. Hilton (ed.), *Legal responses to wife assault; current trends and evaluation* (pp. 188–229). Newbury Park, CA: Sage Publication.

Hamby, S. L. (2000). The importance of community in a feminist analysis of domestic violence among American Indians. *American Journal of Community Psychology*, *28*(5), 649–669.

Hansen, M. (1993). Feminism and family therapy: A review of feminist critiques of approaches to family violence. In M. Hansen, & M. Harway (eds), *Battering and family therapy: A feminist perspective* (pp. 69–91). London: Sage Publications.

Harbord, R. J. (1996). Natural born killers: Violence, film and anxiety. In C. Sumner (ed.), *Violence, culture and censor* (pp. 137–158). Bristol, PA: Taylor and Francis.

Harris, A. (2005). *Gender as soft assembly*. Hillsdale, NJ: Analytic Press.

Hartsock, N. C. M. (1997). The feminist standpoint: Developing the grounds for a specifically feminist historical materialism. In N. Nicolson (ed.), *The second wave: A reader in feminist theory*. New York, NY: Routledge.

Hays, P. (2001). *Addressing cultural complexities in practice: A framework for clinicians and counselors*. Washington, DC: American Psychological Association.

Herman, J. (1992). *Trauma and recovery*. New York, NY: Basic Books.

Ho, C. K. (1990). An analysis of domestic violence in Asian American communities: A multicultural approach to counseling. *Women & Therapy*, *9*(1–2), 129–150.

Hochschild, A. R. (1983). *The managed heart: Commercialization of human feeling*. Berkeley, CA: University of California Press.

Hoeveler, D. L. (1998). *Gothic feminism: The professionalization of gender from Charlotte Smith to the Brontës*. University Park, PA: Penn State University Press.

Hollway, W. (2006). *The capacity to care: Gender and ethical subjectivity*. New York, NY: Routledge.

Hollway, W. (ed.) (2004). *Psycho-social research* (vol. 10). London: Lawrence & Wishart.

Holtzworth-Munroe, A., & Stuart, G. L. (1994). Typologies of male batterers: Three subtypes and the differences among them. *Psychological Bulletin*, *116*(3), 476–497.

hooks, b. (1984). *Feminist theory: From margin to center*. Boston, MA: South End Press.

hooks, b. (1992). *Black looks: Race and representation*. Boston, MA: South End Press.

Horley, S. (1991). *The charm syndrome: Why charming men can make dangerous lovers*. London: Macmillan.

Humphreys, C. (2006). Relevant evidence for practice. In C. Humphreys, & N. Stanley (eds), *Domestic violence and child protection: Directions for good practice* (pp. 19–35). Philadelphia, PA: Jessica Kingsley Publishers.

Humphreys, C., & Joseph, S. (2004). Domestic violence and the politics of trauma. *Women's Studies International Forum*, *27*(5–6), 559–570.

Humphreys, C., & Stanley, N. (eds) (2006). *Domestic violence and child protection: Directions for good practice*. Philadelphia, PA: Jessica Kingsley Publishers.

Humphreys, C., & Thiara, R. (2003). Mental health and domestic violence: "I call it symptoms of abuse". *British Journal of Social Work*, *33*(2), 209–226.

Ieda, R. (1986). The battered woman. *Women & Therapy*, *5*(2–3), 167–176.

Incite! (2005). Gender violence and the prison industrial complex: Interpersonal and state violence against women of color—critical resistance statement with an introduction by Julia Sudbury. In N. J. Sokoloff (ed.), *Domestic violence at the margins: Readings on race, class, gender, and culture* (pp. 102–114). New Brunswick, NJ: Rutgers University Press.

Jacobs, H. A. (1987). *Incidents in the live of a slave girl, written by herself.* Cambridge, MA: Harvard University Press.

Jacobson, N. S., & Gottman, J. M. (1998). *When men batter women: New insights into ending abusive relationships.* New York, NY: Simon & Schuster.

Jaimes-Guerrero, M. A. (1997). Civil rights versus sovereignty: Native American women in life and land struggles. In M. J. Alexander, & C. T. Mohanty (eds), *Feminist genealogies, colonial legacies, democratic futures* (pp. 101–121). New York, NY: Routledge.

Johnson, M. P. (1995). Patriarchal terrorism and common couple violence: Two forms of violence against women. *Journal of Marriage and the Family*, *57*(2), 283–294.

Johnson, M. P. (2006). Conflict and control: Gender symmetry and asymmetry in domestic violence. *Violence Against Women*, *12*(11), 1003–1018.

Jones, A. (1980). *Women who kill.* New York, NY: Holt, Rinehart, and Winston.

Jones, A., & Schechter, S. (1992). *When love goes wrong: What to do when you can't do anything right.* New York, NY: Harper Collins.

Josephson, J. (2005). The intersectionality of domestic violence and welfare in the lives of poor women. In N. J. Sokoloff (ed.), *Domestic violence at the margins: Readings on race, class, gender, and culture* (pp. 83–101). New Brunswick, NJ: Rutgers University Press.

Kanuha, V. K. (2005). Compounding the triple jeopardy: Battering in lesbian of color relationships. In N. J. Sokoloff (ed.), *Domestic violence at the margins: Readings on race, class, gender, and culture* (pp. 71–82). New Brunswick, NJ: Rutgers University Press.

Kelly, R. M., Bayes, J. H., Hawkesworth, M. E., & Young, B. (eds) (2001). *Gender, globalization, and democratization.* New York, NY: Rowan & Littlefield Publishers.

Kempe, C. H., & Helfer, R. F. (1968). *The battered child.* Chicago, IL: Chicago University Press.

Kempe, C. H., Silverman, F. N., Steele, B. F., Droegemuller, W., & Silver, H. K. (1962). The battered child syndrome. *Journal of the American Medical Association*, *181*, 17–24.

Kidder, L. H., & Fine, M. (1997). Qualitative inquiry in psychology: A radical tradition. In D. Fox, & I. Prilletensky (eds), *Critical psychology: An introduction* (pp. 34–50). Thousand Oaks, CA: Sage Publications.

Kingsolver, B. (1989). *Holding the line: Women in the Great Arizona Mine Strike of 1983.* Ithaca, NY: Cornell University Press.

Kivel, P. (1996). Where do batterer's intervention programs fit in?, retrieved from http://www.paulkivel.com/articles/batterers%27%20programs.com

Klein, M. (1952). Notes on schizoid mechanisms. In J. Riviere (ed.), *Developments in pyscho-analysis* (pp. 292–320). London: Hogarth Press.

Klein, N. (2007). *The shock doctrine: The rise of disaster capitalism.* New York, NY: Metropolitan Books.

Klein, R. C. A. (ed.) (1998). *Multidisciplinary perspectives on family violence.* New York, NY: Routledge.

Koss, M. P., Goodman, L. A., Browne, A., Fitzgerald, L. F., Keita, G. P., & Russo,

N. F. (1994). *No safe haven: Male violence against women at home, at work, and in the community*. Washington, DC: American Psychological Association.

Krieger, S. (2002). The dangers of mediation in domestic violence cases. *Cardozo Women's Law Journal*, *8*, 235–259.

La Violette, A. (2002). Batterers' treatment: Observations from the trenches. *Journal of Aggression, Maltreatment & Trauma*, *5*(2), 45–56.

Lamb, S. (ed.) (1999). *New versions of victims*. New York, NY: New York University Press.

Latané, B., & Darley, J. M. (1970). *The unresponsive bystander: Why doesn't he help?* Englewood Cliffs, NJ: Prentice Hall.

Lawson, D. M. (1989). A family systems perspective on wife battering. *Journal of Mental Counseling*, *11*(4), 359–373.

Layton, L., Hollander, N.C., & Gutwill, S. (eds) (2006). *Psychoanalysis, class and politics: Encounters in the clinical setting*. New York, NY: Routledge.

Le Guin, U. (1989). *Dancing at the edge of the world: Thoughts on words, women, places*. New York, NY: Grove Press.

Leisey, M. R. (2008). The multiple meanings of domestic violence: A constructivist inquiry. *Dissertation Abstracts International Section A: Humanities and Social Sciences*, *68*(7-A), 31–50.

Levinson, D. (1989). *Family violence in a cross-cultural perspective*. Newbury Park, CA: Sage Publications.

Lewin, K. (1975, c1951). *Field theory in social science: Selected theoretical papers of Kurt Lewin*. Westport, CT: Greenwood Press.

Littlechild, B., & Bourke, C. (2006). Men's use of violence and intimidation against family members and child protection workers. In C. Humphreys, & N. Stanley (eds), *Domestic violence and child protection: Directions for good practice* (pp. 203–215). Philadelphia, PA: Jessica Kingsley Publishers.

Loseke, D. R. (1992). *The battered woman and shelters: The social construction of wife abuse*. Albany, NY: State University of New York Press.

McBride, D. A. (2001). *Impossible witness: Truth, abolitionism and slave testimony*. New York, NY: New York University Press.

McGillivray, A., & Comaskey, B. (1999). *Black eyes all of the time: Intimate violence, aboriginal women, and the justice system*. Toronto: University of Toronto Press.

Mankowski, E., Haaken, J., & Silvergleid, C. (2002). Collateral damage: An analysis of the achievements and unintended consequences of batterers' intervention programs and discourse. *Journal of Family Violence*, *17*(2), 167–184.

Mankowski, E., & Rappaport, J. (1995). Stories, identity, and the psychological sense of community. In R. S. J. Wyer (ed.), *Knowledge and memory: The real story: Advances in social cognition* (vol. VIII, pp. 211–226). Hillsdale, NJ: Lawrence Erlbaum Associates, Inc.

Marcus, I. (1994). Reframing "domestic violence": Terrorism in the home. In M. A. Fineman, & R. Mykitiuk (eds), *The public nature of private violence: The discovery of domestic abuse* (pp. 11–35). New York, NY: Routledge.

Martin, D. (1976). *Battered wives*. San Francisco, CA: Glide Publications.

Massé, M. A. (1992). *In the name of love: Women, masochism, and the gothic*. Ithaca, NY: Cornell University Press.

Merry, S. E. (2001). Rights, religion, and community: Approaches to violence against women in the context of globalization. *Law & Society Review*, *35*(1), 39–88.

Metaksa, T. (1997). *Safe, not sorry: Keeping yourself and your family safe in a violent age*. New York, NY: ReganBooks.

Mills, J. (ed.) (2006). *Other banalities: Melanie Klein revisited.* New York, NY: Routledge.

Mitchell, J. (1974). *Psychoanalysis and feminism*. New York, NY: Pantheon Books.

Molino, A (2004). *Culture, subject, psyche: Dialogue in psychoanalysis and anthropology*. Middletown, CN: Wesleyan Press.

Morgaine, K. (2007). Domestic violence and human rights: Local challenges to a universal framework. *Journal of Sociology & Social Welfare*, *34*(1), 109–129.

Morrison, T., & Lacour, C. B. (1997). *Birth of a nation'hood: Gaze, script, and spectacle in the O.J. Simpson case*. New York, NY: Pantheon Books.

Mullender, A. (1996). *Rethinking domestic violence: The social work and probation response*. London: Routledge.

Mulvey, L. (1988). Visual pleasure and narrative cinema. In C. Penley (ed.), *Feminism and film theory* (pp. 57–68). New York, NY: Routledge.

Nathan, D., & Snedeker, M. (1995). *Satan's silence: Ritual abuse and the making of a modern American witch hunt*. New York, NY: Basic Books.

Nathanson, C. A. (1991). *Dangerous passage: The social control of sexuality in women's adolescence*. Philadelphia, PA: Temple University Press.

Nelson, K. (ed.) (1989). *Narratives from the crib*. Cambridge, MA: Harvard University Press.

Nicolson, P. (1996). *Gender, power and organisation: A psychological perspective*. New York, NY: Routledge.

Niemtzow, A. (1982). *Six women's slave narratives*. Urbana, IL: University of Illinois Press.

Norton, I. M., & Manson, S. M. (1997). Domestic violence intervention in an urban Indian health center. *Community Mental Health Journal*, *33*(4), 331–337.

Obeyesekere, G. (1990). *The work of culture: Symbolic transformation in psychoanalysis and anthropology*. Chicago, IL: University of Chicago Press.

Okum, L. (1986). *Woman abuse: Facts replacing myths*. Albany, NY: State University of New York Press.

O'Neil, J. M., Helms, B. J., Gable, R. K., David, L., & Wrightsman, L. S. (1986). Gender-role conflict scale: College men's fear of feminity. *Sex Roles*, *14*(5/6), 335–350.

Orme, J., Dominelli, L., & Mullender, A. (2000). Working with violent men from a feminist social work perspective. *International Social Work*, *43*(1), 89–105.

Pagelow, M. D. (1992). Adult victims of domestic violence. *Journal of Interpersonal Violence*, *7*(1), 87–120.

Peltoniemi, T. (1981). The first twelve months of the Finnish shelters. *Victimology: An International Journal*, *6*(1–4), 198–211.

Pence, E. (1989). Batterer programs: Shifting from community collusion to community confrontation. In P. L. Caesar, & L. K. Hamberger (eds), *Treating men who batter: Theory, practice, and programs* (pp. 24–50). New York, NY: Springer Publishing Company.

Pence, E., & Paymar, M. (1993). *Education groups for men who batter: The Duluth model.* New York, NY: Springer Publishing Company.

Perilla, J. L., Bakeman, R., & Norris, F. H. (1994). Culture and domestic violence: The ecology of abused Latinas. *Violence and Victims*, *9*(4), 325–339.

Pizzey, E. (1974). *Scream quietly or the neighbours will hear*. Baltimore, MD: Penguin Books.

Pizzey, E., & Shapiro, J. (1982). *Prone to violence*. Feltham, England: Hamlyn.

Pleck, E. (1979). Wife beating in nineteenth century America. *Victimology: An International Journal*, *4*(1), 60–74.

Pleck, E. (1987). *Domestic tyranny: The making of social policy against family violence from colonial times to the present*. New York, NY: Oxford University Press.

Post, J. M. (1999). The psychopolitics of hatred: Commentary on Ervin Staub's article. *Peace and Conflict*, *5*(4), 337–344.

Preisser, A. B. (1999). Domestic violence in South Asian communities in America: Advocacy and intervention. *Violence Against Women*, *5*(6), 684–699.

Price, J. (1999). Difficult maneuvers in discourse against Latina immigrants in the United States. *Cardozo Journal of International and Comparative Law*, *7*(2), 277–318.

Radway, J. A. (1991). *Reading the romance: Women, patriarchy and popular literature*. Chapel Hill, NC: University of North Carolina Press.

Råkil, M. (2006). Are men who use violence against their partners and children good enough fathers? The need for an intergrated child perspective in treatment work with men. In C. Humphreys, & N. Stanley (eds), *Domestic violence and child protection: Directions for good practice* (pp. 190–202). Philadelphia, PA: Jessica Kingsley Publishers.

Rappaport, J. (1993). Narrative studies, personal stories, and identity transformation in the mutual help context. *The Journal of Applied Behavioral Science*, *29*(2), 239–256.

Rempe, D. (2001). Hidden in plain sight: Secrecy and safety in battered women's shelters. Unpublished Master thesis. University of Arizona.

Renzetti, C. M. (1994). On dancing with bear: Reflections on some of the current debates among domestic violence theorists. *Violence and Victims*, *9*(2), 195–200.

Renzetti, C. M. (1999). The challenge to feminism posed by women's use of violence in intimate relationships. In S. Lamb (ed.), *New versions of victims* (pp. 42–56). New York, NY: New York University Press.

Restuccia, R. (2000). *Melancholics in love: Representing women's depression and domestic abuse*. New York, NY: Rowman and Littlefield.

Richie, B. E. (2000). A Black feminist reflection on the antiviolence movement. *Journal of Women in Culture and Society*, *25*(4), 1133–1137.

Richie, B. E. (2005). A Black feminist reflection on the antiviolence movement. In N. J. Sokoloff (ed.), *Domestic violence at the margins: Readings on race, class, gender, and culture* (pp. 50–55). New Brunswick, NJ: Rutgers University Press.

Ridington, J. (1977–1978). The transition process: A feminist environment as reconstitutive milieu. *Victimology: An International Journal*, *2*(3–4), 463–575.

Riger, S., & Krieglstein, M. (2000). The impact of welfare reform on men's violence against women. *American Journal of Community Psychology*, *28*(5), 631–647.

Ristock, J. L. (2002). *No more secrets: Violence in lesbian relationships*. New York, NY: Routledge.

Rivera, J. (1994). Domestic violence against Latinas by Latino males: An analysis of

race, national origin and gender differentials. *Boston College Third World Law Journal, 231*, 1–22.
Roche, S. E., & Sadoski, P. J. (1996). Social action for battered women. In A. R. Roberts (ed.), *Helping battered women: New perspectives and remedies* (pp. 13–30). New York, NY: Oxford University Press.
Rodriguez, N. M. (1988). A successful feminist shelter: A case study of the Family Crisis Shelter in Hawaii. *The Journal of Applied Behavioral Science, 24*(3), 235–249.
Rose, J. (1986). *Sexuality in the field of vision*. London: Verso Press.
Rosen, L. N. (2006). Origin and goals of the "Gender Symmetry" Workshop. *Violence Against Women, 12*(11), 997–1002.
Rubin, L. (2008). A critical interdisciplinary analysis of domestic violence intervention. *PsycCRITIQUES, 53*(8).
Schechter, S. (1982). *Women and male violence: The visions and struggles of the battered women's movement*. Boston, MA: South End Press.
Schneider, E. M. (1994). The violence of privacy. In M. A. Fineman, & R. Mykitiuk (eds), *The public nature of private violence* (pp. 36–58). New York, NY: Routledge.
Segal, L. (1990). *Slow motion: Changing masculinities*. London: Virago Press.
Sekora, J., & Turner, D. T. (eds) (1982). *The art of slave narrative: Original essays in criticism and theory*. Macomb, IL: Western Illinois University.
Shamai, M. (1996). Couple therapy with battered women and abusive men: Does it have a future? In J. Edleson, & Z. C. Eisikovits (eds), *Future interventions with battered women and their families* (pp. 201–215). Thousand Oaks, CA, London & New Delhi: Sage Publications.
Shepard, M. F. (1999). Advocacy for battered women: Implications for a coordinated community response. In M. F. Shepard, & E. L. Pence (eds), *Coordinating community responses to domestic violence: Lessons of Duluth and beyond* (pp. 115–125). Thousand Oaks, CA: Sage Publications.
Shepard, M., & Pence, E. (eds) (1999) *Coordinating community responses to domestic violence: Lessons from Duluth and beyond*. Thousand Oaks, CA: Sage Publications.
Shuman, A. (1986). *Storytelling rights: The uses of oral and written texts by urban adolescents*. Cambridge: Cambridge University Press.
Siegel, R. B. (1996). "The rule of love": Wife beating as prerogative and privacy. *The Yale Law Journal, 105*, 2117–2207.
Smith, S. (1974). *Where I'm bound: Patterns of slavery and freedom in Black American autobiography*. Westport, CT: Greenwood Press.
Smith, B. V. (2005). Battering, forgiveness, and redemption: Alternative models of addressing domestic violence in communities of color. In N. J. Sokoloff (ed.), *Domestic violence at the margins: Readings on race, class, gender, and culture* (pp. 321–339). New Brunswick, NJ: Rutgers University Press.
Sokoloff, N. J. (ed.) (2005). *Domestic violence at the margins: Readings on race, class, gender, and culture*. New Brunswick, NJ: Rutgers University Press.
Sorenson, B. S. (1996). Violence against women: Examining ethnic differences and commonalities. *Evaluation Review, 20*, 123–145.
Span, P. (1989). Women protest "Hedda-bashing": 300 sign response to Steinberg case. *The Washington Post*, March, 13.

Spence, D. P. (1982). *Narrative and historical truth: Meaning and interpretation in psychoanalysis*. New York, NY: W. W. Norton & Company.

Sprengnether, M. (1995). Mourning Freud. In A. Elliot, & S. Frosh (eds), *Psychoanalysis in contexts: Paths between theory and modern culture* (pp. 142–165). New York, NY: Routledge.

Staeuble, I. (2005). The international expansion of psychology: Cultural imperialism or chances for alternative cultures of knowledge? In A. Gülerce, A. Hofmeister, I. Staeuble, G. Saunders, & J. Kaye (eds), *Contemporary theorizing in psychology: Global perspectives* (pp. 88–96). Concord, Ontario, Canada: Captus University Press.

Stanley, A. D. (1998). *From bondage to contract: Wage labor, marriage, and the market in the age of slave emancipation*. Cambridge, UK: Cambridge University Press.

Stark, E. (2006). Commentary on Johnson's "Conflict and Control: Gender Symmetry and Asymmetry in Domestic Violence". *Violence Against Women*, *12*(11), 1019–1025.

Stark, E., & Flitcraft, A. (1996). *Women at risk: Domestic violence and women's health*. Thousand Oaks, CA: Sage Publications.

Stephens, M. (1988). It's news, but is Steinberg's case really "significant"? *Newsday*, December, 20.

Stevenson, R. L. (1974/1886). *The strange case of Dr. Jekyll and Mr. Hyde*. London: New English Library.

Stout, K. D., & Thomas, S. (1991). Fear and dangerousness in shelter work with battered women. *Affilia*, *6*(2), 74–86.

Strang, H., & Braithwaite (eds) (2002). *Restrorative justice and family violence*. New York, NY: Cambridge University Press.

Straus, M. A. (1973). A general systems theory approach to a theory of violence between family members. *Social Science Information*, *12*(3), 105–125.

Straus, M. A. (2006). Future research on gender symmetry in physical assaults on partners. *Violence Against Women*, *12*(11), 1086–1097.

Straus, M. A., & Gelles, R. J. (1990). *Physical violence in American families*. New Brunswick, NJ: Transaction Publishers.

Straus, M., Gelles, R., & Steinmetz, S. (1980). *Behind closed doors: Violence in America*. New York, NY: Doubleday.

Stubbs, J. (2002). Domestic violence and women's safety: Feminist challenges to restorative justice. In H. Strang, & J. Braithwaite (eds), *Sydney Law School Research Paper 08-16* (pp. 42–61). Cambridge: Cambridge University Press.

Swan, S. C., & Snow, D. L. (2006). The development of a theory of women's use of violence in intimate relationships. *Violence Against Women*, *12*(11), 1026–1045.

Syers, M., & Edleson, J. (1992). The combined effects of coordinated criminal justice intervention in woman abuse. *Journal of Interpersonal Violence*, *7*(4), 490–502.

Thompson, E. P. (1966). *The making of the English working class*. New York, NY: Vintage Books.

Tolman, R. M., & Edleson, J. (1995). Intervention for men who batter: A review of research. In S. M. Stith, & M. A. Straus (eds), *Understanding partner violence: Prevalence, causes, consequences, and solutions* (vol. 11, pp. 262–273). Minneapolis, MN: National Council on Family Relations.

Turner, T. with Loder, K. (1986). *I, Tina: My life story*. New York, NY: Avon Books.

Ussher, J. M. (2003). The ongoing silencing of women in families: An analysis and rethinking of premenstrual syndrome and therapy. *Journal of Family Therapy*, *25*(4), 388–405.

Ussher, J. M., & Pert, J. (2008). Empathy, egalitarianism and emotion work in the relational negotiation of PMS: The experience of women in lesbian relationships. *Feminism and Psychology*, *18*(1), 87–111.

Volcan, V. D. (2009). Large group identity: "Us" and "them" polarizations in the international arena. *Psychoanalysis, Culture & Society*, *14*(1), 4–15.

Volk, P. (2009). The Steinberg Trial: Scenes from a tragedy. *New York Times Magazine*, September, 12.

Volpp, L. (2005). Feminism versus multiculturalism. In N. J. Sokoloff (ed.), *Domestic violence at the margins: Readings on race, class, gender, and culture* (pp. 39–49). New Brunswick, NJ: Rutgers University Press.

Walker, A. (1970). *The third life of Grange Copeland*. New York, NY: Harcourt, Brace, Jovanovich.

Walker, A. (1982). *The color purple*. New York, NY: Harcourt, Brace, Jovanovich.

Walker, L. E. (1978). Battered women and learned helplessness. *Victimology*, *2*(3–4), 525–534.

Walker, L. E. (1979a). *The battered woman*. New York, NY: Harper & Row.

Walker, L. E. (1979b). Behind the closed doors of the middle-class wifebeater's family. *PsycCRITIQUES*, *24*(5).

Walker, L. E. (1984). *The battered woman syndrome*. New York, NY: Springer Publishing.

Walker, L. E. (1988). The battered woman syndrome. In G. T. F. Hotaling (ed.), *Family abuse and its consequences: New directions in research* (pp. 139–148). Newbury Park, CA: Sage Publications.

Walker, L. E. (1989). *Terrifying love: Why battered women kill and how society responds*. New York, NY: Harper & Row.

Walker, L. E. (1995). Current perspectives on men who batter women: Implications for intervention and treatment to stop violence against women: Comment on Gottman et al. *Journal of Family Psychology*, *9*(3), 264–271.

Walker, L. E. (1999). Psychology and domestic violence around the world. *American Psychologist*, *54*(1), 21–29.

Walker, L. E. A. (2006). Battered woman syndrome: Empirical findings. In F. L. Denmark *et al.* (eds), *Violence and exploitation against women and girls* (pp. 142–157). Boston, MA: Blackwell Publishers.

West, T. C. (1999). *Wounds of the spirit: Black women, violence, and resistance ethics*. New York, NY: New York University Press.

Wexler, D. B. (1999). The broken mirror: A self psychological treatment perspective for relationship violence. *Psychotherapy Practice and Research*, *8*(2), 129–141.

White, E. C. (1985). *Chain, chain, change: For Black women dealing with physical and emotional abuse and exploring responses to it*. Seattle, WA: Seal Press.

Williams, K. C. (1994). Mapping the margins: Intersectionality, identity politics, and violence against women of color. In M. A. Fineman, & R. Mykitiuk (eds), *The public nature of private violence: The discovery of domestic violence* (pp. 93–118). New York, NY: Routledge.

Yllo, K. A. (1993). Through a feminist lens: Gender, power, and violence. In R. J. Gelles, & D. R. Loseke (eds), *Current controversies on family violence*. (pp. 47–62). Newbury Park, CA: Sage Publications.

Young, R. M. (2006). Projective identification. In J. Mills (ed.), *Other banalities: Melanie Klein revisited* (pp. 60–76). New York, NY: Routledge.

Zaretsky, E. (2004). *Secrets of the soul: A social and cultural history of psychoanalysis*. New York, NY: Alfred A. Knopf.

Zellerer, E. (1999). Restorative justice in indigenous communities: Critical issues in confronting violence against women. *International Review of Victimology*, *6*, 345–358.

Zizek, J. (2001). *Enjoy your symptom! Jacques Lacan in Hollywood and out*. New York, NY: Routledge.

INDEX

Note: Page numbers in *italics* refer to figures.